HISTORY OF CHRISTIAN MISSIONARIES

HISTORY OF CHRISTIAN MISSIONARIES

A Study in Kurnool District of Andhra Pradesh

By

M. Indira Santhi

KALPAZ

First Published, 2018

Published by

Kalpaz Publications
C-30, Satyawati Nagar,
Delhi – 110052
Ph.: 011-47034999, 9811692060
www.kalpazpublications.com
E-mail: kalpaz@hotmail.com

Printed at: G. Print Process, Delhi

Cataloging in Publication Data—DK
Courtesy: D.K. Agencies (P) Ltd. <docinfo@dkagencies.com>

Indira Santhi, M., author.
History of Christian missionaries : a study in Kurnool District of Andhra Pradesh / by M. Indira Santhi.
pages cm
ISBN 9789353240080

1. Missionaries—India—Kurnool (District)—History. 2. Missions—India—Kurnool (District)—History. 3. Ecumenical movement—India—Kurnool (District)—History. 4. Kurnool (India : District)—Church history. I. Title.

LCC BV3265.3.I53 2018 | DDC 266.0095485 23

Contents

Foreword

History of Christianity in India is viewed as an integral part of the socio-cultural history of the Indian people rather than as separate from it. The history will therefore focus attention upon the Christian people in India; upon who they were and how they understood themselves; upon their social, religious, cultural and political encounters; upon the changes which these encounters produced in them and in their appreciation of the Christian gospel as well as in the Indian culture and society of which they themselves were a part. For the downtrodden Christianity provided a mean of preserving their identities and promoting their interest in the face of powerful forces of change.

The present book ***History of Christian Missionaries: A Study in Kurnool District of Andhra Pradesh*** describes the relentless, selfless and dedicated services to the people of the region. Missionaries treated these people compassion and selfless services. The equal treatment of the untouchables and caste Hindus in the hospitals engendered a kind of social awareness among the latter. Missionaries taught this people cleanliness and infused in them an element of health consciousness. This is the fair description of the work of the major Christian missions in Andhra Pradesh. Drawing their strength and impetus from the religious awakening all over the world during 19th century, these denominations found economically backward, socially downtrodden and religiously deprived community in Andhra Pradesh for their work. Not losing a single opportunity, they concentrated on their goals. They were encouraged even astonished by the stunning and surprising results that their work accomplished in these areas. In spite of the caste policies of the early Christian missions and the exploitation of poverty by later groups, it is clear that Christian missions worked hard to help people from the lower rungs of the caste system, and were, in turn, embraced by them. In this context, the author rightly pointed out that the various Christian organizations lead in bringing higher education and modern medical care to the population by establishing several prominent educational institutions and hospitals in Andhra Pradesh. These elements constitute the history of Christianity in India. This history should, therefore, provide an insight into the changing identity of the Christian people of India through the centuries.

G Godavarthi

Faculty, Department of English
Maulana Azad National Urdu University,
Hyderabad

Preface

Christianity is a monotheistic religion based on the life and teachings of Jesus as presented in canonical gospels and other New Testament writings. Adherents of the Christian faith are known as Christians. Christianity teaches that Jesus is the son of God, God having become human and the savior of humanity. Because of this, Christians commonly refer to Jesus as Christ or Messiah. Christians believe that Jesus is the Messiah prophesied in the Hebrew Bible, referred to as the "Old Testament" in Christianity. The foundation of Christian theology is expressed in the early Christianity. The beauty of a religion is glorified when its firm conviction of brotherhood of man and Fatherhood of God is deep-rooted universally in the form of practical service to mankind. Christian missionaries are known for this kind of selfless service all over the globe irrespective of race, caste and creed.

Jesus instructed the apostles to make disciples of all nations. This verse is referred to by Christian missionaries as the Great Commission and inspires missionary work. The kind of service rendered by the Christian missionaries in Kurnool district is priceless. Be it a church, or an educational institution, a colony or a small village – each one of them stands testimony to the quality of service willingly rendered by them.

The relentless and selfless efforts of the missionaries have come to stay with the needy in a natural course of time and there is no second opinion to the fact that Christianity is now looked upon with conviction and great veneration in India. They tried to weed out social inequalities and developed moral values among the people.

After the London Mission Society S.P.G., A.B.M., and R.C.M. first entered at Nandyal in Kurnool district. These organizations rendered noble service for the progress of education and medicine, thereby gaining prominence among the people. Untouchability, Devadasi tradition, child marriages, child abortions and sati system were a cruel practice of the ancient Indian society. The missionaries fought against these social evils bravely, encouraged widow marriages and created awareness among the people. Thus, their lives full of self-sacrifice leave an indelible impression in the annals of Indian history of reformation. In this background an attempt has been made to study the history of Christian Missionaries and their role in Kurnool district of Andhra Pradesh.

M Indira Santhi

Acknowledgements

The relentless, selfless and dedicated services to the people of the region of Christian Missionaries in the region inspired us to take up this account. We deeply acknowledge the contribution of all Christian congregations that brought socio-economic change in the lives of people in the region.

M Indira Santhi

Chapter - I

Introduction

Social services are a range of public services provided by government, private, and non-profit organizations. These public services aim to create more effective organizations, build stronger communities, and promote equality and opportunity. Social services include the benefits and facilities such as education, food subsidies, health care, job training and subsidized housing, adoption, community management, policy research, and lobbying.[1] **Social service** refers to activities to improve the quality of life of the disadvantaged section of the society. It aims at elevating the living condition of the poor, disabled, elderly, children, women, and depressed section of the society. **Service to mankind is service to God.** There are many people, who believe that "service to man is service to god". They do not let a single day pass without doing some act of charity, however small it may be. The sense of social service comes out of kindness of the heart and depends largely upon character. Many wealthy people live selfless lives. They spend anything for the good of their neighbours.

Christians believe that Christianity is the gift of the Heavenly Father, the God of the universe, Creator of everything that exists, the Master of the History of the universe and the destiny of mankind. Christianity is the revelation of God's unparalleled love for man inspite of man's great revolt and unrighteousness. It is not to be listed just as one of the religions of the world, however ancient, philosophical or comprehensive and complicated they may be. Christianity is the way of life - a new way based on the Truth.

Religions are manmade systems, of rituals and philosophy which try to help man to know God, the unknowable and to get the joy of freedom from the bondage of Sin. Man has endeavoured to discover God through history, culture, philosophy and art, but has failed. Dr. R. Panikar describes religion as 'a path of man following an order to reach the purpose of life'. This being the definition of religion,[2] Christianity does not come under man's effort but it is purely God's gracious attempt in the final stage of man's despair to save him.

The history of Christianity in India is as old as the history of Christianity itself. India being the land of Religions, Christianity being an alien religion, a religion born in middle Europe, travelled to this oriental land and established its influence on the religious, social and cultural thinking of the people of India. Within the First Century after the life, death and resurrection of Jesus Christ, Christianity spread itself into the greater part of the civilized world. The very concept of colonialism started with the voyage of Vasco Da Gama in 1498. However there are ample and undisputed evidences that there were Christians in India on the West Coast of India, namely Kerala and in parts of Tamilnadu more particularly Mylapore-Madras during the first century.[3]

The Indian Caste system is unique in nature and when we compare it with other societies in the world, is still continues to exist in the modern Indian society. The origins of the caste system can be traced to the 90th Sloka of 10th Mandala of Purusha Suktha of Rig-Veda. The seed of caste has grown up with its deep root dividing human society of India resulting in the creation of unequal socio-economic, politic-cultural system. It widened the gap between upper castes and lower castes as well as perpetuated exploitative social relations. This contribution for the heinous practice of untouchability towards Ati-shudras (Dalits) by the upper caste communities. In this process, the people of lower castes i.e., Dalits such as Madiga and Mala were excluded from the main stream of the Indian society.[4] Whenever they entre in to the village for cleaning streets of village and to attend the other works of villagers, they were forced to close their mouth with a small utensil, a long leaf at the back to clean their foot prints and a stick in their hand to make alert the villagers about their entry in to the villages. As per the Hindu religious practices, the entry of Dalits into temple is banned. But they do worship village gods and goddess such as Pochamma, Maisamma and Mahkalamma etc., to attained spiritual satisfaction. The practice of untouchability is continuing even in the democratic society of India even after 69 years of independence. Therefore, untouchable communities were attracted towards other religions like Christianity and Islam where they could get equivalent socio-economic, politico-cultural opportunities.[5] In this study, the conversion of Dalits into Christianity is examined in a long term historical perspectives.

The role of Christian missionaries in religious conversion and socio-cultural change as well as the development of educational, health and self-improvement schemes in modern India has been acknowledged by many historical studies. Recent studies on the growth of Christianity in modern India focused on the interconnection between conversion movements, social reform and social change. Christian missionaries were considering being the great institutions builders, since they pioneered works relating to social reform, language/literature/philosophy, socio-economic development of weaker sections. Hence, Christianity has been described as the "religion of the poor". In fact, education social uplift had become synonymous with Christianity in India. During the latter half of the 19th century, the impact of Christian proselytization and evangelization was left throughout the length and breadth of the country. Thus, Christian have become an integral part of the diverse population of India. It was also during this period that considerable movements of mass conversion took place in south India, including Telugu country. The Christian missionaries have been perceived as the protagonists and patrons of the poor. The image of the missionaries as persons committed to justices and equality and prepared to espouse/champion the cause of the depressed as well as to act as advocates of the underprivileged had certainly caught the imagination of the downtrodden masses and facilitated mass conversion of lower castes into Christianity. Especially, in the Telugu districts of erstwhile Madras Presidency (south India), German and other Protestant missionaries were instrumental in organizing various programmers of socio-economic advancement for the benefit of lower and communities.[6]

As per the Charter Act of 1813, the Christian Missionaries of European continents were permitted to preach their religious gospel to the people of Indian society. While Christianity missionaries were preaching their religious gospel to Indians, they provided education, health and economic benefits and socio-cultural upliftment. In this process, Missionaries constructed schools, Hospitals, dispensaries, Teacher training centers, houses for orphans, hostels for women and children with free boarding and lodging facilities, which the Dalits communities could not enjoy in Hindu religion.

To provide such facilities, American Telugu Baptist Mission, Roman Catholic Mission, London Missionary Society, Canadian Baptist Telugu Mission, American Evangelical Lutheran Mission, Arcot Mission of the Reformed Church of America Godavari Delta Mission, Weslyan Methodist Missionary society, Features of Scotland Mission and, Hermansburg Evangelical Lutheran Mission had come forward to serve Dalits in India.

As per the Subsidiary Alliance agreement between east India Company and Nizam government, the missionary activities spread in to the Nizam's dominion also. As a part of the above American Telugu Baptist Missionary and Roman Catholic Missionary stations were established in Kurnool in 1873 and 1886 respectively. Campbell and Lord Lecrees visited Hanumakonda and started rendering services to Dalits since 1872. This mission had started the construction of school for poor children in 1880 and hospital in memory of Victoria Maharani in 1883. Dr. V. Timpani developed this hospital in a full pledged manner. In the beginning nurses came from America to serve in the hospital as well as orphans. In memory of wife of Luther Ford established Preston institution in Hunumakonda in 1919 and later it had been shifted to Jangaon which was in Nalgonda district in those days.

Hyderabad Vicariate consisting of all Telangana districts and some parts of Coastal Andhra came into being. It developed under PIME missionaries, as a diocese in 1886. Then on-wards the Mission developed even more. The number of Catholics increased in various parts of the diocese and the mission stations. This called for bifurcation of the Uri's in 1933 and converted as a Diocese in 1937. After the bifurcation of Vijayawada diocese, Hyderabad Diocese was left with Telangana District. The study will deal Kurnool district. The Hyderabad - Vijayawada Railway line-work had brought a good number of catholic workers to the main Railway junction / station like Kazipet, Dornakal and Khammam. The Baptism Registers kept at Kazipet reveals the presence of Catholic community the since 1887. During 1890-1930, a good number of Catholics families migrated from Guntur and other part of the Coastal Andhra to Telangana in search of good cultivable land for their livelihood. Wherever they found good black soil, they settled there. The earlyMissionaries helped these Migrant Catholics communities in their settlements and took care of their spiritual needs.

Regarding the literature concerned to this field so much work has been done by the distinguished scholars on the history of Christian missionary services in Kurnool district of Andhra Pradesh. Besides that number of Ph.D. thesis's and dissertations produced on Christian missionary issues, tried to throw light on the Christian missionaries in modern India. Few studies tried to establish a link between the emergence of history of Christian missionary services and relative deprivation, social mobility and reference group theory, though it is inadequate in understanding the Christian movements in its totalitarian perspectives.

It is not purely a theoretical framework, but a systematic, scientific approach and meticulous devices have been formulated to draw certain inferences based on Christian struggle for social justice in Andhra Pradesh in general, Kurnool district in particular. At the same time how they were experienced dexterous problems by upper caste people was another pertinent issue. The study summarizes different views of various writers, eminent scholars like W.P. Hares and Archdeacon F.F. Gledstone and Sundaresan C.S. a renowned Christian intellectual, contributed number of articles and books on Christian missionary perspectives and championed the cause and projected the relevance and need for social change of Christians in Andhra Pradesh.

R. Herbert[7] Lessons from the life of Jesus*: Practical Insights from the Gospelsliving belief books, (2017)*, Rather than simply retelling the story of the life of Jesus, this book focuses on some of the details of the Gospel narratives that are easy to miss, but which can help us to better understand his life and teachings. In each case there are lessons we can learn and apply. Enrich your understanding of the life and work of Jesus and take away lessons you can apply today.

James Elisha Taneti[8] *(2011), History of the Telugu Christians: A Bibliography,*Christian communities in the state of Andhra Pradesh of south India and the Telugu Christians in Diaspora have passed their stories from one generation to the next by oral traditions as well as in scattered texts. These memories have sustained Telugu Christian communities for over four centuries. Yet there has been no significant attempt made to compile a comprehensive history of the Telugu Christians until James Elisha Taneti's History of the Telugu Christians: A Bibliography. This annotated bibliography lists more than 700 published and unpublished textual sources related to the history of Telugu Christians from south India. Opening a window into the histories of 15 mission societies from the North American region, History of the Telugu Christians lists monographs, journal articles, letters, reports, minutes and the proceedings of missionary conferences, unpublished theses, dissertations, souvenirs, and manuscripts. The documents selected by Taneti were written or printed in the English or Telugu languages by native Christians and western missionaries. Aimed to facilitate research and writing on Telugu Christians, Taneti's insightful historiographical analysis and comprehensive list of bibliographic sources offer seminarians, historians of Christianity, and scholars of India the opportunity to study closely the meeting of East and West and the religious history of India through the founding and evolution of this community.

Geevarghese Coorilos Nalunnakkal,[9] *The Joy Of The Gospel Of Life: Contextual Reflections On Mission And Evangelism, (2016)*, Ecumenical missiology has travelled quite far since Edinburgh (1910). It has undergone sweeping changes ever since. The accent on missiology has shifted from colonial modes to postcolonial paradigms; from classical modes to contextual modes; from monolithic Euro-centric ways of thinking and doing mission to polyphonic expressions of missiology; from confessional slants to truly ecumenical perspectives; and from human centeredness to life-centric missiology. It is these shifts in mission thinking that this book attempts to reflect on. "Bishop Coorilos' approaches are not always based on anger and cries alone, but also on the joy that is generated while standing with the oppressed people in fighting for their dignity and liberation; when we are committed to the mission of solidarity with the marginalized, and when we move 'together towards life'. This has equipped him to write this book with a broad vision of the ecumenical movement. It is my humble honor to commend this volume for the purpose of rejuvenating the ecumenical movement and re-energizing mission with 'the joy of the Gospel of Life."

ArunaGnanadason Edwin Samuel Jayakumar,[10] *(2016), The Christian Imperative And A Moral Challenge*, NCCI strongly believes in a corrupt free society. While it challenges the government and its related agencies on issues of corruption, it is important to note that it is time to look into corruption and the corrupt practices prevailing within our churches and its institutions. We need to find mechanisms to address this very critical issue which contradicts and distorts the authentic witness and mission of Christians."

Monodeep Daniel[11] *(2016), Religions in India: the Vision of B.R. Ambedkar*, Dr. B.R. Ambedkar's personality (1891-1956) towers over others as we begin to discover him more and more. He is widely venerated as an icon of the Dalit movement.

Akepogu Jammanna, Pasala Sudhaka,[12] *(2016), Dalits' Struggle for Social Justice in Andhra Pradesh* (1956-2008), The complete alienation of Dalits from resources like land, water, and agricultural implements has led to the collective demand for an equal share in productivity. This book discusses the range of socio-economic and cultural problems faced by the Dalit community. The movement advancing the rights of Dalits took place both before and after independence, however they varied in intensity, and concerned land ownership and fair wages, self-respect, social dignity, and the demand for equal rights. This movement appeared to have significantly changed the very mindset and attitude of upper caste people to restrain themselves and not to resort to any discrimination or humiliation of Dalits. However, this seems to have been only a temporary phenomenon, and the practice of suppression and humiliation continues today. This book explores the circumstances of Dalits in the Indian state of Andhra Pradesh, and the current efforts attempting to achieve more social equality for the caste here.

Godwin Shiri,[13] ***(2015), Christian Dalit Women,*** The book places before the readers the very pathetic condition in which Dalit women live under continued caste and gender oppression in rural areas, especially in the vast drought prone region of Deccan, south India.

Bouvert Regulas[14] ***(2015), Christian Philosophy Of Religion,*** Philosophy of religion is a general term, which includes the study of any religion in the world with philosophical perspective. Philosophy of religion with Christian perspective went through its three important stages in the 20th century.

Jonathan Masih,[15] ***(2015), Contribution Of Missionaries Towards Education In India,*** The book focuses on the nexus between Christian missionary Endeavour and development of modern education in India, a system of education we now take for granted.

Felix Wilfred,[16] ***(2014), Christians For A Better India,*** India means 1.2 billion people, one sixth of humanity, with the largest concentration of the poor in the world. There are competing dreams and imaginations about its future. The book is an attempt to look at the burning issues of today and hope with the poor and the marginalized for a different India Unlike the one the pundits of neo-liberalism imagine.

Dionysius Rasquinha, S.J.,[17] **(2013),** ***The Dalit Quest,*** This book is appropriately titled The Dalit Quest. No doubt, it is a well-documented journey with the Dalits from Brokenness to Wholeness. It traces the path of historical analysis towards theological response.

Monodeep Daniel Helen Everett,[18] **(2014),** ***Christian Studies,*** If our aim is to build an integrated and a cohesive national society, then every religion must inform its faith and practices to general public. One way to start this is with our students.

John C.B. Webster,[19] **(2013),** ***Dalit Pastoral Ministry: A Training Manual,*** The Dalit Pastoral Ministry Training Manual is a great resource for those attempting to pursue a more relevant and meaningful pastoral ministry among Dalit Christians. It has a very practical approach without being shallow, enabling dioceses and institutions to conduct workshops for Pastors among Dalit Christians. Individual pastors and social workers among Dalits will also benefit from reading the manual and can find many insights that they can put into practice in their ministry Dalit Pastoral Ministry provides both a practical training model and some valuable resource materials for church leaders and theological educators to use in training clergy and lay leaders in pastoral ministry to Christian and other Dalits. It is based on two important premises. The first is that, because of the history of untouchability they have had to endure, Dalits" whether in Dalit or mixed congregations "have special spiritual needs and struggles which other Christians do not have. The other is that pastoral ministry to Dalits cannot be a ministry of the pastor alone, but must be a ministry of the congregation as a whole if it is to be healing and empowering. Dalit Pastoral Ministry and the Kolkata workshop that produced it have been built upon earlier works, The Pastor to Dalits (ISPCK 1995) and From Role to Identity: Dalit Christian Women in Transition (ISPCK 1997) as well as upon many prior workshops with pastors and lay leaders.

Thomas Varghese,[20] (2013), ***Abuse Of Women in Indian Christian Families,*** Some Christian women in families face terror on two sides: In their historical culture lie the ill-treatment of women and girls due to inheritance by sons that leads to the dowry system, abortion of the female foetus and the denigration of the women across society. In their present lie the inroads of modern popular culture with the self-saving and selfishness that erode for females the justice God wants for all people. On both sides, there rests a tendency to keep women from the decisions that affect their own destiny, leaving them vulnerable to neglect and abuse in many areas of life-above all in the family.

Samuel Matthew [21](2013), ***Leadership Development and Practice,*** Organisational success In today world depends largely on leadership. Even the Church needs efficient leaders. It is undisputedly true that there is a leadership crisis in the Church today. It may be because of the leaders themselves, the life or organisation of the Church or the particular leadership models, methods, style and strategies employed. Whatever the reasons may be, the Church worldwide— particularly in India is on the quest for revitalised and re-emphasised leadership. This book, which is an expanded and revised version of the author' s book in Malayalam titled, Leadership Models, focuses on what the Bible says about leadership and delegation and gives valuable insights into leadership development in the Church.

Godwin Shiri[22] (2012), ***Dalit Christians,*** Dalit Christians: A Saga of Faith and Pathos is another scholarly well-researched socio-economic, politico-religious and empirical study of Dalit Christians in five villages in Karnataka, namely Hacholli and Beerahalli (in Bellary district) and Talmari, Gangavar and Malkapur (in Raichur district), the two districts bring located in the north-eastern region of Karnataka and generally known to be very backward areas. It is a case study of select rural Dalit congregations.

Pramod Roa,[23] (2013), ***Religio-Cultural Changes and Continuities,*** This book investigates the nature and pattern of religio-cultural continuities and changes in the life of Christian Dalits in Telangana during 1884-1960. In other words, it covers virtually all aspects of religio-culture persistence and transformation of Dalit Christians in Telangana.

Robert Eric Frykenberg[24] (2013), ***Christians and Missionaries in India: Cross-Cultural Communication since 1500,*** The assumption that Christianity in India is nothing more than a European, western, or colonial imposition is open to challenge. Those who now think and write about India are often not aware that Christianity is a non-Western religion, that in India this has always been so, and that there are now more Christians in Africa and Asia than in the West. Recognizing that more understanding of the separate histories and cultures of the many Christian communities in India will be needed before a truly comprehensive history of Christianity in India can be written, this volume addresses particular aspects of cultural contact, with special reference to caste, conversion, and colonialism. Subjects addressed range from Sanskrit grammar to populist Pentecostalism, Urdu polemics and Tamil poetry.

Mary John,[25] (2011), ***Indian Catholic Christians and Nationalism,*** The book focuses on the dilemmas that India's freedom struggle posed for the Catholic Christian community in India. This work brings to light an eclipsed aspect of Indian Christian historiography. It can also be viewed as a contribution to the study of Indian nationalism. By highlighting the role played by the Christian community in India, it makes the nationalist historiography more complete, nuanced and sensitive to the contribution made by the minorities to the Indian society.

Rohan P. Gideon,[26] (2011), ***Child Labour In India: Challenges For Theological Thinking And Christian Ministry In India,*** This book brings to light many of the forgotten concerns of children in our theological thinking and church ministry. While children are very much part of our families, churches, society and God's kingdom, many of us continue to believe that childhood is an insignificant stage. As a result, today's theologies do not give any serious attention to the issue of children's rights. This book challenges these notions in the light of the Scriptures and the recent developments in the field of child theology.

AkhetoSema[27], (2011), *Understanding The Nature And Purpose Of Christian Religious Education,* Christian religious education is holistic in nature and purpose as it views humans in the completeness of their humanity and focuses on their temporal and eternal existence. The book addresses the issues and concerns underlying Christian religious education.

B. Sunil Vara Kumar,[28] (2010), *Dynamics Of Power Sharing Between Mala And Madiga In Church,* In this book, the author focuses on power-sharing between Mala and Madiga Christians in four congregations in the CSI Rayalaseema diocese.

Rowena Robinson[29] (2003), Christians of India,This book is dense with information and well structured. It gives a good overview of the extraordinary variety of Christian life in India and maps out the terrain for further research any serious student of Christianity in India will find this book very valuable. It ought to be read - however unlikely it is for this to happen - by all those who are contesting the place of Christianity in contemporary India' - *Journal of Contemporary Religion* 'This volume, which also provides an excellent select bibliography, is therefore to be welcomed by all those interested in the study of Indian Christianity' - *The Journal of the Royal Anthropological Institute.* Christians of India is an important study on Christian communities in India. Beginning with the authors critical scrutiny on existing literature on Christianity in India, which she feels has suffered from enormous neglect - a neglect that has extended to the study of all non-Hindu communities. The author traces the roots of this neglect to the roots of Sociology and Anthropology, from the moment these disciplines came to India.

Adrian Hastings,[30](2000), *A World History of Christianity,* Christianity is the most global of religions. However, most books on the subject fail to do justice to the history of Christianity outside Europe and North America. This prodigious work provides the first genuinely global one-volume study of the rise, development, and impact of the Christian faith. Written by an international team of specialists, this comprehensive volume covers the full breadth of Christian history while also taking seriously the geographical diversity of the story: extensive chapters cover North America, Latin America, Europe, Africa, India, China and its neighbors, and Australia and the Pacific. Though unified in scope, these chapters each focus on what matters most in the specific time and place covered, ensuring that readers are introduced to the major themes—social, theological, political, and cultural that together constitute Christianity's role in world history. Ideally suited for classroom study as well as for independent reading, A World History of Christianity will serve as the definitive study of church history for the coming generation worldwide.

Abraham Vazhayil Thomas,[31] (1974), Christians in Secular India, it Seeks to explore the role of the Christian community in the Indian secular state. Although the Indian Christian community forms only 2.4 percent of the population, it has played an important part in the social, educational, political, and religious spheres of the recent life of India.

Charles E. Farhadian[32] *(2012), Introducing World Christianity,* This explains the interdisciplinary introduction offers students a truly global overview of the worldwide spread and impact of Christianity. It is enriched throughout by detailed historic and ethnographic material, showing how broad themes within Christianity have been adopted and adapted by Christian denominations within each major region of the world.

W.P. Hares[33] (1952) *published in book entitled* 'A History of the Christian Church' of the First Six Centuries' in which discussed the history of Christian Church during Apostolic age, then followed upto Sixth Century wherein he presented vividly the general obstacles encountered by the Church in its expansion. The whole work concluded with the Christian faith since the early times to the end of Sixth Century B.C.

Archdeacon F.F. Gledstone and Sundaresan C.S.[34] (1956) in their book 'Church History of India and Pakistan' published in Telugu by the Christian Literature Society dealt with the historical evidences of the entgry of Christianity in undivided India and how this religion spread to various parts in India. This book also brought out how the missionaries interacted with native Kings and the persecutions faced by them.

J.W.C. Wand[35] (1959) *in his work the Church Today'* discussed elaborately three important aspects like The Church in Society', 'the Constitution of the Church', 'the Soul of the Church' and answers to some special questions. In Church and Society, he discussed the concept of public welfare and Church and the culture and the Church and politics. In the 'Constitution of the Church' he discussed the growth of organisation, growth of diversity in the Church, the Anglican situation and return to unity. In 'the Soul of the Church', he discussed the idea of Church, worship and evangelism. Finally he concluded the work with answering to few questions relating to Church and History, the origins of the Ministry, tradition and Salvation.

Phillippee Maury[36] **(1959)** ***in his book 'Politics and Evangelism'*** presented a systematic study of the subject of Evangelism and politics. What he had undertaken is, in a way self-examination. The author tried to explain that, through political action, Christians fulfill diaconal responsibility. He believed that social service is the most natural response to the second commandment. "Love thy neighbor". He also says that those, who cannot love his country, cannot love the heavenly abode in which they believe. He added that there is dual citizenship in heaven and on earth.

B.E. Devaraj[37] **(1969)** ***brought out a work entitled 'History of Christianity in India'*** in which he discussed about the history of Christian Church how it spread to eastern countries and the establishment of Roman Catholic Missions. He also presented an interaction of Jessuit Missionaries with Mogul Emperors and services of William Carey and the establishment of Churches belonged Europe and America. He made brief how the Indian Church accepted the responsibility of evangelism in India. However, the work is in Telugu language.

Andre Bieler[38] **(1970)** ***in his book 'Politics of Hope' described man's place in the modern global world,*** and the collective responsibility of Christians for development and discernment. Here the author tried to explain the responsibility of the Church towards the world's suffering. The individual's social relationship, in cultural, economic and political life is also discussed.

M.E. Gibbs[39] **(1972)** ***in his work The Anglican Church in India (1600-1970) discussed the beginning of the Anglican Church in India,*** its Bishops and Missionaries and Bishop Cotton's Missionary work in Coastal Andhra. It also highlighted the independence and Church Union Movement in South India and further adaptation and union movement in North India.The services of missionaries of Anglican Church in the field of Education, Medical and Evangelism and the establishment of various institutions in India were presented in this work.

John Howard Yoder[40] **(1973)** ***in his book presented a discussion about the Kingdom coming,*** Christ and power. The author also presented a principle that the Christian who accepts his subjection to the Government retains his moral independence and judgment. He expressed his view that Government is not self-justifying and whatever Government exists is ordered by God. Christian pacifists hate violence and anticipate the people of the Country to live peacefully.

Paul B. Henry's[41] (1974) ***book 'Politics for Evangelicals'*** is a combination of his academic training, political experience and spiritual commitment. He explains the impact of Christ's life on the political and social conditions. He believed that practicing politics is an art. He explained that a leader in a community, and an activist who gives his time and energy sacrificially for the wellbeing of another, is a Good Samaritan.

Solomon Thanugundla[42] (1977) ***in his work 'Structures of the Church in Andhra Pradesh'*** discussed about Catholic Churches and the steps towards the foundation of the Vicariate of Bijapur, its extension and limitation. In this he presented a brief history of the Telugu land and sowing the seeds of salvation among the Telugus and steps taken towards the erection of the vicariates in Andhra Pradesh. In his second part the work, discussed exclusively the present structures of the Church in Andhra Pradesh and role of Congregations in implantation of the Local Churches and so on.

Andre Dumas[43] (1978) ***began his book 'Political Theology and the life of the Church'*** with a series of lectures which he gave as visiting professor in the University of Lyons. The author is in view that politics is a necessary dimension of the life of the Church. He gave one of Jesus' famous reply to the Pharisees (Holy Bible, Mathew 22: Verses 17-21) Render therefore to Caesar the things that are Caesar's and to the God, the things that are God's. He says that Jesus tells them that they are already Caesar's subjects and urge them to become God's servants. His reply has been understood to establish the basic character of the separation between God and Caesar, spiritual and temporal things.

Mathal Zacharia's(1981)[44] ***'The Christian Presence in India'*** is a collection of essays. He commented on all the forms of the Christian presence in India with theological and sociological insights. He agrees that election is always an opportunity for the people to assert their will and politics is a game of relative choices. He is of the view that expediency, power of money and manipulation have become the order of the day and service, justice, principles and ideology have become nonessential. He is of the opinion that there is need for leaders to foster vision, courage, character and conviction in them.

K. Felix[45] (1985) ***dissertation on 'A Study of Churches in Anantapur District'*** to Sri Krishnadevaraya University, Anantapur wherein he presented very briefly the Art and Architecture of Churches both Protestant and

Catholic Churches in Anantapur Town. He also touched how Christianity spread in Anantapur Town.

Solomon Doraiswamy[46]**(1986)** ***published a book entitled 'Christianity in India - A Unique and Universal Mission'*** presented the true position of the Christian enterprise in India. This work is a response to the misrepresentations, adverse and even erroneous remarks made in a publication under the auspices of the Ramakrishna Mission entitled 'Christianity in India - A Critical Study'. The author never intended this book as an Apologia, but he desired to present the Truth regarding the Christian faith and its mission in and to the world, in a spirit of love - the Spirit of Christ. The book went on in a question and answer format like why Christianity in India? Why Global Ecumenism, Why Christian Mission to the Tribals in India, and so on.

Arthur Mayhew [47]**(1988)** ***in his work 'Christianity in India'*** presented the history of Christianity but briefly touched the contributions of few missionaries like William Carey and the survival of Christianity during certain Movements like Sepoy Meeting and the reactionary influence on Christianity.

Paul D. Wiebe[48] **(1988)** ***in his book 'Christians in Andhra Pradesh'*** brought out the services of Mennonite Church Missionaries in the drought prone Mahaboobnagar District of Andhra Pradesh. The author discussed various aspects relating to the missionary activities, recruitment of Hindus as Christians, Church interaction with community, leadership and development. It is an exclusive study of Mennonite Church in Mahaboobnagar district.

Prasanna Kumari[49] **(1995)** ***in her edited book 'Liberating Witness'*** published in two volumes is a collection of various articles written by Theologians, academicians, ordained Presbyters and other laity. This covered various aspects like the Church and the Congregational life, Role of Church in Society, Evangelism, Theological Education, Mission and Ecumenism, Churches Constitutions, Church and Dalits, women and Church mission, Churches Social Action and so on.

P.Vijayalakshmi's[50] **(1999)** research on 'The Rise and Spread of Church Missionary Society in Krishna District with special reference to Machilipatnam,' presented the history and spread of Christianity in Andhra region and the Church Missionary Society activities in Machilipatnam of Krishna District.

The above review of literature shows clearly that all the above studies were mostly macroscopic and touched vast aspects relating to Christianity, Christian Missionaries and their services. Further, the scope of the above studies did not cover the missionary work done in Andhra Pradesh in general and backward and drought prone Region in particular. So far, no attempt was made to study Church of South India in general and a micro level study specifically on Rayalaseema Diocese of Church of South India in particular. Hence, an humble attempt is made in this thesis to study the genesis, growth and activities of Rayalaseema Diocese of Church of South India.

Kurnool district is one of the backward districts of Rayalaseema region in Andhra Pradesh, with a scheduled caste population 17.81% of the total population of the district. In spite of the constitutional guarantee and safe guards to the Dalit Christians, they never had an opportunity to enjoy the privileges like social equality, access to economic standardization and participation in the political and public life. Atrocities and attacks on Dalit have become a common phenomenon in the district. The oppressive methods imposed on Christian Groups, once again establishes the upper caste dominance and political empowerment of caste Hindus in rural areas of Kurnool district. This clearly speaks, mere constitutional guarantees does not serve any purpose, unless and until the state and civil society feels it as a very important aspect to uplift of the Dalit.Hence, an attempt is made to study the role of Christian Missionaries in Kurnool and the growth and development of Christianity in Rayalaseema region of Andhra Pradesh.

The present study is an attempt to focus on the History of Christian Missionaries in Kurnool district of Andhra Pradesh as mentioned below. Christians and their movements and their struggle for social justice and its influence on the socio-economic life of the people in the Kurnool district of Andhra Pradesh. Any social movement has to grapple not only with the dimensions of genesis, ideology, collective mobilization, organization, and leadership, but also with the conceptual problems relating to social change.

- To trace the origin of Christianity in India, its growth in India from a historical perspective.
- To discuss the growth, development and leadership of Christianity in Andhra in general particularly Rayalaseema region.
- To examine the contributions of Christian missionary services to the development Andhra Pradesh society and culture as well as Kurnool district.

- To highlight the socio-economic contribution of Christian missionaries in the upliftment of downtrodden communities through education, health and employment.

The present study covers different parameters and paradigms of Christian Missionary services and its impact on society and also the role played by various Christian groups in consolidating their position and safe guard their identities and interests. To fulfill the objectives, both primary and secondary sources are used for the present study. The literature brought out by the missionaries, the manuals, annual reports, magazines, souvenirs etc., brought out by the Christian associations are consulted. The secondary sources like books, journals published and are unpublished materials are consulted. Books like The Development of Christianity, History of the world Christian movements, History of Christian Missionaries, Constantine and Pagan Rome, etc are consulted. The present study is confined to Kurnool district of Andhra Pradesh. An attempt is made to study the problem in historical perspective.

Christians have for many centuries occupied a deeply ambiguous place within Indian society. Especially in Andhra Pradesh, it is more rampant because of the ignorance and lack of social exposure resulted in attacks on Dalit Christians from the ages. The Christian community is facing a serious threat from the caste Hindus across the state. As Christians certainly occupy a subaltern position in Indian society, the series could have had a significant impact upon our understanding of Christian history. The fair their strength and impetus from the religious awakening all over the world during 19th century, these denominations found economically backward, socially downtrodden and religiously deprived communities in Andhra Pradesh. They were encouraged even astonished by the stunning and surprising results that their work accomplished in these areas. Under this background an attempt is made to study the role of Christian missionaries in Kurnool district, Andhra Pradesh.

References

1. Azariah V.A. India and the Christian Movement. Christian Literature Society, Madras, 1936.
2. Christian Weiss G. What is Christianity. A back to The Bible Publication, The Good News Broadcasting Society, Inc. 1958.
3. Kuria Kose M.K. Historv of Christianity in India. Source Materials, The Christian Literature Society, Madras, 1982.
4. Ryburn W.M. The Theory and method of Christian Education. The Senate of Seramoore College, the Christian Literature Society, Part Town, Madras, 1960.

5. Thomas M.M. Christian Participation in Nation Buildina. The Christian Literature Society, Madras-3, 1967.
6. ZachariaMathai Christian Presence in India. The Christian Literature Society, Madras,1981
7. R. Herbert Lessons from the life of Jesus: Practical Insights from the Gospels living belief books, 2017.
8. James Elisha Taneti 2011, History of the Telugu Christians: A Bibliography, Scarecrow Press.
9. Geevarghese Coorilos Nalunnakkal, The Joy Of The Gospel Of Life: Contextual Reflections On Mission And Evangelism, 2016, Indian Society for Promoting Christian Knowledge (ISPCK).
10. Aruna Gnanadason Edwin Samuel Jayakumar, 2016, The Christian Imperative And A Moral Challenge,
11. Monodeep Daniel 2016, Religions in India: the Vision of B.R. Ambedkar, Indian Society for Promoting Christian Knowledge (ISPCK).
12. Akepogu Jammanna, Pasala Sudhaka, 2016, Dalits' Struggle for Social Justice in Andhra Pradesh (1956-2008), Cambridge Scholars Publishing.
13. Godwin Shiri, 2015Christian Dalit Women, ISPCK.
14. Bouvert Regulas 2015, Christian Philosophy Of Religion, Indian Society for Promoting Christian Knowledge (ISPCK).
15. Jonathan Masih, 2015, Contribution Of Missionaries Towards Education In India, Ethical & Moral Universal Issues, ISPCK.
16. Felix Wilfred, 2014, Christians For A Better India, Ethical & Moral Universal Issues, ISPCK.
17. Dionysius Rasquinha, S.J., 2013 The Dalit Quest, ISPCK.
18. Monodeep Daniel Helen Everett, 2014, Christian Studies, ISPCK/DBS
19. John C.B. Webster, 2013, Dalit Pastoral Ministry: A Training Manual, ISPCK
20. Thomas Varghese, 2013, Abuse Of Women in Indian Christian Families, The Amazon Book Review
21. Samuel Matthew, 2013 Leadership Development and Practice, Ethical & Moral Universal Issues, ISPCK..
22. Godwin Shiri 2012, Dalit Christians, Dalit Christians: A Saga, ISPCK/NCCI.
23. PramodRoa, 2012, Religio-Cultural Changes and Continuities, Ethical & Moral Universal Issues.
24. Robert Eric Frykenberg 2013, Christians and Missionaries in India, William B. Eerdmans Publishing Company.
25. Mary John, 2011, Indian Catholic Christians and Nationalism, Ethical & Moral Universal Issues, ISPCK.
26. Rohan P. Gideon, 2011, Child Labour in India: Challenges For Theological Thinking And Christian Ministry In India, ISPCK/NCCI.
27. Akheto Sema, 2011, Understanding The Nature And Purpose Of Christian Religious Education, Ethical & Moral Universal Issues.

28. B. Sunil Vara Kumar, 2010, Dynamics Of Power Sharing Between Mala And Madiga In Church, Ethical & Moral Universal Issues.
29. Rowena Robinson2003, Christians of India, SAGE Publications Pvt. Ltd; 1 edition (11 September 2003)
30. Adrian Hastings, 2000, A World History of Christianity, Wiliam b. Eerdmana publishing company /Cambridge, U.K.
31. Abraham Vazhayil Thomas, 1974, Christians in Secular India ,Fairleigh Dickinson Univ Press.
32. Charles E. Farhadian 2012, Introducing World Christianity, John Wiley & Sons.
33. W.P. Hares (1952) published in book entitled 'A History of the Christian Church'Madras
34. Archdeacon F.F. Gledstone and Sundaresan C.S. (1956) in their book 'Church History of India and Pakistan'published by Telugu by the Christian literature society.
35. J.W.C. Wand (1959) The Church Today' discussed elaborately three important aspects like The Church in Society', 'the Constitution of the Church'
36. Phillippee Maury (1959) in his book 'Politics and Evangelism' Doubleday publisher.
37. B. E. Devaraj, History of the Church in India, Telugu Theological Literature Board, 1969.
38. Andre Bieler (1970) 'Politics of Hope', Grand Rapids: Eerdmana, 1974.
39. M.E. Gibbs (1972) in his work The Anglican Church in India (1600-1970), New Delhi
40. John Howard Yoder (1973) about the Kingdom coming, Christ and power.
41. Paul B. Henry's (1974), Politics for Evangelicals valley forge, PA:Judson Press
42. Solomon Thanugundla (1977) 'Structures of the Church in Andhra Pradesh'An historical judicial study (Secundrabad India: Karunasri printers).
43. Andre Dumas (1978) began his book 'Political Theology and the life of the Church' SCM Press,
44. Mathal Zacharia (1981) The Christian Presence in India' Madras
45. K. Felix (1985) 'A Study of Churches in Anantapur District' unpublished M.Phil dissertation, Sri Krishnadevaraya University, Anantapur.
46. Solomon Doraiswamy (1986) 'Christianity in India - A Unique and Universal Mission.Madras pp. 168.
47. Arthur Mayhew (1988) 'Christianity in India'New Delhi.
48. Paul D. Wiebe (1988)'Christians in Andhra Pradesh' Published for Christian Institute for the Study of Religion and Society, Bangalore, by Christian Literature Society, 1988
49. Prasanna Kumari, ed, 1995, Libarating witness :Dr.K.Rajaratnam's Platinum Birthday Anniversary Commemoration VoL-1 Madras Gurukul, p-13
50. P.Vijayalakshmi (1999)'The Rise and Spread of Church Missionary Society in Krishna District with special reference to Machilipatnam'un published M.Phil dissertation, Nagarjuna University, Guntur.

Chapter - II

Christian Missionaries in India

Christianity is one of the ancient religions of the world. It is the religion originated from Jerusalem and derived from Jesus Christ of Nazareth, based on the Holy Bible as sacred scripture and professed by Eastern Roman Catholic and Protestant Bodies.[1] The travel of Christianity from Rome to India was made possible due to historic trade relations between the Roman empire and India in the first century A.D. Strabo, who lived during the time of Augustus, makes reference to trade between the Roman Empire and India.[2] "I was with Gallus at the time he was prefect of Egypt, and accompanied him as far as Syene and the frontiers of Ethiopia, and I found that about one hundred and twenty ships sail from Myos Hormos to India." Pliny the Elder (24/24-79 A.D) also mentions voyages from the Roman empire to India and the Pepper trade between these two countries[3] during the beginning century of Jesus Christ Christianity was brought to India by St. Thomas, one of the twelve disciples of Jesus Christ. These twelve disciples of Jesus Christ in Jerusalem divided the regions of the world that each one of them might go to regions which fell to his lot. Accordingly India fell to St. Thomas (also named as judas Thomas and Didymus) but he did not wish to go saying that through weakness of the flesh he could not travel. "How can I, who am a Hebrew, go and preach the truth among Indians."[4] But the source material speak that the Lord Jesus Christ appeared to him by night and said to him, 'Fear not, Thomas, go to India and preach the word there, for my grace is with thee.' But would not obey and said: 'Send me where thou will but somewhere else! For I am not going to the Indians' And as he thus spoke and thought, it happened that a certain merchant was there who had come from India. His name was Abban and he has been sent by King Gundaphorus and had received orders from him to buy a Carpenter to bring him back to him. On the following morning St. Thomas prayed and be sought the Lord and said; 'I go wither thou wilt, Lord Jesus; thy will be done! and he went off to Abban the merchant.[5]

St. Thomas came to South India through Persia in 52 A.D.and reached Kranganur in Malabar (Kerala State) and started preaching the Gospel of Jesus Christ and converted four Brahmin families namely Kali, Kailankaru, Sankarapuri and Pakalomattam. These were the first Christian families in India during the first century.[6] He preached the word of God for a decade and baptized the people. He built five Churches and set two men over them and then went to Mylapore (Madras) and was proclaiming the word of God. A certain captain of King Misdaeus (Mazdais) had conspired to put him to death.' And arising he took Thomas with him outside the city and a few armed soldiers followed him. And at once the four smote him and slew him and wrapping in fine robes and many fine linen clothes they laid him in the tomb.[7] There is an another version to tell about his death, that he was speared to death by the Purohits when he was preaching the gospel. The body of St. Thomas buried in Mylapore very moderately in the Church which his disciples and followers built for him. Mar Solomon, a Nestorian Bishop in his 'Book of Bee' written in 13th Century A.D. gave an account of the St.Thomas Tradition. The book says, Thomas was from Jerusalem of the Tribe of India. He taught the Pursians, Medes and the Indians and because he baptised the daughter of the king of the Indians the King stabbed him with a spear and he died'. He was buried in Mahluph, a city in the land of the Indians.[8]

Christians in Malabar

Whatever the truth about St. Thomas the Apostle may be, it seems very probable that there were Christians in Malabar before the time of Nestorius. The vigorous trade between the region and the Roman Empire led to the arrival of Christian Merchants. This is confirmed by the tradition of Thomas of Cana or Knaye Thomas, who is said to have arrived at Cranganore with about 400 Christians including several Priests and Decaons, about 345 A.D. His name probably means Thomas the Merchant'. About 522 A.D. another Christian Merchant, this time forAlexandria, visited Malabar. This was Cosmos Indicopieuster. He later became a Monk and wrote in his book some mention of his travels. He said that he found Christians in the land of Malabar, where peper grows and that at a place called Caliani there was a Bishop appointed from Persia. He also a Christian Congregation in Ceylon with a Presbyter appointed from Persia. But this Church perhaps consisting mainly of foreign merchants, did not survive. The Church in South India continued to receive its Bishops from Persia and was consequently Nestorian till 1590.[9]

Destruction of Jerusalem (A.D. 70)

In Jerusalem, James the brother of Lord Jesus Christ was already dead, having been put to death by the High Priest Annas in 62 A.D. as the Jewish Historian Josephus tells us. Jewish discontent with Roman Rule resulted in a great revolt in A.D. 66. After one of the most prolonged and terrible siegas in history, Jerusalem was taken by the Roman genera! Titus, son of the Emperor Vespasian in A.D. 70. The temple was destroyed and the sacrifices finally ceased. It was not till 1947 that a Jewish State again came into existence. The result of the events was the final separation of Christianity from its Jewish roots. Henceforth,the Christian Church stood out as a quite separate, mainly gentile community.[10] After the assassination of St.Thomas in 62 A.D. at Madras,the Christians in India established and maintained religious relations with Christians in other countries like East Syria, Mesopotamia and Pursia.Those Christians who came to South India from Pursia settled down in South India and became Syrian Christians and converted the fishermen who were untouchables in that area into Christianity.[11]

During the Patriarchate of Shahlufa and Papa (295-300 A.D) Dudi (David), Bishop of Basra on the Persian Gulf, an eminent doctor came to India and evangelised many people.[12] During 300 A.D. Pantoenus, a philosopher of the Stoic School was appointed as a herald of the Gospel of Christ to the nations of the Far East and was sent as far as India by Demetrius, Bishop of Alexandria.[13] During 345-410 A.D, Frumentius of Alexandria who visited India as an episcopal authority became a preacher of Gospel and built several Churches in interior India.[14] Cosmas Indicopleustes, a Nestorian travelled to India in 520-525 A.D. He wrote a book namely 'Christian Topography' in which he gave details concerning the Christians he found in Malabar and Sri Lanka...... '. In the country called Male (Malabar), where the pepper grows, there is also a Church'.[15] Isidore's writings reveal the event of European knowledge about India in the Seventh Century A.D. and the tradition that the Apostle Bartholemew came to India. He was also familiar with the tradition of St. Thomas martyrdom in India.[16] In the year 825 A.D, a merchant called Jacob came and dwelt in India with two Syrian Bishops.

Christians were orthodox jacobites in their habits from the beginning of the preaching of the Apostle Thomas. The two sets of Tarisapalli copper plates available with orthodox Church and the Mar Thoma Church, most of these plates were inscribed in Tamil-Malayalam but two plates were written in Pahlavi and Arabic. Both sets, constituting of the earliest details concerning the Christian community in India which also revealed that grants were made by Ayyanadikal, King of Venad, to the new Church at Quilon, built by Marwan Sabriso in 849 A.D and the high social status enjoyed by Christians in that part of the country.[17] Friar Menetillus, a Dominican, forwarded a copy of a letter from John of Monte Cornivo in which the conditions of Christians in India during the period between 1292-1293 A.D is described. 'In the regions by Sea are many saracenes, and they have great influence but there are few of them in the interior. There are a very few Christians, and Jews and they are of little weight. The people persecute much the Christians and all who bear the Christian Name."[18] In the year 1291 A.D John of Monte Corvino departed from Tauris, a city of Persians and proceeded to India.He stayed in the country of India for thirteen months and baptized in different places about one hundred persons.[19] Odoric of Pordenone wrote an account of his travels in India especially Malabar, Pandarani, Cranganore, Quilon and Mylapore in 1324 A.D'. I came to the land, the name thereof is Minibar, and the pepper groweth nowhere else in the world but there. In that forest there were two cities called Flandrina (Pandarani) and the other Cyngilin (Cranganove). In the city of Flandrina some of the inhabitants are Jews and some are Christians and between these two cities there is always internal war, but the result is always that the Christians beat them and overcome the Jews.[20] John de Mariglonni gives an account of his travels through the areas of India occupied by the St. Thomas Christians. "....And sailing on the feast of St. Stephen we navigated the Indian sea until Palm Sunday and when arrived at a very noble city of India called Columbum (Quilon) where the whole world's pepper is produced and the proprietors are Christians of St. Thomas. And these are the masters of the public steel-yard, from which I derived a prerequisite of my office as Pope's legate, every month a hundred gold fan, and a thousand when I left". The third province of India is called Malabar, and the Church of St. Thomas which he build with his own hands is there, besides another which he built by the agency of workmen."[21]

The Portuguese in India

Christianity spread rapidly in India with the arrival of Portuguese. In India, the Portuguese insisted that everyone who lived in their settlements should be a baptised Christian and by encouraging Portuguese soldiers to marry low caste women, they produced the Goans and made of Goa itself a rigidly Roman Catholic Community.In 1599 by the Synod of Diamper, the Portuguese brought about a union of the Nestorian Church of Malabar with Rome. They were allowed to keep their Syriac liturgy of Addai and Mari and some of their other customs, and became a uniat church, distinct from the Roman.

Catholics of the Latin rife who were descended from St Francis Xavier's converts. The Jesuit Archbishops of Cranganore attempted to assimilate the customs of the church more closely to those of Rome, and they were often harsh and overbearing in their attitude. Francis Gorzia, who took over charge about 1636, attempted to introduce the Latin rite. In 1653 the Patriarch of Babylon had made another attempt to get into touch with the Christians of Malabar by sending a bishop called Ahatalia to them. The Portuguese, however, seized the bishop on his arrival, put him on board a ship at Cochin, and deported him to Goa where he was tried by the Inquisition and burnt at the stake. When this became known, thousands of Christians gathered before the large stone cross at Mattancherry near Cochin, called the Coonen cross,[22] to make a protest. Here they solemnly renounced their allegiance to the Church of Rome. As the numbers were so great that all could not touch the cross at once, they connected themselves to it by ropes. The revolt was at the moment complete, but the Roman Catholics succeeded in winning back a large section, who are known today as the Palayakam or old community. Those who persisted in their protest were in a great difficulty, as Portuguese control of the sea prevented all communication with Persia. Archdeacon Thomas, of the Pakalomattan family, was recognised as their leader and consecrated as Bishop by the laying on of the hands of twelve priests.

This was irregular,but in 1655 Mar Gregorious of the Jacobite Syrian church arrived in Malabar where, as the Dutch had taken Cochin in 1663 and driven out the Portuguese, there was no hindrance to his actions. He was welcomed heartily, and consecrated Archdeacon Thomas bishop, thus restoring the regular episcopal succession in the church, which passed from a Nestorian connection to a Jacobite or monophysite connection. This involved, among other things, the adoption of the Syrian liturgy of St.James instead of the Nestorian liturgy. Nestorians and monophysites had represented opposite extremes when these divisions first arose in the fifth century; but the Church in Malabar at this time was not learned, and had never held particularly strongly to Nestorian doctrine, so that the great majority of its members seem to have been quite unaware that any great change was involved.[23]

Jesuit Missions

St. Francis Xavier 1506-1552

Where they could not dominate politically, the work of the Jesuit Missionaries was more wholly admirable. The most famous of them all was St. Francis Xavier, the friend of St. Ignatius Loyola and one of the original members of the Society of Jesus. St. Francis Xavier, who came of a noble Spanish family, arrived in Goa in 1542 on the invitation of John III, King of Portugal. From there he went on to Cape Comorin, where he worked for two years among the Paravas, a low caste of pearl fishers. Although he remained here so short a time and was unable to speak the language of the people, their conversion proved permanent, and the Roman Catholic Church of the Latin rite in Kerala is the result of this mission.[24] From Cape Comorin he went on to Mallacca, the Molucca Islands and Ceylon. In 1549 he landed in Japan, and returned to Goa in 1552, whence he set out in the same year on a mission to China. He never reached China, however, but died on the island of Chang Chien (otherwise St. John's Island) off the Chinese coast.

De Ricci (1552- 1610). De Nobili (1577-1656)

The Jesuit missionaries at the Mogul court attempted, but without success, the method of converting the ruler as a preliminary to converting the people. The Roman Catholic quarter in Agra and the old cemetery there are the result of concessions by the Mogul rulers; but Akbar and Jehangir seem to have been actuated by little more than intellectual curiosity about Christianity in their welcome to the Jesuit fathers. De Ricci in China attempted the same approach; and he also tried to gain a hearing from the intellectual Chinese by introducing them to European knowledge of Astronomy and Geography. Different methods were adopted by Robert de Nobili who began to work in Madura in 1606. He attempted to appeal to the Brahmans by disclaiming all connection with the Portuguese Jesuits and their low caste converts, and by proclaiming himself to be a western Brahmin born in Rome. He wore the saffron robe of a sanyasi, became a strict vegetarian and adopted other Hindu customs; and he proclaimed Christianity as a newly discovered fifth veda. He attained an astonishing knowledge of Sanskrit, Tamil and Telugu and lived a life of considerable austerity till he retired to a monastery in 1648, to die in 1656. Missions on de Nobili's principles were carried on in this area until the methods were condemned by Pope Benedict XIV in 1744. The number of Brahman converts made by these means was never great; and the method involved, not only the maintenance of rigid caste distinctions in the Church, but also fundamental dishonesty. In Japan the alarm caused by the success of the Jesuit missionaries led to the closing of the country to European influence for centuries and the most savage prosecution which stamped out all outward traces of Christianity; and yet when the Europeans returned to Japan in the nineteenth century there were still people who claimed to be Christians there.[25]

Beginning of Protestant Mission in India

The whole complex of religious movements in the Western Church in the sixteenth and seventeenth centuries which are known as Reformation and Counter reformation constitute one of the most important events in the history of the Church. The protest movement spearheaded by Martin Luther (1483-1546) in Germany against the Roman Catholicism on certain issues resulted in division in Christian religions as Roman Catholics and Protestants. Those who followed the sacraments and cannons advocated by Martin Luther were termed as Protestants and this Protestantanism had rapidly spread to other parts of the world. As stated earlier, consequent of the Reformation, Protestantism took birth and these Protestants fall into four main divisions viz., Lutherans, Reformed or Presbyterians, Anglicans and Separatists.[26]

The Danish Mission in Tranquebar [1706]

Schwartz 1750-1798

Frederick VI King of Denmark (1699-1739) was a pious Lutheran ruler. The Danish East India Company had established itself at Tranquebar, and the King felt that it was his duty as a Christian ruler to start a mission there. He found his missionaries among the disciples of Franke at Halle, and in 1706 Bartholomaus Ziegenbalg and Henrich Plutschau landed at Tranquebar. This was the beginning of Protestant missions in India. Ziegenbalg learnt Tamil and produced a translation of New Testament and of part of the Old which, though crude and imperfect, was the first to be made into any modern Indian language.[27] A little later Fabricius (in India from 1742-1791), a great Tamil scholar, produced improved translations of the scriptures, which are the basis of all later Tamil translations, and of many Germany hymns, as well as a Tamil grammar and dictionary. Much the most famous of the Tranquebar missionaries, however, was Christian Friedrich Schwartz, who landed in India in 1750 and never left it again till his death in 1798. Schwartz's sterling character led him to the generally trusted in the troubled political life of the period; and he became for a time, at the end of his life, the guardian of Saraboji, the minor Rajah of Tanjaore, a descendant of Shivaji's brother. In spite of this, Schwartz continued to live extremely simply, and to carry on his work of teaching in the school and preparing catechumens for baptism.[28]

Later History of the Danish Mission: From 1709 the Society for Propagation of Christian Knowledge (S.P.C.K) contributed towards the funds of this mission, and after 1734 the main responsibility for the mission outside Tranquebar rested on them. This part of the work was called the English mission, though the missionaries were Lutherans, mostly Germans, sent out from Halle by Franke and his son and successor. In India they were very independent, organized the Church much as they liked, and exercised an absolute authority over their converts. At the end of the century the influence of Pietism weakened at Halle, and Europe became involved in the Napoleonic Wars; and the mission fell into decline. In 1826 the S.P.C.K. handed over its responsibilities to Society for Propagation of Gospel (S.P.G) In 1813 the first Church Missionary Society (C.M.S) missionaries arrived in South India, and in Tinnevelly the C.M.S. missions soon became more numerous than the older missions. These first C.M.S.missionaries were also German Lutherans; but by this time there were Anglican Bishops in India, and though the Anglican societies accepted the Lutheran orders of the existing missionaries and Indian clergy, they required that in future all ordinations should be in accordance with Anglican practice.

Another difficulty which arose at this time was the question of caste within the Church. The Danish mission had adopted a very tolerant attitude to this, partly following the usages common in the Roman Catholic Church, partly perhaps because the implications of caste were at first very imperfectly realised by the European missionaries. At first only sudras were ordained as pastors; pariah Christians has to sit apart from the sudras in Church, and to receive the holy communion only after all the sudras had communicated; and pariah catechists when there were any, were only acceptable in churches composed entirely of their own caste fellows. But this tolerance was now felt to be an abuse; and in 1835 Bishop Daniel Wilson, the first Metropolitan of India, arranged a communion service at Trichinopoly at which both European and Indian clergy assisted; and English, sudras and pariahs came up to the communion table together in a carefully prearranged order. This led to the secession of many of the sudras, clergy as well as laity. Some of these became attached to the Leipzig Lutheran mission, which earned the reproach of other Protestant missions for its lax attitude to caste.[29]

The Moravians of Herrenhutt

Nikolaus Ludwig von Zinzendorf (1700-1760) was a Saxon nobleman who was a pupil and godson of Franke at Halle. In 1722 he gave refuge on his estate at Herrenhutt to the Bohemian Brethren, a group of Christians who had originally been followers of John Huss and who had managed to survive the prosecutions which accompanied the Thirty Years War. Zinzendorf and his friends, who came to be known as Moravians, attached the same importance as the Pietists to direct personal experience of Christ; but they stressed more exclusively the actual moment of conversion, and were therefore accused by Pietists of the school of Franke of antinomianism. The Bohemian Brothers had been organised as a church with bishops for whom they claimed the historic succession; but their last bishop, Commenius, a famous educationist far in advance of his time, had died in 1671. They continued, however, to insist that they were not Lutherans, and the episcopate was restored among them in 1735, though a Moravian bishop has no administrative authority. The Moravian church continues to the present day, and has been active in missionary work out far out of proportion to its small numbers. In India proper, however, there have been no Moravian missions. Some Moravians came out to Tranquebar in the eighteenth century, but were not allowed by the Danish mission, who distrusted their orthodoxy, to undertake evangelism. A Moravian mission in Ladakh was for a long time almost the only Christian work in that part of the world, though Jesuit missionaries visited Tibet in the seventeenth century. The Moravians of Ladakh are now included in the United Church of North India.[30]

The Modern Missionary Movement

William Carey (1761-1834)

A result of the evangelical movement was to rouse the Church to its missionary obligations. The real originator of the modern missionary movement among Protestants was William Carey. A shoemaker by trade, Carey taught himself Latin, Greek, Hebrew, Dutch and French, and became a Baptist preacher. At a meeting of Baptist ministers at Kettering, Northamptonshire in 1792, Carey read a paper insisting that God intended Christians to fulfil his command to preach the Gospel to every creature. It seems strange that anyone should ever have doubted this, but the prevailing Calvinistic theology suggested that, if God had wished other peoples to be

Christian, he would have provided the means himself without human agency. The immediate result of Carey's paper was the founding of the Baptist Missionary Society (BMS) and Carey's own departure for Bengal as its first missionary.[31] In 1795 Anglican evangelicals joined with Congregationalists, Presbyterians and Methodists to form the London Missionary Society (LMS) which is nowadays mainly Congregational. But the Anglicans were dissatisfied with the undenominational basis of this society; S.P.G. was not very active at this time, and was closely connected with the predominant 'high and dry' party in the church which was not very favourable to evangelicals. The consequence was the formation of the Church Missionary Society in 1799, John Venn being the first President. In 1805 members of the Clapham Sect were active in forming the British and Foreign Bible Society on inter-denominational lines. In 1807 the mainly non-conformist British and Foreign Schools Society was founded, and in 1811 the Anglican National Society, both for the education of poor children in England and Wales, where there was as yet no system of state education. These two societies differed in the type of religious instruction given in their schools; the British Society taught the Bible only, the National Society the Prayer Book catechism as well. In 1789 Robert Raikes began to gather the poor children of Gloucester together on Sundays, to teach them scripture reading and other elementary subjects. His example was followed by Hannah More (1745-1833), a formidable maiden lady who came to be closely connected with the Clapham sect. In 1803 the Sunday School Union was formed. At this time illiteracy was general among poor people, and many of the children who attended Sunday Schools were working during the week. The Sunday Schools therefore found it necessary to teach reading, and sometimes even writing and arithmetic, as well as giving purely religious instruction. Another famous society formed about this time was the Religious Tract Society (RTS).[32]

General William Booth (1829-1912)

William Booth originally a Methodist, founded a mission chapel in Whitechapel, a poor London district, and finding that ordinary methods made little impression.He dressed his congregation in semi-military uniform, and called them the **Salvation Army** and himself the General. A brass band accompanied hymns sung to catchy tunes at open-air meetings. The Salvation Army incurred a great deal of criticism for its crude theology and sensational methods, and a great deal of opposition from toughs; but it grew into a world-wide organisation. The Salvation Army found that religious conversion alone did not solve the problems of the criminals, drunkards and down-and-outs whom they were trying to help; and so hostels were organised, where the homeless could be received, and schemes devised to put former wastrels in the way of earning an honest living. The Salvation Army considers itself a mission rather than a church, and therefore administers no sacraments; but in practice almost all its members consider themselves to belong to the Salvation Army as other people belong to a religious denomination. In India the Salvation Army works among criminal tribes and does much other work. The methods of the Salvation Army were copied, but in close connection with the Church of England, by the Church Army, founded by PrebendaryCarlile in 1882.[33]

India William Carey (1761-1834)

William Carey, who arrived in 1793 was not the first Protestant missionary in India as already seen something of the work of the Danish Mission in Tranquebar. Carey experienced great opposition from the East India Company, who feared for their newly established authority in India if non-Christians were offended by Christian missionary preaching. He eventually settled in Serampore, then a Danish settlement. The missionaries at Serampore were pioneers in the translation of the Bible into Indian languages; they set up the first vernacular press and published the first vernacular newspaper. Unfortunately much of this work had the faults of a pioneering effort. It was done in too much of a hurry, and on the basis of insufficient knowledge of the languages concerned, so that none of the original Serampore translations is in use today. Carey himself, however, became a good scholar in Bengali and Sanskrit, and was later appointed professor of these languages in Fort William College, which was set up by the East India Company to train its young civilians. The college which grew up at Serampore was empowered by the King of Denmark to grant degrees; and it is still the only institution in India which can grant degrees in Christian theology.[34]

Henry Martyn (1781-1812)

One of the first offers of service received by the C.M.S. was from Henry Martyn, a brilliant Cambridge scholar and a disciple of Charles Simeon. Circumstance, including the hostility of the East India Company to missionaries, led to Martyn's coming to India as a chaplain; but in his short stay before he was compelled by advancing tuberculosis to leave the country, he achieved an Urdu translation of the New Testament which was immediately recognised as superior to the Serampore translation, and which is the basis of the modern Urdu New Testament. Martyn attempted to go back to England overland, and spent a year in Persia, disputing with the the Persian maulvis and making a Persian translation of the New Testament. He then continued his journey, but died in Armenia through fatigue and exhaustion, and was buried by kindly Armenian monks, Martyn made one convert, a Moslem of good family who had led a wild life in the disordered India of the early nineteenth century. Hearing that Martyn was in the habit of preaching to beggars on Sundays at Cawnpore (Kanpur), he came to scoff, but was so much impressed by what he heard that he got himself employed as a proof reader for Martyn's New Testament. The result was his baptism in Calcutta, under the name of Abdul Masih. In 1813 Abdul Masih arrived in Agra with Martyn's friend and fellow-chaplain, Daniel Corrie; and this was the real beginning of Protestant missions in this part of India.[35]

The Anglican Episcopate

Middleton (1814-1823) and Heber (1823-1827)

When the East India Company's Charter was renewed by Parliament in 1813, the influence of Wilberforce, Lord Teignmouth and Charles Grant, with all members of the Chapham Sect, brought about free admission for missionaries and the appointment of a Bishop of Calcutta. Bishop Middleton, the first to hold this office, founded Bishop's College and entered into friendly relations with the Jacobite Syrians in the South. His successor was Reginald Heber, a man of saintly and lovable character, the author of some well-known hymns, Bishop Middleton found he had no power to ordain Indians and doubted whether he had any right to license the C.M.S. missionaries who first arrived in India at this time. This legal difficulty was removed before Heber took up his appointments, and he ordained Christian David, a Tamil catechist from Ceylon, and Martyn's convert, Abdul Masih.[36]

Anglicans And Syrians [The Mar Thoma Church]

Colonel John Munro, the British Resident in Travancore and Cochin, an earnest evangelical, took a warm interest in the welfare of the Syrian Christians. He persuaded the reigning Maharani to give him land in Kottayam for a college for Syrian deacons and others, and invited the help of C.M.S. missionaries. The Metran, Mar Dionysius II, who was conscious of the low level of education among his clergy, accepted this plan and took up his residence in the college. Of the missionaries, Joseph Fenn was in charge of the college, while Henry Baker translated the Bible and Prayer Book into Malayalam. Unfortunately a later Metran, Mar Dionysius IV was less anxious for reform. He ordained mere boys on payment of a fee; and at the same time new missionaries who were intolerant and tactless hadreplaced the earlier ones. Cooperation with the C.M.S. therefore came to an end in 1836, but some Syrian church asked to be received as Anglicans. Apart from this, there continued to be a reforming party in the Syrian church, of which the chief leader was Abraham Malpan (1796-1846} who had been on the staff of the college at Kottayam. They revised the liturgy so as to omit all prayers for the dead, all invocation of the Virgin Mary and the saints, and other practices deemed superstitious. The communion was to be administered in each kind separately, instead of by intinction, as had previously been the custom, and Malayalam was to be substituted for Syriac as the language of worship. To ensure the triumph of his reforming views, Abraham Malpan obtained the consecration in 1842 of his nephew, by the Jacobite Patriarch at Mardin in Syria, under the title of Mar Athanasius Matthew (1843-1877). The result of all this was a long dispute between Mar Athanasius Matthew, who returned to India in 1843, and the recognised Metran, Mar Dionysius IV, who was supported by the more conservative party. After long litigation judgment was given against the reformers, who now recognised as their Metran Mar Athanasius Thomas (1877-1888), whom Mar Athanasius Matthew had consecrated to succeed him. The decisive judgement was given in 1889, and the reforming party became the independent Mar Thoma Church. The Mar Thoma Church has been distinguished by its zeal for evangelism and social reform, and is now in full communion with the Anglican Church.[37]

Bishop Daniel Wilson (1833-1858)

After two very short episcopates, Bishop Daniel Wilson arrived in India as fifth Bishop of Calcutta in 1833. By this time the impossibility of administering a diocese which included not only the whole of India and Ceylon, Malaya, Australia and New Zealand as well, had been realized, and when the East India Company's Charter was renewed in 1833, the sees of Madras and Bombay were created, and the Bishop of Calcutta became Metropolitan. In 1846 the see of Colombo was created.In 1836 the first Bishop was consecrated for Australia, and in 1841 the first Bishop of New Zealand. Wilson was an active promoter of missionary work. His energy in promoting church building led to the construction of the cathedral in Calcutta, and of very many of the large cantonment and civil lines churches which are to be found in most of the cities of India.[38]

Christian Colleges

Alexander Duff (1806-1878)

Christian colleges were started in Bengal, at that time the higher castes among Bengalis were eager for western education, in result, Hindu College in Calcutta was founded by David Hare, a free thinker. When Alexander Duff, a Church of Scotland missionary, arrived in Calcutta in 1830, he saw that advantage could be taken of this demand for western knowledge to found a Christian College, in which the teaching of secular subjects should be combined with the proclamation of the Christian faith and founded Scottish Churches College. It is the prototype of all later Christian Colleges; and some of Duff's converts provided leadership for the Church in the whole of North India. The Church of Scotland became responsible for the foundation of Wilson College at Bombay and Madras Christian College at Madras. The C.M.S. followed the same example, the first of their colleges being St. John's College, Agra, whose founder, Thomas Valpy French (1825-1891) a pupil of Arnold's at Rugby, and a scholar who had a notable future before him at Oxford, was afterwards first Bishop of Lahore (1877-1887) and finally died in exhaustion at Muscat in trying to start a Christian mission in Arabia.

Seepoy Mutiny [1857]– Christian Missionaries

The generation following the Mutiny of 1857 was that of the most rapid Christian expansion in India; for the faithfulness of Christians at a time when British rule seemed to be crumbling was proof of their sincerity. They were obviously not, as had previously been thought, mere hangers-on of the British government. Early in the nineteenth century there was a remarkable movement towards Christianity among low caste people in Tinneveliy, and towards the end of the century similar mass movements began in other places. The success of the Christian missions among tribal people was also marked. There were a few noteworthy Brahman converts, such as Pandita Ramabai, Nehemiah Gorch and the Marathi poet, Narayan VamanTilak. But these conversions did not lead to any general movement towards Christianity among the higher castes, and Christians tended to form another, somewhat westernised community. Yet Christian ideas began to spread, especially through the influence of the Christian colleges; caste rules tended to become less rigid and the position of women was improved; whilst girls' education was almost entirely the work of missionaries.

During the month of May, 1857 great excitement has been produced throughout India by the meeting of several of the Sepoy (Native Soldier) in the North of India. Nearly a dozen regiments, located at Meerut, Ferozepur, Mean, Meer and Delhi, rose in open revolt, the cause being as is said, the introduction of new catridges, the paper of which was really or was imagined to be prepared with the fat of beef or pork. Thus, caste prejudices were offended, and the Seepoys, in their ignorance and superstition, imagined that the English Government was attempting to overthrow their religion and interfere with caste observance, of which they are so very tenacious. At Meerut ten or fifteen European Officers and three or four of their wives and children were barbariously murdered. After committing the ravages, the mutineers took possession of the ancient and fortified city of Delhi.[39] The following are the few names of Missionaries, Chaplains and Indian Christian workers killed during the Rebellion of 1857 [40]

The Europeans who were killed during Mutiny are, Rev. M.J.Jennings, Chaplain of Delhi and Miss Jennings.Both killed in their house on the gate of the palace. Rev A.R. Hubbard of the Propagation of Gospel Society killed by the mutineers in Delhi Bank. Rev. Mackey of the Baptist Missionary Society Delhi defended himself with several friends in Col. Skinner's house for three or four days, when the roof of the Cellar in which they had taken shelter was dug up by the order of the King and they were all killed.Mr. Cocks and Mr. Louis Koch, both of the Propagation of Gospel Society, killed by the Mutineers in the Delhi Bank.Mrs. Thompson, widow of the Rev. J.J.Thompson formerly Baptist Missionary in Delhi, and his two adult daughters. All three were killed in their own house in Delhi. Rev. Thomas Hunter, Missionary of the Church of Scotland, Sialkot, Mrs. Hunter and their infant child were killed in their buggy while fleeing to the fort. A ball passing through the face of Mr.Hunter, entered the neck of his wife; a goal warder completed the murder with a sword killing the child also. Rev. J.E.Freeman and Mrs. Freeman; Rev. D.E. Campbell, Mrs. Campbell and their two children, Rev. A.O. John and Mrs. John; Rev. R.M.Mullen and Mrs.M.Mullen, of the American presbytarian Board of Missions, Futtehgur. All were killed by the Nava at Bihoor. Rev. W.H-Heycock, of the Propagation of Gospel Society, Cawnpore Kanpur and Mrs.Heycock his mother, both killed at Caunpore Kanpur. Mr.Heycock was shot just as he was entering the intrenchments.Rev. H.E. Cockey of the Propagation of Gospel Society, Caunpore Kanpur, was wounded in the thigh by a musket ball and afterwards was shot on the parade ground at cawnpore, together with other Europeans in the presence of the Nana.

The Indian Christians who were killed during the Sepoy Mutiny are, Willayat Ali, Catechist of the Baptist Mission, Delhi was killed by a party of Mohammedans in the streets of Delhi, at the time of the outbreak. Thankoor, Catechist of the Propagation Society Mission, New Delhi was killed by troopers in the streets of Delhi. Dhokul Parashad, Head Teacher of the Futtehgur Mission Schools,his wife and four children - all were killed in company with the Europeans in the parade at Futtehgur.Ram Chandra Mitter, Head Master of the American Presbyterian Mission School was murdered at a near Futtehpur.

Rebellion in Travancore

According to tradition the low caste Shanar women of Travancore were not permitted by the upper castes to wear any clothing above the waist. When Shanars were converted to London Missionary Society Missionaries, they were requested to wear clothing on the upper portions of their bodies. When the Shanar women started doing so, it led to a widespread conflict with the higher castes that came to be known as the 'Upper Cloth Rebellion'. Though the missionaries were undoubtedly motivated by their own Western notions of propriety, the agitation infact took on the character of a social movement. Madhava Rao, the Dewan of Travancore also wrote a letter to Gen. Cullen, the British resident describing the situation.[41] Latter, four missionaries wrote to Lord Stanley, the Secretary of State dated 26 March, 1859, concerning the upper-cloth rebellion in Travancore, and this exhibits the level of missionary interest in the matter.[42]

Establishment Of Rajasimla Church In Assam (1867 A.D)

For more than thirty years the American Baptist-Mission had worked with only limited success on the plains of Assam. The establishment of Church at Rajasimla, the first of that mission among a hills tribe, led to an increasing concentration upon missionary work in the hills.[43] Omed, a member of the Garo tribe of the present Meghalaya, was the first important convert among the Baptists from among the hills tribes of North-East India. A year following his Baptism, which took place at Gauhati on February 8, 1863, he became an evangelist among his own people. His successful work influenced the Mission to take up the work in other hill areas - a work review led to the establishment of large Christian communities in that region. Similar work was done by the Welsh Presbyterian Mission among the Khasis and Mizos.[44]

Godhula, an Assamese evangelist, was the first to undertake a successful Christian work among the Nagas. After an exploratory journey into the hills occupied by the A.O. Nagas in the winter of 1871, he spent the winter months in the village of Dekha Haimong (Molungkimong)during the succeeding years. There he gathered the first Naga Christian Congregation.[45] The first All India Missionary Conference (at which it was decided to hold such Conferences every ten years) was held at Allahabad from December 26, 1872 to January 1, 1873. 136 persons attended among whom were 28 native members. Several persons read out several papers on various aspects relating to Christianity and the Churches. Papers by W.T.Santhanadhan, on 'Native Church in South India', R.Jardine on 'the Brahmo Samaj', J.Barton on 'Mutual relation of Indian Churches', K.C.Chaterjee on 'the Relations of the Missionaries to converts in secular matters', and the resolutions on Mutual non-interference of Missionary Societies' were read out.[46]

In 1879, the Missionary Conference of South India and Ceylon was held at Bangalore and in that Conference passed a Resolution in support of foreign support and guidance. The conference while convinced of the great importance of promoting by every judicious means the self-support and self-government of the Native Church, desires to place on record its conviction that the native Church is no part of it as yet in a position to dispense with European guidance and support; and that any premature step in this direction would be highly injurious to its healthy development and ultimate stability".[47]

Mission Movement Of Conversion In Ongole

In a letter written to American Baptist Missionary Union in the summer of 1876 J.E.Clough, the only Missionary in the field, describes the beginning of the great mass Movement at Ongole (Andhra Pradesh). Some Madigas had become Christians before a severe famine during which Clough had secured work. The baptisms reported here took place after the famine period. It is clear that the converts did not gain any material benefit by becoming Christians.[48]

South India Missionary Conference, Madras (1900 A.D)

The South India Missionary Conference was held at Madrason 2-5 January 1900. In this Conference it was re-emphasized the opinion that congregations of long standing should support their own pastors, and that in other congregations some arrangements had to be made for the partial fulfillment of this duty. The Conference also recommended for more responsibility to be placed upon pastors and people, in each Mission a well organised system be established by which the Christian laity in the congregations could be trained to take more interest in the affairs of the

Church [49] This Missionary Conference also recommended for Constitution of a National Missionary Society (NMS) in India.[50]

Shortly before the formation of National Missionary Society, a Survey was taken among missionaries to determine their reaction to the formation of such an Indian Agency. In the various meetings where the plan was suggested, it was not only unanimously approved but received invaluable aid from suggestions offered in those conferences. The majority strongly favoured the plan and believed that the time had come for its inception. The object of this society was to evangelize the unoccupied fields in India and to lay upon our fellow countrymen the burden of responsibility for the evangelization of this land. The general direction of affairs were to be placed in the hands of a Council, composed of representative Indians elected by the members from missions and one or two missionaries who had deeply at heart the interests of the Indian Church,

The fourth All Indian Decennial Missionary Conference was held at Madras in 1962 which was the last of the important field conferences in India. This Conference discussed and resolutions were passed to represent the culmination of missionary thinking during the second half of nineteenth century, the formation of 'the National Missionary Council which was later emerged as National Christian Council (NCC) and so on.The National Missionary Society (Bharat Christyan Sevak Samaj) was finally founded at a meeting of Indian Christians held in Sevampur from the December 24-28,1905. By the end of the first century there were Christian churches in several cities of Palestine, Syria, Asia Minor, Cyprus and Greece; in Rome and Puteoli in Italy; in Alexandria in Egypt and in Cyrene in Lybia. All the books of the New Testament had already been written except second Peter; but they had not yet been collected into a New Testament to place beside the Old Testament as Scripture. The last of the generation who had known Lord Jesus Christ in the flesh had passed away, and the Church was passing into a new age with new conditions and new problems.

The evangelical movement was strong in personal devotion to the Lord Jesus Christ; it brought about a new Puritanism in morals after the laxity of the early eighteenth century; it was strong in its evangelistic emphasis and in the practical application of Christianity. Besides the great societies mentioned, it was the evangelicals, William Wilberforce and his successors who brought about the abolition of the slave trade (1807) and ultimately of slavery itself throughout the British Empire (1833). The influence of Wilberforce with Charles Grant, both evangelicals, led to the opening of India to missionary work when the Charter of the East India Company was renewed in 1813. Charles Grant's influence on appointments on the Board of Directors resulted in the arrival in India of evangelical officials who played a large part in transforming British government from the corrupt and predatory system it had been when it was first established, to the incorruptible and benevolently despotic bureaucracy it became in the course of the nineteenth century. In a later generation, the evangelical Earl of Shaftesbury (1801-1885) was a pioneer in improving conditions in the factories and coal mines, and in many other good causes. But evangelicals took a low view of the Church and the sacraments, though it was they who began the movement for more frequent communion - once a month instead of three times, or sometimes only once a year, as had been customary. They took little interest in the actual conduct of public worship; and above all, they had almost no contribution to make to the development of Christian thought.The Missionary Movement in India in general and South India in particular during the early years of twentieth century and the series of Conferences held and the deliberations out of them, all paved way for strengthening Church Union Movement in South India and consequent formation of Church of South India are discussed in the successive chapters.

References

1. Solomon Doraiswamy, Christianity in India. Madras: The Christian Literature Society, 1986, p. 2.
2. Holy Bible, New Testament, Matt. 28:18-20.
3. Stephen Neil, A History of Christian Missions. Madras: CLS and ISPCK, 1972, p. 3.
4. Kuriakose, M.K., History of Christianity in India - Source Material.Bangalore: Indian Theological Library, 1978; p. 2.
5. Hennecke, Edgar, The New Testament Apoerypa., (Ed) by Wilhelm Schneemelcher, Philadelphia: The Westminister Press, 1965, Vol.ll, p. 11.
6. Thomas, P., Christians and Christianity in India and Pakistan. London: George Allen and Unwin Ltd., 1954, p. 7.
7. Kuriakose, M.K., Op.cit., p. 3.
8. Mar Solomon, 'Book of Bee' P.105 cited in Mathew, C.P. and Thomas M.M. The Indian Churches of St. Thomas. Delhi: ISPCK, 1967, p. 9.
9. Kuruvilla, K.K. Jerusalem to New Delhi. Madras: CLS, 1951, p. 59.
10. *Ibid,* p. 20.
11. Devaraj, B.E., History of Christian Church in India. Rajahmundry: Andhra Christian Sabha, 1969, pp. 20-21.
12. Ibid, p. 23.
13. William G.Young, Hand Book of Source Material for students of Church History. Madras: CLS 1969, p. 27.

14. Kuriakose, M.K., Op.cit., p. 7.
15. Perumalil, A.C. The Apostles in India. Patna: Xaviour Teachers Training Institute, 1971, p. 65.
16. Kidd, B.J. Documents illustrative of the History of the Church. London: SPCK, 1941, Vol.lll, p. 31.
17. Cherian, C.V., A History of Christianity in Kerala. Kottayam: CMS Press, 1935, pp. 112-115.
18. Yule Cordier, Cathay and the Way Thither (Taipei Chen-Wen Company, 1966), Vol. I, p. 63.
19. *Ibid.,* Vol. III, p. 45.
20. *Ibid.,* Vol. II, p. 132.
21. *Ibid.,* Vol. III, pp. 216-218.
22. That is the Crooked Cross.
23. Kuriakose, K.K., Op.cit., pp. 203-204.
24. Priolkar, A.K., The Goa Inquisition, pp. 22-23 quoted by Kuriakose,M.K., Op.cit., p. 34.
25. Cronin Vincent, A Pearl to India, The Life of Roberto Nobili. London:Libra Books, Dorton, Longman and Todd, 1966, p. 136.
26. Kuruvilla, K.K., Op.cit., p. 207.
27. Fenger, Fred, J., History of the Tranquebar Mission. Tranquebar: Evangelical Lutheran Mission Press, 1863, p,303.
28. Pearson, Hugh, Memoirs of the Life and Correspondence of the Rev. Christian Schwartz. London: J. Hatchard and Son, 1835, Vol. II, pp. 115-119.
29. Kuruvilla, K.K., Op.cit., p. 222.
30. Richter J., A History of Christian Missions in India. London: Oliphant, Andersen and Ferrier, 1908, p. 150.
31. Smith George, The Life of William Carey. London: John Murray, 1887, pp. 94-95.
32. Kuruvilla, K.K., Op.cit., p. 225.
33. William G.Young, Op.cit., p. 72.
34. Rouse, Ruth and Stephen Neil (Ed.), A History of Ecumenical Movement. London: SPCK, 1954, p. 355.
35. Grimes, C.J., Towards an Indian Church. London: SPCK, 1946, p. 246.
36. Kuruvilla, K.K., Op.cit., p. 108.
37. Mingana, A., Easily Spread of Christianity in India. Manchester: University Press, 1926, pp. 50-53.
38. Keay F.E., A History of the Syrian Church in India. Delhi: SPCK, 1960, pp. 81-82.
39. Gazette and Courier from Malur and Madhura. dated 15th June, 1857.
40. Paul R.D., They kept in Faith' (Lucknow: Lucknow Publishing Home), 1968, pp. 45-48.

41. Official Papers sent from India touching the recent disturbances in Travancore, 1859, pp. 8-10.
42. *Ibid.,* p. 3.
43. Baptist Missionary Magazine, Vol. XLVIl (1867), pp. 445-447.
44. *Ibid.,*Voi. XLVIII (1868), p. 454.
45. *Ibid.,* Vol. LIII (1873), pp. 51-53.
46. *Ibid.*
47. Report of the Missionary Conference: South India and Ceylone. 1879, Vol. (1), pp. 293-421.
48. The Baptist Missionary Magazine, September 1878, p. 348.
49. Report of the South India Missionary Conference. Madras: 1900, pp. 16-70.
50. The National Missionary Society of India. Madras: NMS Press, 1905, pp. 94-95.

Chapter - III

Christian Church Union Movement

Christian Missionaries came to India in response to famine and poverty. People who came to faith were frequently put out of their own communities with no place to go but to the mission. Many children were orphaned by famine and they also became dependent on the mission. Missionaries while providing service started attracting them towards Christianity. In 1930 one mission reported that 80 percent of their converts were financially dependent on the mission. These factors removed the converts from their own culture and they became strangers in their own land. These new Christians were perceived as giving allegiance to a foreign land and culture.

India is the homeland of 83 percent Hindu, and the rest are minorities, with 180 million Muslims, 70 million tribal people, 60 million Sikhs and uncounted millions of others. Each of these groups represents a potential voting bloc in India's democracy. However, Christians are not in significant numbers to be catered to by the national politicians. Christians in India are discriminated against in certain government programs. The government has a program of reservations for jobs and university education. This program gives preference to the people of the lower castes and the downtrodden communities. To qualify for these benefits, applicants must state their caste origin. Christians, having denounced caste, are unable to do this. Yet many Christians come from the very groups for whom these programs were devised. This represents a major loss to these people struggling for education and jobs.

Government jobs are widely sought and highly valued. The perception of many Christians is that they do not have an equal opportunity for these jobs and subsequent promotions. On the other hand, some Christians benefit by being perceived as more honest, resulting in more rapid promotions. Despite minority status, Christians are seen as leaders in medical care and education. This reflects the emphasis of many foreign missions. There are disproportionately more Christian doctors and nurses compared to the general population. It is estimated that more than 30 percent of the nurses in India are Christian. The quality of medical care and education in Christian institutions is believed to be higher than that available through government institutions. Indians concede that the conditions for Christians in the south differ from the north. Christians in the north go about their business quietly. The programs of some churches appear to be aimed at survival more than an open involvement in the larger community.

Christians in southern India date their origins back to the landing of Thomas on their shores. Thomas established churches throughout southern India. Catholic missionaries came in 1505 with Vasco de Gama and instituted changes including penance, prayers for the dead and the confessional. Two hundred years later church leaders became aware of their history though the help of British missionaries. Subsequently a reform movement started from within the church. These reforms represent a return to the original tenets of the church prior to 1600. Southern Christians have a strong sense of continuity from the first century to the present. Their liturgy is 2000 years old. Members are happy to be known as part of the church. There is a strong lay movement. Since government workers are required to retire at the age of 55, an impressive amount of social work is done by lay members of the church. The church in India is a mosaic of places where the church is thriving and places where it is merely surviving. Christians face the future with caution of persecution, and hope in a loving God.

The Christianity as a religion though it came to India some two thousand years ago but it never crossed the borders of Malabar and Travancore. But it was only after fifteen hundred years the attempts to spread this religion to other parts of the country were made. In the first instance the Roman Catholic Churches started spreading Christianity and the conversion of non-Christians into Christianity took a very slow pace.Later in Eighteenth Century the Protestant missionaries arrived India and started their preaching of Christian Gospel. The simple understanding methodology adopted by the Protestant missionaries in preaching the gospel made very easy to reach the illiterate common man in Indian society and thus made them to accept Jesus Christ and prompted them to slowly join as members of the Church. In this way, the Churches established by foreign Christian missionaries replaced the traditional Hindu religious customs and traditions including idol worship. The Indian Christians also started adopting and following the foreign and westernized Christian traditions and procedures in all their religious practices, worship, church constructions including their dress and language.

The Christian Church which was founded in the first Century in Rome slowly divided itself into three sects and divisions namely Eastern Church, Western Church and Coptic Church. Under Eastern Church Division, the Churches formed in the countries like Palestine, Syria, Asia and Greece were grouped. In Western Church Division, Italy, Germany, France, Spain, Holland and British Islands Churches were included. The Church in North Africa was called as Coptic Churches. The Bishop in Rome slowly expanded his influence and power and entitled himself as Pope and then started exercising his authority on the Churches in Western Division. This position continued for few hundred years and the Popes started misusing their authority. Then there broke out a threat and protest movement in Germany under the leadership of Martin Luther, a Catholic monk and protested the papal authority and his doctrines in 1517. Later many Christians got convinced his philosophy and followed Martin Luther. Consequently the Catholic Church under Pope divided among itself and new Churches like Lutheran, Calvanist, Anglican Zynglivian, Baptist and so on Churches were formed in addition already to the then existing Catholic Church. Later some new Churches were further formed consequent on the divisions among these Churches and all these Churches spread throughout the length and breadth of the world.

Christians worshiping one God, one religion and one salvation but keeping themselves divided as different Churches and denominations was against to the commandment of Jesus Christ. Bible speaks unity, love and sacrifice and the Jesus Christ gave his commandment to all his disciples to 'go and preach the word of God to the whole world'. This emphasised the unity among all for a single mission. Otherwise it is against to the principle. This was realised by the Missionaries as well as Church elders and leaders and thus they started advocating for Churches unity and oneness of Christians. The desire for unification of Churches was discussed for the first time by the Anglican Bishops in 1867, the Methodists in 1881, the old Catholics in 1889 and so on. Even the Young Men Christian Association (YMCA) formed in 1854 which comprised of Christians of various Churches and denominations also worked in this direction. The Student Christian Movement (SCM) which was formed with Christian students of various Churches and denominations also contributed their might for this noble cause. The Christians in foreign countries also formed 'Missionary Societies' for propagating the Gospel of Jesus Christ in their respective countries. These societies travelled to various other countries including India and established Christian Churches by preaching the Gospel of Christ. These Christian Missionary Societies also felt the need and urgency of unification of Church for the purpose of spreading the Gospel of Christ as quickly as possible and to reach nook and corners of the world.

In December 1900, the Founders of National Missionary Society tried for the unification of Churches into one United Church and it resulted in the efforts for Churches Union Movement in India.[1] Although the Union Movement had proceeded in a delayed manner, as far back as 1902 informal colloquies had taken place with missions. While forming part of the Church Union, in most cases the sacrifice was gladly made, and indeed someone both the sides felt that the new basis was more suitable for Indian Church than either of the systems it replaced. While addressing the World Missionary Conference at Edinburgh, in 1910 A.D, Bishop V.S. Azariah of Dornakal was one of the two non-Westerners participated and highlighted the need and urgency of Churches relation and Churches cooperation. Moreover, Indian Christians living in the midst of non-Christian majority, were naturally much more conscious of the things which united them than of those which divided them. It shocked converts to discover that they could not be baptized simply as Christians but had to become Anglicans, Methodists, Baptists, Presbyterians and so on. Out of these conditions the Movement for Church Union was born[2]

Formation of South India United Church (1908 A.D)

The South India United Church (SIUC) was formed with the Churches of Madura and Jaffna Missions, and those of the South India District Committee and the Travancore Mission of the London Missionary Society, in their organised capacity as 'The United Churches of South India and Ceylon on the one part; and the Churches of the Arcot Mission of the Dutch Reformed Church and those of the United Free Church Mission of Madras in their organised capacity as The South India Synod of the Presbyterian Church' on the other part. The first General Assembly of the South India United Church was held at Madras from 25th to the 27th of December 1908. The formation of this Church was an important step in the developing of Church Union Movement in India[3]

The above two bodies determined to and agree on a common basis of Union which has been accepted by the Church which they represent.

Although the negotiations for this kind of Union were begun less than ten years ago, preparatory work went on without which the subsequent rapid progress of the movement would have been impossible. The idea of a United Church was first in the minds of the missionaries who came from distant lands and then arouse in the minds of Indian Christians. The idea that 'why Christians of different Missions should worship apart, although they might live in the same town? Thus the way for a union was being slowly prepared. In fact, sundry attempts to affect a Union had actually been made as far as 1883, when Presbyterian Churches in India should unite. Two years later, the matter was brought before the Northern India Synod of the American Presbyterian Church by the Rev. Dr. Morrison and a Committee was appointed to correspond with the different Presbyterian Churches in India. As a result of this correspondence, a conference took place at Allahabad in 1887; and six years later the Indian Presbyterian Alliance came into being. In the year 1888, the subject of Union was brought before the general Synod of the Reformed Church in America by one to whom the Union cause owes much - Dr. Jacob Chamberlin - and the Synod called upon its representatives in South India - the classics of Arcot - to initiate such measures 'as shall tend to bring together the Churches of the Presbyterian politics in India'. Later in the same year, a Conference of Representatives of the Mission Boards of the Presbyterian Churches of the United Kingdom was held in Edinburgh. The resolution of this body gave effect to formation of this Union.[4]

In South India an attempt was made on different lines. In 1886 some Christians in Madras leaving the Churches with which they had been connected and combined under the title of the 'National Church of India'. In 1900, the 'South Indian Missionary Conference' met in Madras and discussed about the cooperation among the Churches. Within two months of the close of this Conference, a Committee was constituted with the representatives of 'American Arcot Church of Scotland' and 'Free Church of Scotland Missions' and applied itself to the two-fold task of leading the Missions into cooperation and the Churches into one organic Union. In less than two years a basis of Union was agreed upon, the missions and 'Presbyteries of the Arcot' and 'Free Church Mission' and secured the approval of their home authorities. In the case of the Church of Scotland the scheme was approved locally, but the Home Committee did not at the time see its way to sanction more than the cooperative part of the plan. The other two Churches resolved to proceed, and the first Synod of the 'South India United Church' was held in September, 1901 under the moderator ship of Dr. Chamberlin.[5]

The steps leading to the formation of the South Indian United Church were eagerly watched by the Members of London and American Madras Missions. The idea of a wider union such as has been now effected, was suggested but it was thought best to let each of these ecclesiastical families complete its own union first. Accordingly, in 1903, a Committee of Representatives of the London and Madras Missions was constituted. In little over as a year, it had a scheme ready which received with general favour. The union included not only Churches of the American-Madura Mission, and the majority of those of the London Mission, but also the Churches founded by the American Board of Ceylon. In 1905, the first General Assembly met at Madura under the Presidency of Dr. Duthie.[6] The Report of the Second General Assembly of SIUC held at Trivandrum in December 1909 revealed the continuing interest is wider Church Union in relation to both South India, Sri Lanka and the Union as a whole.[7]

Missionaries and Church Union

The Edinburgh (Scotland) Conference (1910)

In what was then called the mission field, the lesson of Christian Unity was also being learnt. C.F.Andrews once said that when he was in England he knew why he was an Anglican, but in India he knew why he was a Christian. Faced with the non-Christian world, missionaries learnt how much all Christians have really have in common, and began to realise the scandal and handicap of the divisions of Christian-down. One of the first results of this was the World Missionary Conference at Edinburgh (Scotland) in 1910, under the Chairmanship of John R. Mott and J.H.Oldem as Secretary, This was largely a Conference of Missionaries with very few delegates indeed from the younger Churches.It began an era of much greater cooperation between missionaries and was the real starting point of the economical movement.[8]

The Edinburgh Conference of World Missionaries was convened to discuss another aspect of 'how to spread the Christianity throughout the world. It is to be noted that this Conference was attended mostly by American and British islands representatives. This Conference has finally given birth to three important Churches Movements namely...[9]

1. International Missionary Movement,
2. Movement for faith and order,
3. Movement for Life and work

V.S. Azaraiah's Address in Edinburgh (Scotland) Conference

V.S. Azariah was one of the two non-westerners and members of younger Churches to give major addresses at the World Missionary Conference held at Edinburgh. He was born in a Tamil Christian family. His comments on the subject, the problem of cooperation between Foreign and Native Workers' made deep impression on the delegates, '......the problem of race relationship is one of the most serious problems confronting the Church today. The bridging of the gulf between East and West, and the attainment of the greater unity and common ground in Christ as the great unifier of mankind is one of the deepest needs of our time. This is not only my own impression, but what I have gathered from a large number of my Indian brethren; and even a ten European Missionaries'. He said.[10] V.S.Azariah was elevated to the episcopate as Bishop of the newly formed diocese of Dornakal in 1912 A.D, was the first Indian Bishop of that tradition and it was an important steps in the Anglican Communion.[11] Followed by the World Missionary Conference in Edinburgh, the first International Missionary Conference was also held at New York in 1912. Sixty one delegates representing 14 countries attended the Conference and resolved to coordinate the efforts for missionary movement, working together in Missionary activities, printing of required Christian books, and bringing solidarity and unanimity in respect of Christian's opinion on international affairs. Later this Council met at Jerusalem in 1928, Tambaram (Madras) in 1938, Ghana (Africa) in 1958 and finally in 1961 it got merged with World Council of Churches at Delhi (India).

The Conference for Movement for faith and order was convened first at Laussane (Switzerland) in 1927 which was attended by 335 delegates from 108 Churches. Later in 1937 at Edinburgh (Scotland), its Second Conference was held and finally merged with World Council of Churches in 1948 at Amsterdam (Holland).The Conference for Movement of Life and Work was first convened at Stockholm in Sweden in 1925 which was attended by 600 delegates from 37 countries. Its Second Conference was convened in 1938 at Utrecht and finally this was merged with World Council of Churches in 1948 at Amsterdam.

World Council of Christian Churches

The two Movements which originated from Edinburgh Conference in 1910 namely 'the Movement for Faith and Order and the Movement for Life and Work started functioning as separate movements. But the Churches elders and leaders felt that it would be good and advantageous if these two movements work together. Thus these people contemplated to unite these movements and form 'World Council of Churches'. Finally it was decided in Life and Work Movement Conference held at Utrecht in 1938 to form the 'World Council of Churches'. The first Conference of World Council of Churches was held at Amsterdam on August 23rd 1948. As many as 351 delegates from 147 Churches and 44 Nations attended the Conference. The Second Conference of World Council of Churches was held in 1954 at Evanston. At the third Conference held in 1961 at Delhi, all the International Missionary Councils merged with this 'World Council of Churches'. The fourth Conference was held at Sweden in 1968. The Roman Catholic Churches, however did not exhibit interest in joining in this 'World Council of Churches'.[12]

The Headquarters of 'World Council of Churches' is located in Geneva, Switzerland. There are seven sections in this Council each under one President elected at the time of Conference. The seven sections are (1) Faith and Order (2) Laity Affairs (3) Youth Affairs (4) Financial Affairs (5) Gospel Work (6) Congregations and Churches (7) Inter Cooperation of Churches. Later one Regional Branch was opened at New York for the convenience of Churches in U.S.A. This Council has no authority on any Church. It cannot make Legislation or rules pertaining to any Church but it is only an advisory body on Churches problem at international level. However, this Council played a major role in unification of Churches in all countries in the world.[13]

Christians snd the Indian National Movement :

The First All India Conference of Indian Christians which brought together various provincial Indian Christian Associations (AICIC) was held in 1914. The leaders of the AICIC who counted among their number the most highly qualified and influential Indian Protestant leaders of the pre-independence period were committed nationalists. But they were often reserved their attitude towards the Indian National Congress. One of its resolutions stated 'In view of a State of flux in the principles and Constitution of Indian National Congress, it is the opinion of the Conference that Indian Christians should reserve judgement as to the advisability of either joining or refraining from joining the Indian National Congress'.[14] In its 1921 year resolutions, the AICIC reiterated its opposition to the Non-Cooperation Movement of Gandhi, it also illustrated the fact that for Indian Christians the National Movement had ecclesiastical as well as political implications. The Indian Church like the Indian Nation should be liberated from foreign rule. The Conference had also opined that 'the time has come' when

Protestant missions as such should be completely merged in the Indian Church and that in future all foreign Missionaries should be related to it.[15] Gandhiji while writing on the subject of conversion of non-Christians as Christians and the life style and attitudes of Indian Christians, he appealed to them not to equate Christianity with denationalization. He also expressed the opinion that Christianity has made little positive contribution to National Life in India.[16]

Indian Church Act (1927 A.D)

On 22nd December 1927, the British Parliament acted in consequence of the Indian Church measure already passed by the National Assembly of the Church of England. This was an Act to make provision incidental to and consequential on the dissolution of the legal union between the Church of England and the Church of England in India, The Act stated that The Governor General in India in Council with the sanction of the Secretary of the State in Council of India, with the concurrence of Bishop of Calcutta may make rules:

(i) regulating the licensing, posting, discipline, ministrations, duties and supervision of chaplains.

(ii) the Indian Christian Marriage Act, 1872 shall apply to the Indian Church on and after the date of the severance in like manner in all respects as it applied to the Indian Church before the date of Severance.[17]

The Roman Catholic Church

The Lateran Treaty of 1929: One of the most important events in the history of the Roman Catholic Church in this period was the agreement made by Pope Pius XI with the Italian state in 1929, by which the estrangement which began with the Italian occupation of Rome in 1870 was brought to an end. This was the more necessary for the Pope because by this time there was no longer any Roman Catholic great power in Europe to which he could look for support. France had become a secular state, and the Austrian Empire had broken up into a number of comparatively owerless succession states. By the Lateran Treaty the Pope received a small area, including the palace of the Vatican and St. Peter's cathedral, in full sovereignty, with the right to independent diplomatic representation. The Establishment of the Vatican City makes the Pope a citizen of no earthly state, but it is too small to have the disastrous effect on papal policy which was exercised by the former States of the Church.

Roman Catholics and Other Churches: The attitude of the Roman Catholic Church to other Churches in the twentieth century has been rather ambiguous. On the one hand, the decree on the Immaculate Conception of the Blessed Virgin Mary (1854), making an essential part of the faith a matter for which there is no reliable historical evidence whatever, and which was denied by medieval thinkers like St. Thomas Aquinas, the decree of papal infallibility (1870) and the pronouncement on the Assumption of the Blessed Virgin Mary (1950) are undoubtedly additions to the faith once delivered to the saints, and make reunion between Roman Catholics and other Christians more difficult; on the other hand, the misfortunes of the twentieth century have led Roman Catholics to join with other Christians to withstand non- Christian forces; and this had led to better relations. Soon after the First World War, the Malines Conversations (1921-1925) took place between Anglicans and Roman Catholics. The initiative on the Anglican side came from Lord Halifax (1839-1934), the leading Anglo-Catholic layman of the Church of England; and on the Roman Catholic side, from Cardinal Mercier (1851-1926) who had been a centre of Belgian national resistance during the German occupation. The conversations ended without agreement. They also suffered from the fact that the Anglican participants represented only the 'high' or 'catholic' school of Anglican thought; but it was wonderful that they should have taken place at all. The Roman Catholic Church suffered the same kind of persecution under the Nazi regime in Germany as the Protestants did, and proved in some ways better equipped for resistance; and the relations between the Roman Catholic Church and the State in Germany are still regulated by the Concordat of 1933, negotiated with Hitler. Moreover, since the beginning of the ecumenical movement, the non-Roman Christian world no longer presents the unedifying spectacle of divided churches, most of which have few dealings with one another, and some of which are actively hostile; and so the unity of the Roman Church becomes less impressive than it used to be by contrast.[18]

Reforms Within the Roman Catholic Church

In the Roman Catholic Church, there is an important liturgical movement, particularly strong in north Italy and parts of France. This involves making the mass more congregational by supplying the laity with books in which they can follow the Latin mass in a parallel vernacular translation; reading the epistle and gospel in the vernacular; and encouraging more frequent lay communion. The laity is now being encouraged to study the Bible in vernacular translations, of which one of the best is the English translation of R.Knox (1888-1957).[19] Of late years too, the Roman Catholic attitude to biblical scholarship has become less rigidly conservative, and good work has been done by Roman Catholic scholars in this field. Besides this, a noteworthy series of papal encyclicals has attempted to define the attitude of the Roman Church to modern social and industrial problems. An interesting experiment was tried in France, in order to win back the industrial working class to the Church. Worker-priests took jobs in factories like ordinary workmen, in order to get into touch with their fellow workmen. The experiment, however, was abruptly stopped by higher authority, as it was felt that the worker-priests were getting too much involved in left-wing politics. To these misunderstandings must be added the ignorance of one another in which the divided churches live. Even where, as in most towns of any size in the English-speaking world, churches of a wide variety of denominations stand side by side, many of their devout members never in their whole lives think of sharing in the worship of a denomination to which they do not belong. Further, divided churches acquire property, institutions and organisations which provide additional practical problems for reunion, and often vested interests against it. Besides this, divided churches grow apart. A more lively appreciation of what Wesley was trying to do in the Church of England, and more patience on his part, might have kept the Methodists within the Church of England in the eighteenth century; but the problem of reunion between Anglicans and Methodists is now much more formidable. In countries like India, where Christians are in a small minority of the population, and many of them are the result of fairly recent conversions, these non-theological factors are less formidable. Very many Christians move about a good deal, and constantly find themselves in the position of having to join in public worship with a denomination to which they do not belong or else refrain from public worship altogether. Yet in India too, non-theological factors, such as doubt about continued support from parent churches after reunion, and questions about the right to property, complicate the question.

The Roman Catholic Church: Its progress

Nevertheless, some progress in understanding has been made, even where it seemed most difficult, between the Roman Catholic Church and other Christians. The Roman Church is now prepared to recognise all the baptised as at least fellow-Christians, and to speak of them as 'our separated brethren'. Some Roman Catholic scholars are keen students of the oecumenical movement. A French priest, the Abbe Couturier (1953) was the promoter of a movement of prayer 'that our Lord would grant to His

Church incarnate on earth that peace and unity which were in His mind and purpose when, on the eve of His Passion. He prayed that all might be one'. This 'Octave' of prayer, the week between January 18th and 25th has been officially accepted by the World Council of Churches' Commission on Faith and Order. When, in 1958, Pope John XXIII succeeded Pius XII, a new spirit seemed to inform the Vatican. But there has been no abating of the claim that, apart from the uncovenanted mercies of God, salvation is impossible for those out of communion with the see of Rome; and no doubt there is sufficient recognition on the Roman side of the great difficulties for Protestant Christians which have been created by recent Roman additions to the faith. Pope John XXIII has announced his intention of calling a General Council; and while this Council would be, like that of 1870, a Council of the Roman Church only, observers were to be invited from other Christian communions. Meanwhile a notable event was the tour of Arch bishop Geoffrey Fisher of Canterbury, which was one of the last acts of his primacy, before he resigned in 1961. On this tour he met and had friendly conversations, not only with the ecumenical Patriarch at Constantinople and the Patriarchs of ther churches of the Middle East; but he was the first Arch Bishop of Canterbury since the Reformation to meet the Pope. Too much importance must not be attributed to courtesy calls; but there is certainly a new atmosphere in the Christian World to make them possible at all.[20]

Church Union in South India

In 1929, a London Missionary Society Missionary, A.H. Legg, made critical comments on the proposed scheme of Church Union in South India. When this Scheme was published which was put forwarded by negotiators representing the South India United Church, the Anglican Church, and the British Methodist Church. A.H.Legg spoke for a number of persons both within SIUC and abroad who felt that union on the proposed terms was sacrificing too much Christian liberty. He published a pamphlet entitled 'An Examination from the congregational point of view, with some suggestions'. In fact this Scheme advocated that an attempt has been made to conserve for the United Church the elements of value in each of the traditions that are to be brought together, and the scheme itself contemplates application with amongst others, the World Union of Congregational Churches. He criticized that in the United Church as outlined in the Scheme, seems that the emphasis on importance of the individual congregation and individual Church member would disappear. They would be swamped in a vast and complex organisation and would become mere cogs in the machine.

A Church would not be able to call its own minister or suspend its own backsliding members. The Bishop or the Diocesan Council might often act in accordance with the wish and judgement of the congregation, but they might also often act contrary to them.[21]

The English Methodists : Of all the Church bodies negotiating Church Union in South India, the English Methodists had the least difficulties accepting it, both in India and in England. The pastoral session of the English Methodist Conference held at Leads in 1930 represented a positive reaction to the first edition of the Scheme of Union (1929). The resolution stated The Conference has received with profound thankfulness the proposed scheme of Union prepared by the 'Joint Committee of the Church of India, Burma and Ceylon. The South India United Church and the South India Provincial Synod of the English Methodist Church for presentation to the governing bodies of these Churches in India and elsewhere". This Conference authorised the South India Provincial Synod to continue the consultations with the representatives of the other Churches concerned, and would watch with the most sympathetic interest the further process of such consultations.Later in 1931 A.D the All India Conference on Church Union was convened at Nagpur in accordance with the resolution of the Round Table Conference held at New Delhi in 1930. It met to consider the principles that would be accepted in the formation of a United Church for India and thus brought together those involved in Church Union discussions in both South and the North.[22]

In 1943 the All India Conference of Indian Christians during its meetings gave attention to the political situation of that time and demanded for assurance of independence to India following the end of the war and also demanded that Christians be given due share in appointments made on a communal basis, though they would prepare that appointments should not be made on that basis.

Formation of Church of South India (CSI)

The year 1947 was marked by two epoch making events; the first being India's Independence and the second was the inauguration of the Church of South India. After lengthy negotiations that began in 1920s, the Church of South India was formed on 27th September 1947. The decision to unite was made by the autonomous Indian Churches that had been historically related to these traditions through mission societies. It brought together the Churches of the Anglican, English Methodist, American Reformed

(Presbyterian), British and American Congregational and Basel (Lutheran reformed) traditions.

The birth of this new united church marks a sacred and significant land-mark in church history. It was rightly hailed by Christians and ecumenical leaders from all over the world as a great and momentous event in the history of the church union movement, as significant and epoch-making as the Sixteenth Century of Protestant Reformation Movement of Martin Luther. The significance lies in the fact that for the first time, episcopal and non-episcopal churches joined together to form the new united Church of South India. The inauguration of the Church of South India at a solemn and moving service in St. George's Cathedral, Madras, on that day brought to a glorious consummation the devoted labours of many Indian Christian leaders who worked hard to see the fulfillment of Church Union.

The desire for church union had been there ever since the various Christian missionary societies started their work in India in the 19th Century. Even as far back as 1806, William Carey called for holding missionary conferences once in ten years. Such Decennial missionary conferences had been held regularly since 1892. Those conferences provided a forum for the mission bodies and churches to discuss ways and means of fostering and promoting co-operation and co-ordination among the churches and missions in India. The South India Missionary Conference was another such organisation which tried to bring together the different churches and missionary societies in India for mutual conservation and support. Later on the National Missionary Council, and the National Christian Council together with their regional branches also did valuable spade work in this regard. Further, ecumenical institutions like the Madras Christian College, Vellore Christian Medical College and Hospital, the United Theological College at Bangalore and several others in different parts of India represent the experiments in positive and constructive inter-denominational and inter-missionary relations and cooperation in various fields of Christian Mission and ministries. But in all these discussions and ventures, there was much missionary initiative and involvement, and very little presence of Indian Christian leadership. Moreover, they were limited to co-operation and joint action in certain specific projects and programmes without venturing into any serious discussion of doctrinal issues pertaining to church union.[23]

However, it must be admitted that those decennial missionary conferences and other inter-denominational organisations and institutions did pave the way for the emergence of certain interdenominational united churches. For instance, in 1901, the Presbyterian Missions in South India, the United Church of Scotland Mission and the American Arcot Mission of the American Dutch Reformed Church formed themselves a Federal Union. Those missions were of the same doctrinal background. In 1904, another church union took place between the Congregational churches of the American Mission in Madurai and Jaffna, and the Congregational churches of the London Mission, South Travancore as it was known then. Those two bodies joined in 1908 to form the South India United Church (SIUC). Subsequently, the Telugu congregational churches of the London Mission also joined the SIUC. All these unions were really the fore-runners of the Church of South India. But in all these cases, church union was limited to the churches subscribing to the same doctrine and belonging to the same tradition.

The first serious and major step in the direction of a wider union between Episcopalian and non-Episcopalian churches was taken in 1919. This was in response to the political and socio-cultural changes taking place in India at that time as well as the growing awareness among the Indian National Christian leaders of the need to search for church unity. The Indian National Movement which was spreading fast and acquiring a broad popular mass base under the dynamic leadership of Mahatma Gandhi, resurgent Hinduism over the prospects of India achieving swaraj as a British Dominion in the near future challenged the Indian Christian leaders to think about the future of the Indian Christian community which was microscopic minority in independent India and made them realise the need to close their denominational differences over divisions, and come together to safeguard their legitimate rights in the impending dispensation of freedom and independence of India. They also realised that such closer union was needed to facilitate the continued participation of the Indian Churches in nation-building.

As far as the Indian churches were concerned, there was positive change in their attitude to and relations with one another. Under the impact of the Missionary Conferences, National Christian Council and other ecumenical institutions, the old inter-denominational rivalries and bickering which marked the missionary enterprise in the nineteenth century, had begun to gradually yield place to mutual appreciation and understanding, and respect for one another's doctrine, tradition and church polity. In fact, they were eager to enter into negotiations for church union. For instance, the Anglican Church in India and the South India United Church were anxious to start such negotiations because of S.I.U.C. presbyters felt that the Episcopalian elements of the Anglican Church were needed for the S.I.U.C. while the

Anglican priests realised that they needed the elements of individual freedom, lay participation and evangelical zeal of the S.I.U.C. Moreover, Indian Christian leaders like Bishop V.S. Azariah of Dornakal, Rev. Santiago of the S.I.U.C, Rev. M. Theophilus of the CBM and several others began to question the theological validity, and national and cultural relevance of the denominational labels branded on the Indian Churches by their respective parent churches and missionary bodies in Great Britain, Europe and U.S. They wanted that the Indian churches should become truly Indian by shedding their foreign denominational, indigenising their forms of worship, music and orientation, striving for self-reliance and financial self-support, and making evangelism and mission of the churches relevant to the socio-cultural milieu of India. They were also keen to acquire Indian national identity for the churches and equip them for effective participation in nation building. There was also a growing awareness among the laity as well as the clergy about the weakness and ineffectiveness of Christian witness by a divided church, especially at a time when Indian nationalities and leaders of the resurgent Hinduism were highly critical of the foreignness and dependence of the Indian churches on foreign Mission Boards. It was also hoped that a united church would add strength to the Indian Christian minority community to unitedly represent the problems of the community to the government and secure redressal for their grievances. All these created a congenial and hopeful atmosphere for the leaders to meet as friends and colleagues in the Mission of Christ and negotiate for forging unity among all Protestant churches.

It was under such circumstances that 33 Christian leaders, all Indians except two, representing the Episcopalian and non-Episcopalian churches met together under the leadership of Bishop V.S. Azariah of Dornakal at Tranquebar to share with one another the burden they were carrying in their hearts for the unity of churches. After careful deliberation and prayerful consideration, this small group of Indian Christian leaders issued a statement at the end of the conference setting forth the following points as the basis for church union negotiations. They appealed to all churches in India to enter into negotiations for union on the basis of those points. This came to be known as the Tranquebar Manifesto of 1919. The following points contained in the Manifesto were to form the basis for church union negotiations.[24]

- The Holy Scriptures of the Old Testament and the New Testament as containing all things necessary for salvation.
- The Apostle's Creed and the Nicene Creed.

- The two sacraments ordained by Christ Himself - Baptism and the Lord's Supper.
- The Historical Episcopate locally adopted.

The S.I.U.C. was the first to agree to negotiate for union on the basis of the Tranquebar Manifesto in 1919. The Anglicans decided to enter into negotiations with the S.I.U.C. in 1920. These two churches set up a Joint Committee consisting of their respective representatives in order to facilitate church union negotiations. Later in 1925, the British Methodists also nominated their representatives to the Joint Committee and joined the negotiations. In 1937, the Joint Committee appealed to all the churches in India to join union negotiations. The discussions made good progress in all issues except in the problem of the maintenance and continuance of the historic episcopate. The single issue defied a solution for a long time and stalled the birth of the church union for more than a decade. As a matter of fact, the Joint Committee held twenty meetings between 1937 and 1947 to find a solution to this problem. Several solutions were suggested but finally this obstacle was overcome by introducing the formula of initial mixed ministry, the pledge and the thirty year experimental period. With agreement reached on this seemingly intractable issue, the stage was all set for the inauguration of the new united church called the Church of South India, which took place on the twenty-seventh of August 1947.

Bishop Azaraiah of Dornakal (1874-1945): It was on the basis of the Lambeth Quadrilateral that the Anglican Church entered the negotiations which resulted in 1947 in the formation of the Church of South India, an event which has implications for the Christian world far greater than the actual numerical strength of the united church. The initiative for this union came from one of the most remarkable Indian Christians of his generation - Samuel Azariah. Azariah was born in a Tamil Christian family, and was one of the few members of the younger churches present at the Edinburgh Conference. The Indian Missionary Society of which he was a founder had begun to work in Dornakal where mass movements were taking place among the lowest castes. In 1909 he had been ordained for work in this mission, and in 1912 he has consecrated Bishop of Dornakal. He thus became the first Indian to be an Anglican diocesan bishop. Bishop Azariah built up his diocese from the very foundations, for most of his people were now converts; he built a remarkable cathedral which is a daring attempt to apply Indian architectural traditions to the purposes of Christian worship; and he was concerned from the beginning with the developments of the National Christian Council which turned out to be the most successful and influential of the national councils which resulted from the Edinburgh Conference. In 1919 Bishop Azariah was one of fifty Indian Christians with one or two missionaries who met in retreat at Tranquebar; and the result was that thirty-three of them, including Azariah, issued a passionate appeal for church union. It took nearly thirty years, however, for this appeal to bear fruit, and Azariah himself died in January 1945, just on the eve of its accomplishment. The uniting churches were the Anglican church, which accounted for about half the membership, the Methodists of the British connection, and the South India United Church which had resulted from a previous union between Presbyterians and the mainly Congregationalist churches founded by L.M.S. In South India, the historic episcopate was conveyed to the united church through the existing Anglican bishops, who consecrated the first bishops of the Church of South India, using the Anglican ordinal; but all existing ministers of the uniting churches were received immediately as presbyters of the united church, whether they had received episcopal ordination or not; though all future presbyters were to be ordained by the bishops, and after thirty years, the church was to decide its future relations with its parent churches abroad. This concession has led to some difficulties in the relationships between the Church of South India and the Anglican Communion; and a somewhat different plan has been adopted in the proposed unions, likely to be realised in the near future, in north India and Pakistan and in Ceylon. Here at the inception of the union, all ministers received authority by mutual laying on of hands. This is not to be interpreted as preordination in the sense of the denial of any grace of ordination which has already been received by the ministers of the separated churches; but it meant that the whole ministry of the united Church would at once be placed on the same footing; and enable those Anglicans who considered episcopacy to be of the esse of the Church to accept them all as having been validly episcopally ordained.[25]

Another significant personality who also played an important role in the Church unification and formation of Church of South India was Rev. J.S.M. Hooper, M.A., who, as Secretary of the Joint Committee on Church Union and later as the Secretary of the Continuation Committee and Treasurer of the Synod of C.S.I, had played a great part in bringing into being the C.S.I. and guiding it in its first critical years. When Rev. J.S.M. Hooper was leaving India to Britain after his service all the members of the Synod, on 10th January 1950 at Madras presented him a brief illuminated address with the signatures of all its members. The following is the text of the address which shows the Yeomen service of Rev. Hooper and the sentiments filled gratitude of the Synod members.[26] "We who are so closely associated with you in the fellowship of the Church of South India cannot let you leave India without some expression of our gratitude and of our affection. You have spent forty four years in this land in the service of one common Lord and Saviour. Your service more particularly, your labours for Church Union in South India during many years that we now think. Those most closely associated with you in the work of the Joint Committee and after the unforgettable experience of September 27, 1947 in the Government of Church of South India are of one mind in thanking you for all that you have done. 'With your God given gifts of spiritual insight, tenacity moral courage, without which the Church of South India could not have come into existence".[27] After the formation of Church of South India (CSI) the Constitution was drafted in 1947. The Constitution says that this United Church is called by the name 'Church of South India' and constituted by Union in 1947 of the Madras, Madura, Malabar, Jaffna, Kannada, Telugu and Travancore Church Councils of the South India United Church: South India province of the Methodist Church, comprising the Madras, Trichinopoly, Hyderabad and Mysore Districts, and the dioceses of Madras, Dornakal, Tinnevelly and Travancore and Cochin in the Church of India, Burma and Ceylon to which in 1950 was added the North Tamil Church Council of the South India United Church. The Constitution also says that the Church of South India recognises that the episcopal, Presbyteral and Congregational elements would have their place in the order of life.[28]

Constitution of Church of South India

The Church of South India was started in St. George Cathedral on September 27, 1947. The Resolutions made and the Act prepared for the unification of the Churches was ratified by the Church Councils of SIUC, Anglican and Presbyterian in 1945, 1946 and 1947 respectively. The church of South India was formed with the strong promise of 'That they all may be one'. When the Constitution of the Church of South India was drawn up it was decided to include as Appendix-I, the 'Basis of Union' which had been drawn up earlier by the negotiating Churches. This was done for the historical record and to fulfil the desire of the Constitution that 'Full regard shall be paid to the Basis of Union as a permanent record of the intentions and desires of the Churches by the Union of which the Church has been formed. The Uniting Churches affirmed that the purpose of the Union was carrying out the God's will as expressed in the Holy Bible.

The United Churches recognise that they must aim at conserving for the common benefit whatever of good has been gained by each body in its separate history. The uniting Churches also agree that they should have right to be free in all spiritual matters from the direction of interposition of any civil government. Further this Church must be an autonomous church and free from any control, legal or otherwise of any Church or Society external to itself. At the same time they remember that the United Church, on account of its origin and history must have special relations with the Churches in the West through which it has come into existence, and they are confident that it will regulate its acts as to maintain fellowship both with those Churches and with other branches of the Catholic Church with which the uniting Churches are now in common.[29]

Synod of Church of South India

In the beginning of formation of Church of South India, the C.S.I.was divided into 14 Dioceses and wanted 14 Bishops (vide Table 3.2). But by that time there were already three Anglican Bishops functioning and thus they were allowed to continue. Additionally 10 new Bishops were consecrated. At present there are 21 Dioceses in the Church of South India. At the time of formation of Church of South India, the strength of members of Church were a total of 10,25,000 comprising of 5,00,000 Anglicans, 2,25,000 Wesleyans, 3,00,000 S.I.U.C.[30] Since, then, the Church of India completed as many as 55 years of age and has grown leaps and bounds both in respect of its organisation, membership and activities. The CSI has its Headquarters at Chennai (Madras) Tamilnadu with 21 Dioceses, each Diocese headed by one Bishop. The following are the names of the dioceses under Church of South India.[31]

Its reveals that during the period of formation of Church of South India all the highest positions like Moderator, Deputy Moderator including the Treasurer were held by Europeans. Even in respect of the positions of Bishops and Dioceses also, these positions were headed by Europeans. It shows out of 14 Bishops 9 Bishops were Englishmen. Same was the case inrespect of the Governors of various standing committees. Out of 16 standing committees shown only four were Indians and the remaining twelve were Europeans. But later slowly the domination of Europeans came to a close and the present position is no European is found in any important positions in the Synod or in 21 Dioceses of Church of South India.

Organisational Structure of Church of South India

The basis of 'Union and Constitution of Church of South India' were contained in a booklet called 'Scheme of Church Union in South India' published by the Christian Literature Society in 1941. In1952, the Church of South India with its constitution embodying some alterations of the original constitution which received the approval of the Synod upto December 31, 1951 was published. Subsequently the Constitution of Church of South India as amended in the following years, 1956,1963,1972,1982 and of late in December 1992 was adopted.[32]

Synod: The Church of South India is headed by a Governing body called the 'Synod' which is Supreme. Its headquarters is located in Chennai, Tamil Nadu State. This is also a legislative body of Church of South India and is the final authority in all matters pertaining to the Church. It has power to make rules and pass resolutions and take executive action as may be necessary from time to time for the general management and good government of the church and of the property and affairs.

The Synod is the top management body responsible for implementing the objectives of the Church Union as well act as a coordinating and unifying agency. The Synod has a definite role to play and cannot be dispensed with. It is an ecclesiastical governing as well as sometimes advisory body. It is also a governing body of an Episcopal province. The Synod is composed of one Moderator, one Deputy Moderator, one General Secretary, one Honorary Treasurer,[33] Bishops of 21 Dioceses, 42 delegates two from each Diocese and three nominated members with a total of 70 members. The Synod is headed by a Moderator elected by the Bishops of all 21 dioceses of Church of South India spread over to the four States of India namely Andhra Pradesh, Tamil Nadu, Karnataka and Kerala and Jafna Province of Sri Lanka and other delegates. According to the rules of the election adopted by the Synod, the election of the Moderator would be without nomination. That means, the members were free to vote for any Diocesan Bishop of their choice. The Moderator is assisted by one Deputy Moderator, who is also one from among the Bishops of 21 Dioceses elected. In addition to these officers, there is one General Secretary and one Honorary Treasurer who are nominated by the Nominations Committee. The Executive Committee of the Synod, consists of all 21 dioceses Bishops, 42 delegates two from each Diocese and three other delegates nominated by the Nominations Committee. There is also a provision to send other persons as delegates from the dioceses as substitutes if the officially elected delegates from each diocese do not turn up to the Synod elections. The term of Synod, Moderator, Deputy Moderator, General Secretary, Honorable Treasurer and the delegates from each Diocese and the three nominated members is two years. However the Bishops of each Diocese will continue as members of the Executive Committee of the Synod till their retirement. The General

Secretary of the C.S.I. Women's Fellowship is also the exofficio Member of the Synod.[34]

Every diocese is represented in the Synod by not less than two Presbyters and four laymen and will have one additional Presbyter and one additional lay representative for every complete 10,000 Baptised members in the Diocese above the first 10,000 up to a maximum of 6 Presbyters and 8 laymen representing any one Diocese. Out of the total representatives from a diocese to the Synod, at least 25% from among the Presbyters and at least 25% from among the laymen must be youth. Out of the total lay representatives from a diocese to the Synod at least 25% will be women.

The Moderator also authoritsed to appoint to the Synod on the advice of the Executive Committee not more than ten and not less than three persons as additional members of the Synod. Every Diocese Council will hold a fresh election of the ministerial and lay representatives of the diocese in the Synod for each ordinary meeting of the Synod, and these representatives hold the office till the completion of the next ensuing election of such representatives.

Synod Departments and Boards: There are thirteen other Departments and Boards under the Moderator. Each Department is headed by a Chairman and a Director. The Chairman will be generally any Bishop of the 21 Dioceses and the Director will be any one of the Presbyters (Pastors) from any C.S.I. Diocese. (1) Department of Christian Education, (2) Department of Mission and Evangelism, (3) Department of Pastoral Aid, (4) Department of Communication, (5) Department of Youth, (6) Board of Diaconal Ministry, (7) Department of Dalit and Adivasi Concerns, and (8) Laity Department.

The Department of Christian Education was started in the year 1990 and is headed by one Chairman and a Director both are clergy. The main motto of this Department is To nurture God's people for Christian service'. This Department since the time of its establishment and for the last ten years initiated several of its programmes to nurture at the Diocese, Region and Synod level. These programmes included the training programmes for material, Peter Cator scripture examination and several other special progrmmes like conduct of special schools for children, teachers and so on. With the help of Bishops, Diocesan Coordinators and selected resource persons from the Dioceses the Department could enlarge the Christian Education activities for a comprehensive nurturing ministry of the Church. The term of this committee is two years and after completion of the term new office bearers are nominated.[35]

The Department of Mission and evangelism started was in 1954 with the motto of "pray, proclaim and participate". This department is also headed by on Chairman and one Director, the Chairman happened to be one of the Bishops of the C.S.I. Dioceses and the Director is also from clergy. The functions of this Department are to coordinate the work carried on by the dioceses. It is also entrusted with the responsibility to arrange for the missionary work of the Church of South India outside the CSI area in India and also in other countries. It designs programmes to stimulate the evangelistic and missionary zeal in the Churches with a view to challenging every Christian become an active witness to Jesus Christ. It also organises Conferences, Seminars, Workshops, Consultations and Bible Studies in order to equip the people of God to take part in God's Mission which is a participatory and holistic one. This Department develops more relevant and need based curriculum materials for use in the missionary or evangelistic training centres in the dioceses.[36]

The Department of Pastoral Aid was started in 1950 with the main motto of 'Servants of the Servant Lord'. This Department is organising various programmes for Church Pastors, like Pastor's continuing education, publication of Bible study material, Sermon Almanac, organising Pastors summer family conferences, Pastor's study and reflection programme, and so on. It also organises special programmes like workshop on Music, Bhajans, Lyrics and Communication, training in counselling, journalism, homlitics and worship, management training to ministers, etc.[37]

The Department of Communication is a unique department attached to the Synod which develops communication network system connecting the Churches, dioceses and the Synod and also with the Churches overseas - Partner Churches CWM, CCA, etc. It establishes communication centres, cells in all dioceses and provide necessary equipment, train communicators through these centres. It organizes Seminars, Conferences on communication, technological development, innovative methods in media and gospel communication. It also conducts courses on effective communication, communication skills, dynamics of communication etc. It also publishes the C.S.I. monthly magazine namely The South India Churchman'. It also points the Joint Diary for CSI-CNIMTC Churches. This Department was started in 1958.

The Department of Youth which was started in 1962 with a vision of 'to enthuse the young people with a new vision and a passion. Vision about Church and Society, passion for Christ and his gospel rooted in Justice and truth. It conducts programmes for youth at Synod level, regional level, and

Diocesan level including ecumenical programmes. The objectives of this department are to ensure that all the youngsters of the age group 13-35 feel 'belonged' to the Church, actively and constructively participating in the life and witness of the Church. It helps youngsters of different social clusters to come together for fellowship and joint action. It also organises specific thrust programmes relating to education, health and basic amenities to the people, Human Rights, preferences to combat poverty, illiteracy and unemployment, democracy, civil society and empowerment of life in community and so on.

The Church of South India created the 'Board of Dioconal Ministry' to promote hope, meaning and self dignity in the life of people living amidst forces of darkness so that they may see the light of a new dawn... life in all its abundance. The Dioconal Ministry is an initiative of the Church of South India, part of its faith, commitment to facilitate transformation and empowerment of those subsisting on the very edges of society. It is promoting a process of sensitisation and capacity building of the Church, and involvement in creative action of affirming the identities and facilitating the empowerment of Dalits, Adivasis, women, children, displaced and so on. The uniqueness of this Board is that it is chaired by the Moderator of Church of South India himself.

The Department of Dalit and Adivasi concerns, a department of recent origin was started in the Church of South India in the year 1992 with various environed programmes like - empowering the C.S.I. congregation which are victimised by untouchability, caste atrocity, encroachment of agricultural lands and enable them to overcome forces of marginalisation. To work towards the prioritised forces of girl child among dalits and Adivasis in all the workings of the Department. To impart skills among dalits and Adivasi boys and girls in gainful employment. To encourage Dalit and Adivasi members to become award of the socio-political realities and equip them enter public life and enable them to run for public offices and so on. This department joins with secular organisations to lobby for the inclusion of the plight of the Dalits in India.[38]

Synod Boards / Committees and Councils : There are as many as Twenty Seven different Committees and Councils in the Synod constituted through nominations by the Nominations Committee which function under the control of the Moderator of the Church of South India. Each Board/ Committee or Council have one Chairman and one Convenor. All those bodies are constituted both with clergy as well as laity. Each Board / Committee / Council is represented by one delegate from each Diocese and the strength of each Board is twenty three members which include 21 delegates from 21 Dioceses and the Chairman and the Convenor. The Chairman of all these Boards / Committees / Councils are clergy and the Convenor may either be a clergy a laity.[39]

Governing Bodies: The Church of South India also runs good number of Theological Colleges, Theological Societies, Educational Institutions, Medical Colleges and Hospitals and other Service Centres. All these institutions are managed by respective Governing Bodies constituted by the Synod and functions under the control of the Moderator of Church of South India. The following are the Institutions.[40]

1. The National Missionary Society : The Director of C.S.L Council for Mission and Evangelism is the Chairman.
2. Madras Christian College (MCC). Tambaram : The Governing Board of this College consists of six members of which one is the Moderator of C.S.I. who is the Chairman of the Board.
3. United Theological College (UTC), Bangalore : This is a Theological College which offers various Theological Courses like Bachelor of Theology, Bachelor of Divinity, Master of Theology etc. The Governing Body of this College comprise of five members of which the Moderator of the C.S.I is the Chairman and all other members are clergy.
4. Christian Literature Society (CLS). Chennai: This is a society which is involved in preparing Christian theological literature and made available to the readers. The Governing Body of the Society is comprising of five members drawn each one from one Diocese.
5. Women's Christian College. Chennai : This is also an educational Institution which imparts secular education to those who got admission into the College. The Governing Body of this College is comprising five members drawn from the Dioceses.
6. Christophers College. Chennai : This is an secular educational institution located at Chennai and it has a Governing Body with five members.
7. Christian Medical College (CMC), Vellore : This is a Medical College attached to a Super Speciality Hospital at Vellore. Its Governing Body consists of five members of which the Moderator of CSI is the Chairman.

In addition to above, there are other institutions like Ecumenical Christian Centre, Whitefield, American College, Madurai, Community

Service Centre, Chennai, Christian Counselling Centre, Vellore, Meston Training College, Chennai.

Council for Technical and Vocational Training (CTVT)

The Council for Technical and Vocational Training, best known as CTVT, has been functioning since, 1980 as a Development arm of the CSI Synod with the primary objectives of facilitating capacity and perspective building of the Dioceses on Development and Skill Training issues; and assisting them in planning and implementation of need based programmes through its accompaniment services; as also liaisoning between the Overseas Partners and the Dioceses in matters relating to accountability and stewardship. Another significant thing that happened was that through concerted and sustained efforts, this Council succeeded in starting Rural Community Polytechnics on the Yellareddy model in four of the five Andhra Dioceses. Programmes around issues such as Dalits, Sustainable Agriculture, Environment and Ecology, Street Children, Urban Labourers, Women etc., were attempted, thus slowly registering a shift towards issue-based initiatives. The Council also enlarged its service activities involving itself in projects and programmes supported by Overseas Church Agencies other than its traditional partners.

Vision for Equipping the Local Congregation in Mission (VELCOM): 'VELCOM' as a programme, has been introduced to bring out not only guided development through its four tenets, Agape, Agenda, Analysis and Action but also changes in attitude, outlook, goals and aspirations. Efforts are being made by the VELCOM contact persons, one in each diocese, and the small action groups they have formed, to orientate congregations in rural and urban areas towards emerging new values of sharing, caring, serving and praying communities.

Church of South India Women's Fellowship (CSIWF):

The C.S.I. Women's Fellowship is an important wing of the Synod which was created in February 1948 just one year after the formation of Church of South India. The Women's Fellowship at Headquarters level has a Central Committee with five members of which one is the President and the one is the Vice-President. One member act as General Secretary. This Women Fellowship is spread to nook and corner of CSI jurisdiction. The Women Fellowships are organised at Diocese, and Local Church levels including remotest congregations. These Fellowships have their programmes like conduct of Bible study,Fasting prayers apart from social programmes like Hospital and Jail visits and helping the helpless like widows, lepers etc. Many women Fellowships are engaged in developmental activities, and providing a platform for the women to learn amongst and thereby earn a living. The Women Fellowships in the CSI are also involved in activities like running of 250 innovative pre-schools which provide facilities for nearly 10,000 children, oldage homes, sewing schools, pottery work units, handicraft centres, day care centres, Creches, Typewriting institutes etc. Ladies Hostels and pre-marital counselling centres are also run by these Women Fellowships.[41]

Order of Sisters : It was in June 1952 on Whit-Sunday that the Order of Sisters came into being. Twenty seven Sisters were Commissioned and ten Probationers were admitted in Bangalore. The Order had grown year by year. A total of one hundred and thirty seven have joined the order during the forty five years. At the moment there are seventy three Sisters, fifty active and twenty three retired in the fifteen Dioceses. Eleven have resigned for various reasons. Sisters while representing the Order wear a white sari with a blue piping or a white dress with blue piping. A silver badge of a cross within a circle or a sari pin or the same design is given to the Sister at the Admission Service when she is admitted as a Probationer. On reception to membership of the Order of Sisters at the Commissioning Services the Sister receives a wooden cross on a silver chain similar to that of the Bethel Sisters. These are not in any way to distance the Sisters from the others. When they are not taking a Service or not officially representing the Order they wear ordinary clothes.

Church of South India Trust Association (CSITA):

The Church of South India Trust Association was incorporated on 26th September 1947 - the day immediately proceeding the inauguration of the Union. The Association was established primarily for the purpose of holding in trust the properties vesting in the Church of South India or the properties henceforth acquired by it. This association consisted of the Moderator, the Secretary, the Treasurer and Twelve other members elected by the Synod. There is a Committee of Management consisting of six members elected by the Members of the Association. The Committee of Management on the 10th November 1947, resolved that to cover the expenses incurred in Management one percent be charged on all interest from investments held by the Association as 'bare trustee'.

The First Meeting of this Association was held at the American College, Madura on the 9th March 1948 when the Committee of Management was elected and the budget was approved for the time being, the Synod appointed Attorneys to act on behalf of the Association in the matter primarily of acquisition of properties for the association. Accordingly the Bishop, the Secretary and Treasurer of the respective Dioceses were appointed to function as Attorneys on behalf of CSI Trust Association.[42]

In Andhra Pradesh there are two Regional Offices namely Khammam covering three Dioceses, and Kurnool covering three Dioceses. Karnataka has one Regional Office at Mysore covering North Karnataka and South Karnataka Dioceses. Kerala has one Regional Office at Kottayam covering North, South, East and Madhya Kerala Dioceses. In Tamilnadu there are two Regional Offices one at Salem covering Coimbatore, Madras and Vellore Dioceses and one at Dindigul covering Trichy, Tanjore, Madhurai Ramnad, Tiruchirapalli and Kanya Kumari Dioceses.

The Church of South India is the Church constituted by the Union in 1947. It was in the year 1919 an appeal by thirty three Christian leaders of which thirty one of them were Indians, was issued after a Conference at Tranquebar. In the same year the South India United Church which was formed earlier decided to open negotiations on the basis outlined in the appeal. Then in 1920, the Anglicans came forward to negotiate for unification. Later in 1925 the Methodists also joined in the negotiations. Then in the year 1929, the first edition of the scheme of the union was released and in1941 the Seventh edition of the scheme of the Union was ready. This scheme was approved by Methodists in 1943 and in the year 1945 the General Council of the CIBC (Anglican) approved. In 1946 the South India United Church General Assembly approved the unification scheme and finally on September 27, 1947 the Church of South India came into existence with its headquarters at Madras. At the time of formation, there were only thirteen dioceses and today there are 21 Dioceses spread over to four States of South India including Jafna area in Sri Lanka.

The Church of South India is run by 'Synod' which is its governing body headed by 'Moderator'. This Church has been functioning with the help of various Departments, Boards, Committees and Councils and performing both Religious, theological, educational and other social activities. Of these 21 Dioceses Rayalaseema Diocese is also one of the oldest Dioceses formed in the year 1950 with a series of historical developments. The formation of Church of South India Rayalaseema Diocese from a historical perspective is dealt in the succeeding chapter.

The Church in South India: The first recorded visit of the Portuguese to Tamil Nadu in 1517 and gradually a Portuguese colony arose in and around Madras. In 1516-17 there took place the great mass conversions of the fishermen on the Parava coast of Cape Comorin. The early slender roots of Christianity in Tami Nadu went back to the 16th Century, few records survived. The roman Catholics had concentrated among the Paravas at the pearl fishery coast, the Mukkuvars near Cape Comorin, Pondicherry and some places in the Carnatic region as well as in Mylapore. The Protestants had smaller Churches of the Tranquebar or Danish Hall Mission, many of them supported by the Anglican Society for promotion of Christian knowledge, which concentrated in the Tanjore and Tiruchirapalli area.[43]

Tranquebar mission had by 1771 reached Palayamcottah. Where Tamil Christians from Tiruchirapalli and Tanjore were working in the service of British army stations. In 1795. A young lad Sundaranandan of the village of Kalangadiwas baptized and from 1796 he worked as an assistant to Satyanandan who was the Pastor or the Church at Palamcottah from 1790. In the following year David (formerly Sundarandan) had gathered a Christian group among the relatives and friends of the Shanar caste at the village of Vijayaramapuram between Tirunelveli and the coast and founded a small congregation of Christian worshippers there and at Mudalur (1799), Jerusalem (1802), Bethlehem (1802) and Nazareth (1804).[44] Around the same time Maharan, a Sambavar (Aidravidan) of the village of Mayiladi a staunch saivite was baptized as Vedamanikam, who in turn started a small group at Mayiladi. The Jesuits established their centres at Madras, Madurai, Santhome, Cauvery and Mylapore etc.

While the great majority of the Christians of the interior of Karnataka lived in the Southern districts, Northern Karnataka had only a few Christians during 17th century. The history of the Christianity in Southern Karnataka is mostly the history of the Mysore mission. Fr Leonard Chinnami, an Italian priest was the first person to start work in inland parts of Mysore territory in 1649, where he put on the robe of a sanyasi. Frchinnami made the first convert, a potter at a place called Bassanapura. He was able to baptize about 40 people. In 1653 Fr Chinnami was able to return to Mysore and set up residence at Rampura, which became the first centre of the Kannada Mission. A few Christian communities in villages such as Ankel, Harabale and Kankanahalli. At the beginning of the 18th century, there were about 190 Christians in Hassan and its environs. Since 1687 Sira had been the capital of the area south of the Tungabhadra River. It seemed that Christianity arrived there about 1715, which stated with a dhobi washerman called Paul, from Sira itself who was brought into the Church. A few others followed him. In 1735, Father Francis Mucci arrived at Sira and founded a Chrch.[45] In Bangalore, a Church was built at Billiakipaati sometime before 1780 and another Church was also built at Gangaumachery. In Bejapur, Richur, Gulbarga and Ballary etc regions established Christian Church.

Christianity in Andhra Pradesh: The first to arrive in the Telugu Territory were the Roman Catholic's. followed by Baptists and Lutherans. The earliest report of Missionary work among the Telugus was in 1500 when a Franciscan Frior, Luis de Salvador, converted some gentiles in the Kingdom of Vijayanagar. Perhaps these were the first Telugu Christians. The Jesuits arrived in India in 1542. Francis Xavier found the Andhras inimical to Christianity and it was reported that one missionary was killed in 1549. In spite of this set back The Jesuits did not give up their gospel work. Freancisco Ricci, one of the Jesuits, who came to work among the Andhras, had already translated the Christian Doctrine into Telugu by 1600. But the progress they made was not very impressive.[46]

Later evidence of Missionary work came from Francisco, Manco who made Machilipatnam as his head quarters in 1640. He established Christian communities in Mechilipatnam and constructed a Church for the community at Bheemilipatnam which was the first constructed in the Kingdom of Golconda. Later there were evidences of Churches in Narsapur, Srikakulam, Vishakapatnam and Hyderabad constructed by Augustians by 1652. In 1701 Evangelists from France and Catholic Missionaries belonging to the Jesuits were preaching the Gospel in Punganoor village of Chittur district. In 1701 Padal Manduit baptized one family, from Velama caste. Thus Punganur became the cradle of the Telugu Christians in the 18th Century. From there they moved towards the North and established their stations at Krishnapuram and Ananthapur.[47] Calmette, S.J. reported that the first Kamma Christians were baptized at Gudikondaseema in Cuddapah district. For the first time in 1843, the Andhra Mission had come under on Vicariate. i.e Vicariate of Madras. In 1845 Vishakapatnam was created as a separate Vicariate. Meanwhile, new Churches were being planted in the places like Macherla, Kurnool, Parakala, Sullurpeta, Thalamus etc. the Telugu press in Nellore published at first edition of the Gospels and acts in 1914. On 2nd November 1875 the first four Mill Hill Missionaries arrived in Madras. After a stay there they were appointed to the Mission in Phirangipuram in December. At the end of the year, the missionaries took a census of Guntur and counted a total of 5,700. 1902 was a famous year in the annals of Mill Hill in India. Twelve new priests arrived from Europe who was quickly called the "Twelve

Apostles". It was given in the official reports that in 1930-1935 over 10,000 Telugus became Catholics. By 1940, total Catholic population had reached 49,000.[48]

The London Missionary Society[49] Gospel came to South India and preached at Travancore, Bellary and Vishakapatnam in 1805. Rev. George cross and Rev. Augustine Granges worked in Vishakapatnam area. Another Missionary Rev. John wands arrived in Ballary in 1810 and established the mission there. Later in 1822 he established another mission in Cuddapah and in 1832 a prominent Church was built there. Rev.Howell dedicatedly preached in Pulivendula area and singificanly one Brahmin by name Veerappa converted as a Christian. From 1835 to 1844 Rev. Edward Porter with his wife worked in Vishakapatnam and built a Church there. They extended their work to such places like Palakonda and Srikakulam.

Initially in 1826, Rev. john Henracide who was the first S.P.G. Missionary[50] in India started his work in Cuddapah. Later about 50 members of the London Mission had joined the S.P.G. in Rudravaram 30 People became Christians. In Giddalur, Nandyala, Jammalamadugu, Kalasapadu villages intensive Gospel work was undertaken by Rev. Wood, Rev. John Clay etc., Realising the shortage of preachers in Muthyalapadu, a bible training center was established. As a result in seven years 12 villages had accepted Jesus as the Saviour.

For a long time all the Anglican Missions in Kurnool district were under the control of Bishop Whitehead. But in 1922, all these Missions were handed over to Bishop Azaraiah. As per the 1945 census there were 50,000 members in these Missions. In 1947 when Church of South India (CSI) was formed it Was expected that all the Anglican Missions would join the C.S.I. but only 10,000 of them joined.[51] Since 1799, in Hyderabad British troupes were stationed and there were some Indian Soliders in them. To serve them Chaplain with ford from England came to Hyderabad in 1841. He had done impressive Gospel work in Secunderabad, Bollaram, Thirumalagiri and Hyderabad. In 1854 a first Muslim took up Christianity followed by many others later. He served for about 20 years and built up Saint Thomas Church in Secunderabad in 1854 with seven thousand rupees.

The American Baptists had commenced their work[52] in 1840 and with the success, they met in the districts of Krishna and Kurnool, they established themselves firmly in Kurnool. Rev. Samuel S. Day, an American Baptist arrived in India to preach among the Andhras as early as 1836. Ongole had witnessed Gospel work in 1854 with the dedicated sevices of Lyman Juliet couple supported by Rev. Clough. In 1865 a Dalit, Yerraguntla Peaiah became a Christian and made many others to come closer to Jesus. It is remarkable to note that in a single day he gave baptisms to 2,222 in Gundla Kamma River. American Baptist Missionaries seved the Southern parts of Andhra Pradesh with match less Zeal in places like Allur, Athmakur, Udayagiri, Kavali, Sattennapalli, Guruajala, Kurnool, Kambbham, Markapur, Nandyala, Gadwal etc.

The Campbells and Rev. Clough served at Ongole under the American Baptist Missionary in 1874 and later moved to Secunderabad in 1875, to establish the Telugu Baptist Mission. In addition to serving the soldiers, they extended their work to such places in Telangana like, Hanumakonda, Nalgonda, Jangoam, Suryapeta and Madhira etc.The Canadian Baptist Mission Gospel work started in[53] India in 1868 under A.T. Timpany. Rev.Jewet who was already working in Nellore. While doing the Missionary work he established a school of theology in Ramayapatnam. Rev. John B.Meclarin with his wife came from Canada and joined Rev. Clough in Ongole in his gospel work. In 1874 Rev. Mcclarin with Rev. Timpani moved to Kakinada to establish Canadian Baptist Mission. Within a short period their work, extended to Bheemini Patnam, Bobbili, Yalamanchili, Ramachandrapuram, Rayagada, Samarlakota and Sompeta.

Church Missionary Society work[54] in Andhra under Rev. Robert Burlington Noble and H.W. Fox came to Machilipatnam in 1811. In St. Marry's Church Rev. Fox was ordained by the Bishop of Madras. Later a small mission was established. In 1844 there were two baptisms followed by five. Those were the first Christians Chilakalapudi, Guduru, Kurukulapadu, Golapalli, Nidumolu and Bezawada witnessed the proselatization activites. In 1847 Kondapalli, villagers were preached the gospel and in 1851 the Dalits were also preached the word of God. The Church Missionary Society activities continued in Polsanapalli, Nayudugudem, Pedapadu, Sirirwada, Nuzividu, Kanumoul, Bhimadolu and Chintalapudi villages. Later C.M.S. seved in the Dummugudem and Khammam areas. The C.M.S. in 1941 celebrated the one hundred anniversary of the arrival in Machilipatnam of their pioneer Missionaries Reverends Nobles and Fox.

The church of England Zenana Missionary Society working in Khammam ,Machilipatnam, Bezawada and Eluru. The South Asia Methodist Mission activities were confined to Telangana including Hyderabad and Secunderabad.[55] The Pentecostal Church of India Activities started at Vijayawada, Eluru, Kakinada, Vishakapatnam, Rajahmundry, Amalapuram and Mandapeta etc. in addition Narasapuram,[56] Palakollu, Agarthipalem, Chettipeta, Tanuku, Kyyalagudam,[57] Prathipadu, Amalapuram, Ambajipeta, Dhavaleswaram, Antharvedipalam, Kothapet, Nidadavolu. These places under the Godavari field actively engaged in the Church working. The Christian Missionaries played a vital role in the service of the downtrodden and Dalits in Andhra Pradesh.

References

1. Donald Fosset Ebright., The National Missionary Society of India (1905-1942)' Doctoral Thesis submitted to the University of Chicago, 1944, p. 76.
2. Gibbs, M.E., The Anglican Church in India, (1600-1970). Delhi: ISPCK, 1972, p. 335.
3. The Report of the First General Assembly of SIUC held at Madras during December 25-27,1908 A.D., pp. 3-4.
4. *Ibid.*
5. Kuriakose, M.K., History of Christianity in India, Bangalore: Indian Theological Society, 1978, p. 297.
6. The Report of the First General Assembly of SIUC, Op.cit., p. 5.
7. Minutes of the Second General Assembly of the SIUC held at Trivandrum in December 1909, p. 14.
8. World Missionary Conference 1910, Vol.IX, pp. 306-315.
9. *Ibid.*
10. *Ibid.*
11. Grims, C.J., Towards an Indian Church. London: SPCK, 1946, p. 242.
12. Devaraju, B.E., History of Christianity in India. Tenali: The Telugu Theological Literature Board, Andhra Christian Council, 1969, pp. 209- 211.
13. *Ibid.*
14. Report of the VII All India Conference of Indian Christians held at Calcutta, December 28-31; 1920, pp. 32-36.
15. Report of VIII AICIC Conference held at Calcutta, 28-30 December, 1921, pp. 40-42.
16. Young India, August 20,1925.
17. Grimes, C.J., Op.cit., pp. 209-218.
18. Kuruvilla, K.K., Jerusalem to New Delhi, Op.cit., pp. 302-303.
19. *Ibid.*
20. *Ibid,* p. 305.
21. Arangadam, J., Church Union in South India. Masalve: Basel Mission Press, 1947, p. 35.
22. *Ibid.,* pp. 74-75.
23. Abel, M., 'Beyond Organic Union' in 'Liberating Witness' Vol. 1 (ed), Prasanna Kumari, Chennai: Gurukul Theological College, 1995, p. 326.

24. *Ibid.*
25. Kuruvilla, K.K., Op.cit., pp. 299-300.
26. Minutes of the Second Session of CSI Synod held at Madras from 7- 11 January, 1950, p. 1.
27. *Ibid,* p. 27.
28. The Constitution of Church of South India, Chapter-I.
29. *Ibid.,* Appendix-!, pp. 87-101.
30. Church of South India, Proceedings of First Synod Executive Committee, 1948, p. 20.
31. *Ibid.,* Proceedings of Twenty Eighth Synod Executive Committee Meetings, Melukavu, East Kerala, 2000, p,211.
32. Foreword written to the Constitution of Church of South India, P.1.
33. CSI Constitution, Chapter IX, Rule (6).
34. *Ibid.,* Chapter IX, Rule(1).
35. Proceedings of the CSI 28th Session of the Synod, January 11-15, 2000, HRD Centre, Melukavu, East Kerala.
36. *Ibid.*
37. *Ibid.*
38. *Ibid.*
39. Res. No.2002-9 of Church of South India Synod 2002.
40. *Ibid.*
41. CSIWF, Golden Jubilee Souvenir, 1948-98.
42. CSI, Minutes of the Proceedings of the Second Synod, Madras, 7-11 January 1950, p. 38, CSI, Synod 28th Session, Report by Frederick William, Treasurer
43. (K.M. George; Christianity in India through the Centuries, op-cit., P.124.
44. E.C.Hambaya; History of Christianity in India, Vol.III, the Church History Association of India, Bangalore, 1997, P.27.
45. K.M. George; Christianity in India through the Centuries, op-cit., p. 133.
46. K.E. Raj Pramukh; Dalit Christians of Andhra, (Under the Impact of Missionaries), Serials Publications, New Delhi, 2008, P.31.
47. *Ibid.*
48. *Ibid.,* P.33.
49. It was established on 18th of January 1795 in London.
50. In 1698 Thomas Brown, a Missionary, Founded Christian Scientific Development Society with a view to spread the Gospel to other nations.
51. K.E. Raj Pramukh; Dalit Christians of Andhra, op-cit., P.34.
52. In 1814 some of those who had Zeal for Gospel work formed into American Baptist Union. In 1835 they sent Rev. Samuel S. Day to India.
53. Dr. Moorduck Founded the Canadian Baptist Mission in 1867.
54. In 1799 Members of the Church of England founded C.M.S. to Preach the Gospel in India and other Asian Countries.

55. K.E. Rajapramukh; Dalit Christianity of Andhra, op-cit., p. 39.
56. K. Jobe Sudhershan; Goppa Sakshi Samuham, Godavari Delta Cristava Sanga Charitra, Jeevan Jyothi Press and Publishers, West Godavari, A.P. 1986, pp. 124-142.
57. *Ibid.,* pp. 204-211.

Chapter - IV

Christian Missionaries in Andhra

The history of Christian missions in India, shedding light on the arrival of Portuguese and Protestant missions into the country. The Missionaries from the U.S. and the European Continent came to India primarily for evangelical work, they rendered substantial services for the weaker sections of the sun to which they were not accustomed in their native lands, frequent visitations of plague, cholera, smallpox, enteric fever etc., the Missionaries rendered yeomen services to the people of India, it is prudent to make a brief but graphic account of the missionary entry into the Andhra districts and their early trails and travails though their intention is to Christianise entire India.

Christians in India are considered as colonial agents because of colonial rule and Christian missionaries, which worked hand in hand. As far as the history of church in India is from the Colonial period and it is the most important period which made a significant impact on Indian society. Christian missions made a positive impact in several areas such as education, medical service, eradication of social evil practices, technology development etc., Especially English education brought renaissance in India which led to Nationalistic movements. Some of the missionaries encouraged Indian nationalistic movements during freedom struggle. Along with their positive impact there are several negative areas that remain as black spots in Indian Christian mission history. Christian mission has always given a wrong impression thinking that mission is always from the superior West to the inferior East and rich North to the poor South. Even though political colonial dominance is over; still the shadow of colonialism is chasing the south by its dominance. It is a fact that Christianity is growing in south, but still its church is under the dominance of western superior power for its theology and mission praxis.

In nineteenth century the Indian castes are depicted as timeless, fixed communities whose customs, rituals, and occupational specialities evolved at an unidentifiable point in the distant past and it has now been shown many castes are of relatively recent origin.Historians have been able to trace the economic, political, and religious changes which acted to form individual caste groups during the colonial period.[1] Several recent works on India have argued that the agglomerations of artisans and cultivators described as castes by the British ethnographers and Census reports had no real cohesion and there were often no more than unstable political alliances or 'administrative fictions'. In this background, it was the misconceived European notion of castes as rigid competing corporations which stimulated the formation of many south Indian castes after I880.[2]

The church history in India helps us to understand that Vosco da- Gama prepared a way for the establishment of colonial Christianity by his arrival to Calicut on May 20, 1498. The Dutch, English, and Danish merchants first represented Evangelical Christianity in India and especially in south India beginning with the 17th Century.(Lehmann 1956: 12). All these groups of Europeans brought their chaplains and the missionaries were accused of having made a business out their piety and turned their activity to profit. The Dutch East Indian Company was not interested on Christian mission and in fact they could not make any efforts for the growth of the church in India. Their main focus was on trade and they could only translate. The Danish colonial power settled in Tranquebar in1620 and at Serampore in 1676. The main purpose of the Danish is to trade, but the Lutheran protestant King Fredrick IV has sent Bartholomew Ziegenbalg and Henry Pluetschau for the Christian mission to work in India. The British Colonial government openly supported missionaries and their activities. Christian mission under British made a great impact in the country in different areas such as education, medical, literacy, technology, eradication of social evil practices etc.,

Indian Christianity

In Christianizing the Hellenic world of the first few Christian centuries, Christianity became pretty largely Hellenized, especially in its apologetic and dogmatic formulas. Fortunately for the Christians of Greece-Roman culture, those who introduced them to Christianity did not introduce the new faith in the form of creeds and dogmas. The missionaries to that world were men of contagious faith and heroic adventure, whose lives were joined by vital links to Jesus Christ. Their contribution to the Hellenic world was a living religion of redemption, and not a system of theology. There is always constructive Christian thought in process. It is psychologically necessary that such thinking be in terms of the imagery of the environment, chronological and social.It is the glory of the Christian faith that it is always so vitalizing that strong men feel the urge to interpret its great facts, especially its greatest fact, Jesus Christ, in terms of the current philosophy of life. This is one of the reasons that its redemptive influence continues throughout the ages to suffice for peoples of varying mould of thought.

The missionary is at best a stranger in a strange cultural environment. Sometimes his task takes him among people whose culture is decidedly primitive. At other times he finds himself planted on the soil of an environment with a culture with greater claims to antiquity than his own. In any case he comes among the new peoples, the heir to a wealth of social imagery that has supplied the tools for all of his past religious thinking, but which is foreign in many respects to the thought processes of his new neighbours and friends. He cannot escape the disadvantage of clothing his message in intellectual moulds other than those common to his hearers. In spite of an overwhelming desire to do full justice to the gospel which he bears, in his hands it invariably presents some aspects of a foreign religion. It is for this reason, that the missionary, enterprise is increasingly being realized as the task of building up strong churches with intelligent leaders, native to the soil and the culture, so that the religion of Jesus may assume a more indigenous character everywhere.[3]

It is of no small significance that the majority of the converts to the Christian faith have been from the depressed and backward classes. It is not my place to discuss at this point the particular phase of Christianity that has proved most attractive to these peoples. The point to be noted is that, until they were given greater cultural advantages than they had enjoyed hitherto, they were not in a position to make much contribution to the task of rendering an Indian interpretation of their new faith. Now that we are getting to the third and fourth generation of Christians in some localities, the situation is rapidly changing. Christians, whose forefathers a few generations ago were the victims of a system that gave them few of the advantages of education, are today graduating and graduated from the various colleges of general and technical learning throughout the land.

There is the added fact that, though less common, there is a good number of Christians from caste communities who bring with them to their adopted faith the heritage of their ancient civilization. In many cases the thought processes have been more active and the emotional element less prominent than in the case of the conversions from the backward classes. Hinduism has very little to offer the non-caste man. So when the claims of Christianity are presented, he has to choose between the traditional religion which proposes to perpetuate his disadvantages and the new faith which promises amelioration for his wrongs and a democracy of spiritual privileges. It is somewhat different with the caste man. He and his ancestors, for millenniums perhaps, have been in the enjoyment of the rights and privileges of Hinduism. When he becomes a Christian he does so because he has deliberated and reached the conclusion that the new religion has more to satisfy his felt needs than the old. The psychological process in the conversion experience of the average caste man has included more of the cognitive element than in the experience of the average non-caste man.

The Christianizing of India will involve an Indianizing of Christianity, as surely as the Christianizing of the Greco-Roman world involved the Hellenizing of Christianity. It is undeniable that India has as much right to interpret the world and to interpret Jesus as Hellenism had. The truth is that India is going to make her own interpretations whether the West likes or dislikes it. Surely Western Christendom should welcome the process as the harbinger of a day of larger significance for Jesus to the life and culture of the Orient.

The experience of God in human life is the consciousness of moral delinquency, the realization of salvation, and the redemptive influence of Jesus are facts too large to be confined within the logical categories of any human group. It is not a token of decadence but a sign of vitality that men are continually making new statements, new interpretations, and new evaluations in terms of the prevailing social consciousness. It is because Christianity is a religion of redemption and not simply a philosophy of religion or a system of dogma that men are never content to accept someone else's theory as doing justice to their own experiences. The reality of the matter is that all of these facts are transcendent facts, refusing to be confined to any definitions or theories, be they never so logically devised. The best that we can bring of mental as well as spiritual vigour to the task of realizing the meaning and worth of Jesus is all too little honour for that peerless life which we would proclaim as the world's Redeemer.

Christian Missionaries

To understand the Christian missions in India in terms of Western missionary expansion. As stated earlier, India had a hoary tradition of tolerance and assimilation. This tradition was the creation of the syncretise

Hindu mind eager to be in touch with all other thought currents. "Let noble thoughts come to us from all sides"[4] was the prayer of the Hindu sages. The early converts to Christianity lived cordially in the midst of Hindus respecting one another. This facilitated the growth of Christianity in the Indian soil perfectly as an Indian religion.

The cordial relation between Christian community and non-Christians was received from the famous Synod of Diamper. Latin rites and ordinances were imposed forcefully and a new world of Christendom was threatened to be extended without caring to understand the social peculiarities of the place where it was expected to grow and prosper and ignoring the religio-cultural sensitivity of the people amidst whom the new religion was to exist. As pointed out earlier the central thrust of the activities of the Jesuit missions established in India during the second half of sixteenth century was proselytizing the native population to Christianity. In Goa mission became an instrument for conditioning the native people to accept to Portuguese rule and to assimilate their culture. Christianity was identified with changing over to Portuguese names and dress, beef eating, wine drinking and loose living. That missionary enterprises almost everywhere served the colonial political power was a characteristic feature of that time, the progress of Jesuit mission activities began to decline when the temporal power of the Portuguese began to decay.

The missions brought with the Portuguese are an attitude of moral superiority of the Christians and a claim in their own exclusive righteousness. The doctrine of the monopoly of truth and revelation as claimed by the missionaries were alien to Hindu mind. The claim of Christian sects that they alone possess the truth and others are condemned seemed unreasonable. The Christian association of missionary work with aggressive imperialism. Colonial culture and its ideologies were imposed upon India by a dominant class of evangelicals and bureaucrats from England. There was no serious effort from the side of the missionaries to understand oriental institutions, learn natives literature deal with the religious and cultural sentiments of Indian people. Missions believed that introduction of western science and Christianity alone would redeem the people of India from their cultural predicament. The missions believed that India was consigned to the lowest rung of the ladder of civilization because of its barbarous and superstitious religion. The educational activities of the missionaries stressing the glories of European culture only led to the identification of the work of mission with western cultural aggression.

The missionaries who preached against caste were themselves perpetrators of the cultural superiority of the west, perpetrating the caste sin in a different way. Though it was taught that in Christ all people are utterly equal the European Christians were more equal, to use an Orwellian expression. There were even instances of English missionaries vehemently opposing efforts by Indian Christian leaders to form indigenous missions. This showed that even missionaries were not free from racism. It is indisputable that in order to interpret the (revealed) message of any religion properly the living situation of the people has to be understood thoroughly. Cultures, languages and traditions must be taken seriously. It could be seen that in this respect also the missions failed. In other words they failed to contextualise the gospel message. It appeared that the missionaries were concerned with ensuring that Indian people received the correct pattern of behaviour, right set of doctrines, and the true model of society, which were developed in Europe. It has been pointed out that the European missionaries failed to understand that authentic mission is true identification with the struggles of human beings for self-expression and self-emancipation, active participation in their struggle for freedom and total involvement towards liberation. Colonial mission failed even in conveying properly the Christian message of hope to the native peoples within context of their sufferings and struggles.

This is not to ignore the fact that there was something basically appealing about the sacrifices of certain missionaries and evangelicals and the efforts they took in bringing the Gospel meaningful and in providing education and knowledge to people in India. Their activities would have been commendable if missions acknowledged the richness of the religious pluralism, communal harmony and the magnificent hierarchy of human relationships prevalent in India. The refusal to accept native cultures deprived the chance of the Gospel being preached in its contextualizing nature and of its dynamics of penetrating every human society.

The Britishers helped missionaries financially in the construction of Churches. The Christians were exempted from drawing procession cars-chariots-in Hindu festivals. They were appointed as civil judges and donations were provided for missionary schools this kind of attitude among the Indians created an impression that British rulers intended to Christianize India.[5] Many of the laws enacted in the princely state of Travancore were in favour of Christians. Converted Christians were exempted from all duties connected with the temples and they were permitted free use of public streets while for other low caste people use of public roads near temples were prohibited.[6]

The work of Christian missions among the depressed classes and tribal is worth examining. The stigma of untouchability that rested upon them for generations had led them to a sub-human level of existence. They were systematically exploited and kept down for centuries by caste Hindus. For many who got converted to Christianity it represented liberation from the de-humanising conditions of their existence. They were also benefited by the educational felicities provided by missions, the converts from the underprivileged groups made striking progress in their social and cultural life. Bulk of the people converted in the nineteenth-and twentieth century's were all tribes. The Bhils and Gonds in Chotanagapur, the tribal of North East India are examples. Besides general education, missions gave technical education to tribal youth. In the field of health and hygiene also the missions rendered substantial service by providing medical aid to women and children.[7]

Since most of the new converts came from the economically and socially backward classes, several industrial and agricultural projects were established to improve their conditions. The Basel Mission on the west coast of south India became well known for its tile making and textile industries. Carpentry, furniture making and other crafts were taught to the poor Christians in south India. There was great emphasis on rural education and reconstruction programmes in the Protestant missions' social agenda. Some of the outstanding Christian schools and colleges of India are the result of the pioneering efforts of missionaries. The Christian educational work for girls served as a model for government and other agencies to found schools for girls' education. St. Stephen's College Delhi, Madras Christian College Madras, and St. John's College at Agra are only a few of the many institutions of higher education started by the missionaries. Pioneer work in the field of women's education was done by Pandita Ramabhai a Christian convert. She worked indefatigably for the progress of women's education. Ramabhai founded an institution called **Mukti** for helping widows and others[8]. Women's Christian College Madras, Isabella Thoburn College Lucknow, Sarah Tucker College Palayamcottah etc. are notable in the field of women education. In addition to these there were schools for the deaf and the blind. The Arya Samaj, Theosophical society, Ramakrishna Mission and other agencies began to take interest in womens' education following the lead given by the Christian missions. The Christian colleges exerted great influence on Indian education and Indian thought. The terrible inadequacy of medical facilities in India induced Christian missions to start hospitals and dispensaries in cities and villages. Zenana Medical Mission (ZMM) was founded to bring medical aid to women and children in India.

The missions' medical work also included establishing several Tuberculosis sanatoriums and leprosy asylums. Tuberculosis(TB) sanatoriums at Arogyavarum and Christian Medical Colleges at Velloore in Tamil Nadu and Ludhiana in Punjab are important medical institutions started by missions.[9]

The movements initiated by the educated Hindus to reform their religion may be listed as the most important positive impact of the work of Christian of missions. The flow of knowledge and education from the west did not brainwash the educated class so as to consider Christianity as a substitute for Hinduism. On the contrary, it helped them to examine and evaluate their own religion in a new light. The western impact and the resultant awakening were pervasive and had its effect upon Indian politics, art and literature besides religion. The Hindus even used the gift of English education in opposing missionaries. Thus the rational criticism and historical analysis which the missionaries themselves employed to dislodge Hinduism were adopted by the Hindus to defend their religion and critique the doctrines of Christianity[10]. The entire nineteenth-century, especially the second half of it was a period of cultural and religious ferment in India under the influence of western culture and missions. Whether they meant it or not, Christian missions by familiarizing the Indian mind with certain European concepts helped in reviving the dormant Indian spirit which in time created new schools of thought. The social activities of Christian missions were directed towards bringing about moral reforms in Indian society and helped in the emancipation of individuals from their age old superstitions and other social evils like untouchability and caste discrimination. Missions demanded legal support from the British government in support of their vigorous fight against social evils and superstitious practices associated with Hindu religion such as widow burning or Sati, child marriage, drowning of children in sacred rivers etc. With the support of liberal Hindu leaders and missionaries Governor General William Bentick introduced several legal measures of social reforms.[11]

Finally during second half of nineteenth-century the educational endeavour of Christian missionaries played an important role in the social liberation of the lower castes particularly in the South and in the North Eastern parts of India. The missionaries strove to secure equal rights for them. Missionaries did much to free them from evils like bonded labour, unjust taxation etc. and also for the rights of the women to wear upper cloth. Here missions played the role of a socio-religious movement, which indirectly gave birth to neo-Hindu reformist movements. J. Waston Pickett has also surveyed the Christian mass movements in India and has spelled out the impact of missions in the social emancipation of the depressed classes.[12]

Activities of Christian Missionaries

Alexander Duff, Charles Trevelyan and Thomas Macaulay formed the triumvirs of English education in India. The evangelicals in England and missionaries in India were the prime movers behind the spreading of English education in India. The missionary educators in India trusted in the transforming power of western education and the universality of English literature. They were bent upon civilizing the people of India by Christianizing and westernizing them. Their assumption was that nineteenth-century Britain was the ideal paradigm of Christian culture and society. They presumed that God has laid upon Britain the solemn duty of civilizing and Christianizing the whole pagan world i.e., the non-Christian world. Governor-Generals like Lord Wellesley and Lord Bentick were in open alliance with Christian missions for introducing English education. They had the dream of destroying the pagan religious system of India and implanting evangelistic beliefs and European cultural practices.[13] Both the missionaries and colonial administrators believed that the introduction of European knowledge and civilization was the remedy for all social evils in India. To Quote Arthur Mayhew: "large and continuous doses of western knowledge would not only purge (India) of Hindu and Islamic religion, but also build up a new India with an essentially Christian constitution".[14]

After the introduction of English education in India the subcontinent experienced a proliferation of English medium schools and colleges, mostly run by missionaries. A conservative estimate would give a total of 180 English institutions and 30,000 students in attendance in 1854. After the opening of the universities, English historical and philosophical works penetrated every corner of British India. In Bombay, Calcutta and Madras Macaulay's scheme of English education was implemented, conditioning the converts culturally to accept the Christian spirit.[15] As the English education introduced in India lacked moral content, and the missionary educators reasoned that mere introduction of western science into academic curriculum was not enough. Science in itself was value neutral, or amoral. It should include moral and ethical teachings, by which was meant Christian instruction.[16] For Charles Grant an important member of the Court of Directors of East India Company, Hinduism was a degrading idolatry with all its rubble of impure deities, its monsters of wood and stone, its false principles and corrupt practices, its delusive hopes and fears, its ridiculous ceremonies superstitions, its lying legends and fraudulent impositions.[17] William Wilberforce while speaking on Indian society and religion declared in the House of Common: Our religion is sublime, pure and beneficent. Theirs' is mean licentious and cruel.[18] John Stuart Mill a utilitarian for example, argued that, his views on Europe could not apply to India because Indian people were civilizationally inferior. In the final chapter he argued that Indian's civilization had 'not attained the requisite degree of development' and his views about Europe could not be applied to India[19] The rulers and evangelicals, in fact, were only articulating the inmost feeling of the self-conscious Britons who in the nineteenth century possessed the inflated self-image of being the most highly civilized people on the earth. They advocated a totally western educational scheme for India and believed in the possibility of disintegration of Hinduism and Indian culture consequent on the widespread introduction of English education. And the spread of English education facilitated intellectual ferment, which produced a new class of Indian nationalists. These educated Indians who came out of the schools and universities, knew Christianity as the spiritual and cultural sources of western civilization and the liberal political institutions of the west. These nationalists had read writers and thinkers like John Stuart Mill, Charles Dickens, Voltaire, Rousseau and missionary educators such as Macaulay,

Alexander Duff, et. al. who idealized western culture and Christianity and poured contempt on Indian culture and religions. They were also watching the Anglicising process that the British under the influence of the evangelicals and the utilitarian had thrust upon India. Further, in the streets of Calcutta, Bombay and Madras, the new educated classes were hearing Christian missionaries from the west criticising Hinduism as the cause of the cultural, social, and political degeneration of India. The challenge of Christianity and western culture was felt by the Indian psyche. At the same time it was forced upon the nationalists that their identity would be sustained by reaffirming the tradition of India, a tradition that might need reinterpretation to guide Indian's life in the modern situation. It was this situation where western culture and Christianity on the one side and Indian culture and Hinduism on the other confronted each other under the shadow of colonialism that led to the emergence Hindu religious renaissance. And the resurgent Hindu religious fervour responded to the challenges posed by the English missions.

Christian Missions in India

There are two views among scholars about the origin of Christianity in India. According to one, the foundation of the Christian church in India was laid by Saint Thomas, one of the twelve Apostles of Jesus. The other view would ascribe the arrival of Christianity in India to the enterprise of Christian merchants and missionaries belonging to the East Syrian and Persian churches. But it has been widely believed that India was St. Thomas' sphere of work. As Cardinal Tisserant says there was a very ancient evangelization started by St. Thomas, the Apostle and mainly in South India.[20]

At the dawn of Christian era there were trade routes connecting West Asia and the East. The land routes reached parts of North India, while the Sea routes reached the coast of Kerala and other parts of South India. Then, one can accept the possibility of the Apostle finding an easy passage to India. Jewish settlements and trade connections with Malabar was an added attraction to the Apostle for his missionary journey.[21] Modern scholarship has advanced evidences and testimonies to prove the historicity of St. Thomas apostolate in Malabar.[22]

The British Period

The British Government had three roles in India, first that of a trader, second that of ruler and then that of a Christian propagandist. British rulers held and professed Christianity. Consequently British rule was equated with Christian domination. In the early years of its rule the Company had taken a position of neutrality with regard to the religious and social affairs of its subject. The East India Company decided not to interfere with the traditional cultures of the people by supporting missionary work. The company's policy was non-interference in Indian education but favouring traditional Hindu or oriental learning. The non-interference probably based was on the fear that missionaries through English education expecting to aid conversions might offend the Hindu subjects of the company and create unrest.[22] This policy of non-interference with the customs and traditions of the natives and lack of support for missionary work were reviewed after the Company Charter was reviewed in 1813. Finally in 1833, the policy of the company was changed under pressure from the Evangelicals in England. This marked the first decisive step of missionary work in India. A spokesman of the Evangelicals declared: "The true cure of darkness is the introduction of light. The Hindus err because they were ignorant and their errors have never fairly been laid before them. The communication of our light and knowledge to them would prove the best remedy for their disorders".[23]

The Charter of 1833 approved the permanent presence of missionaries in India and made provision for Anglican hierarchy at Calcutta. With the expansion of the British Empire missionaries began to arrive and Christianity began to spread by establishing dioceses at Madras and Bombay. Ever since there existed a renewed cooperation between the missionaries and the colonial power in helping one another in their missions.[24] By the end of the eighteenth century a new wave of the spirit of evangelization permeated Protestant Churches. In 1792 the English Baptists organised the first Anglican mission Baptist Missionary Society. Later Protestant missionary operations were undertaken on a large scale by LMS and CMS. Alongside the older societies there have come into the field a bewildering number of missionary organisations. The characteristic feature of nineteenth century missions was the enthusiasm for the multiplication of missionary efforts. The priority of the colonial missions was conversion. Conversion of individual souls was considered the sole end of mission. To a European missionary non-Christian religions and Eastern cultures were non-slavific and that Christianity alone would redeem them. The British rule had provided favourable atmosphere and necessary infrastructure for the missions to work even in the remotest mountain villages without confronting much opposition. Julius Richter says that, it would be hard to find any land possessing so great an attraction for the missionary societies.[25] The mood of mission societies and missionaries were summarized in the following words: "The content of their (missionaries) hope was not merely a conglomerate of individual conversions but a comprehensive revolution in heathen Society in which every aspect of that society would be praised from the grip of satanic domination and submitted to the liberating lordship of Christ".[26]

After the Charter of 1833 was renewed, missionaries were allowed freely to come to India. Missionary teams became powerful and their style of work changed. By this time a new set of missionaries rooted in 'the iconoclastic zeal of extreme Protestantism'[27] began to arrive. These missionaries, soon through letters, reports and stories, created a much distorted image about the people and culture in India. They were imbued with the western 'imperial sentiments' and the sense of cultural superiority and agreed with Charles Grant, the spokesman of the Evangelicals in England, that it was not any inborn weakness that made Hindu degenerate but the nature of their religion. For the evangelicals India was in darkness and would need the light present in the western world. Claudius Buchanan another spokesman of the evangelicals who had been a missionary in India said: "The missionaries asserted that since God laid upon Britain the solemn duty of evangelizing India, the Government should not hesitate to throw its weight into the struggle. They demanded above all open Government patronage of Christian education and vigorous warfare upon the abuses associated with Hindu religion".[28]

The Evangelicals and other mission societies made a combined attempt to change the policy of the British Government and demanded the introduction of legal and social reforms in India. It was thus that William Bentinck in March 1835 issued his resolution intended mainly to promote European literature and science and utilize funds mainly for English education.[29] The study of Indian literature and oriental works was admitted to be of little intrinsic value and the opinion was that these literatures inculcate the most serious errors on the subjects. Also the customs and traditions and the religious beliefs of the subject people were considered by the missionary educators and their societies in England as a sign of depravity and futility. The remedy was the introduction of English education.[30]

Alexander Duff, Scottish missionary and leading educator whose ideas can be considered representative of the majority of missionaries in the nineteenth century, thought that though Hindu philosophical discourse contained lofty terms in its religious vocabulary what they conveyed were only vain, foolish and wicked conceptions. According to Duff, Hinduism spread like a dark universe where all life dies and death lives.[31] The Christian task for him was to do everything possible to demolish such a gigantic fabric of idolatry and superstition. Needless to say, such an attitude prevented any positive encounter between Christianity and Indian culture. Duff, Buchanan, Trevelyan, Macaulay and others had great influence on the missionary thinking. The missionaries and civil servants who came to India were so prejudiced that they did not see anything good in India society.

The missionaries and their societies subscribed to the view that civilizing the Indian people would prepare the primitive religious people to embrace Christianity. Nineteenth century Protestant missiology could be understood against the background of Christianisation and civilizing as two sides of the same coin. Missions were unwilling to understand the complexities of Indian cultural variants. Deeply entrenched in them was a sense of superiority of European civilization and that coloured their approach to people of other cultures and religious faiths.[32] The missions and colonial administrators asserted that Hinduism would die away soon and the whole nation could be civilized and Christianised. English education was a means towards this goal. That is to facilitate change from exterior to interior, from trade to religion, a cultural revolution for the betterment of the natives by disseminating knowledge of Christianity and make them loyal to the British.[33] The comment of Arthur Mayhew is worth mentioning: "The evangelical supporters of Anglican mission were far more interested in the dissemination of the Bible and baptismal statistics than in any measure for the general enlightenment of India".[34] The primary interest of the Raj was to keep control over India. The dominant interest of missions was to work for the conversion of Indians to Christianity. But in the colonial situation they found themselves in need of one another and so mutual support was but natural.Although the missionaries worked hard and suffered a lot for bringing education and awareness of social justice to the people living in the rural areas of India, as they were associated with the colonial-imperial powers, the significance of their selfless service was either overlooked or misunderstood. The response this approach evoked need to be looked into detail. The fourth chapter is an attempt to do this. If Indians really lived under the influence of the pagan religion and were uncivilised, they would have whole-heartedly welcomed the missionary enterprise.

Christian Missionaries in Andhra

From the history and tradition we know that small Christian communities existed in the west cost of India in the early centuries of Christianity. St. Thomas, the Apostle preached the gospel in Malabar area.[35] But the gospel of God did not spread to the interior parts until the arrival of the Portuguese missionaries. The very first contact with Telugus started at the beginning of 16th century with Louis d Dalvador, one of the Portuguese Franciscan missionaries who is also acclaimed as the first martyr to the shed his blood in the Telugu land. The next Franciscan missionaries enjoyed the honour of preaching gospel among Telugus until the Jesuits came to India in 1542. With the arrival of these Portuguese Jesuits missionaries in India, the very first attempt on evangelization of southern Andhra started. From 1599 to 1611 the missionaries tried at the court of King Venkatapatiraya II in Chandragiri, but the attempt was not so successful. Therefore they were obliged to close the mission, and as a result the work of evangelization in this area was postponed to another century.

In 1689, the French Jesuit has crossed over to Pondicherry from Siam and in 1700 planned to start their own mission, quiet independent of the Portuguese province of Madurai. They planned to start in Karnataka which to them meant work among the Telugu people and started what in Karnataka what is called Carnatic mission, through the Franciscans, Capuchins, Augustinians, Oratorians and other Portuguese Jesuit missionaries sporadically worked in the area, it was also with Carnatic mission founded by the French Jesuit; the presented day Andhra church's roots had begun to take shape.Clement Bonnad was looking after the whole mission from Nellore to Machilipatnam, who was known as the father and the apostle of the Telugus because of his missionary activity in the Telugu districts.[36]

In 1843, the Telugu area, south of Krishna consisting of Phirangipuram, Kilachery, and Punganur in the south, Hyderabad and Visakhapatnam in the north was cut off from Pondicherry and attached to the vicariate of Madras. Since then Phirangipuram, Cuddapah, Kurnool, Ananthapur and Nellore came to be looked after by the priests of Madras. Now the entire work is carried out.

In 1928, the diocese of Nellore was born comprising of six Telugu district: Nellore, Guntur, Ananthapur, Kurnool, Cuddapah and Chittoor and was entrusted to the mill hill society. In 1929, William Bouter was appointed as the first bishop of Nellore. Eleven years later the civil district of Guntur was detached from Nellore and made into a separate diocese with Bishop Thomas Pothakamury as its pastor. When bishop Bouter died in 1970, Bishop Thumma Showry, who was his co-ordinator since 1967 and succeeded him as Bishop of Nellore.

The first efforts at evangelizing in Andhra districts, says Martin L.Dolbeerjr., who has done extensive research on this aspect, came from the French Jesuit of Pondicherry. M. Manduit of the Society of Jesus started missionary work in Chittoor district. His first converts came from Punganur in 1701[37]. But, according to Dolbeer, Manduit's labours did not mark the beginning of Christianity in Andhra districts they however, intensified the earlier efforts by Franciscan missionaries in converting 300 Telugu speaking people in the sultanates of Bijapur and Golconda.[38] With these elementary beginnings, activity of missionaries gained ground slowly, but steadily. Bartholomew Ziegenbalg and Benzaman Schultze did some good work among Telugu people. Schultze translated some scriptures and the new-testament into Telugu. Thus, the Telugus were introduced to Christian literature.

However, the London mission society was given the privilege of opening of Andhra Desa to the influence of Christian missions. In 1805 George Cran and Augustey des Granges of London mission society arrived in

Visakhapatnam. They were credited as leaders in the contribution to Telugu Christian literature.[39]

Rev. Robert T. Nobel of the church missionary society began his work among Telugus at Masulipatam on October 28, 1841. Impetus for this mission had come from John, Goldingham collector at Masulipatam, who had since 1836 urged first the 'society for the propagation of the gospel' and the 'Chrruch Missionary Society' to depute missionaries to the Andhra Desa.[40] Nobel made Masulipatam his headquarters because of its location and importance. As with other missions in Andhra Desa, converts were few and far between in the early days.[41]

To Rev. Christian Frederic Heyer of the United States goes the credit of establishing the Andhra. Evangelical Lutheran Church in Guntur. Every day dozens of poor,maimed, blind and helpless beggars used to flock to him to receive alms. He took the opportunity to read the scriptures to them in Telugu; teach those hymns and gospel verses; the Ten Commandments; and always closing with prayers. By his benevolence, he attracted persons belonging to low castes and more especially out castes. His wife Judge Walker helped him in many ways.[42] Rev. Walter Gunn took up the work left by Heyer.[43] Rev. August Milius of Germany did missionary work in Nellore, Gudur and Sullurpet.[44] The Baptist mission made headway in Ongole and its surroundings under Rev. and Mrs. Lyman Jewett and John Erevatt Clough and the latter's wife, Harriet john E.Clough wrote a volume called from darkness to light, which was a story dealing with Indian life. But the letters and reports he sent home U.S. are more informative although the head of Ongole affected Clough adversely, he seldom sought the cooler climate of the hills during summer. A perusal of his letters reveals Ramayapatnam, a village on the coast of bay of Bengal, some twenty five miles south of Ongole.[45]

No wonder, these early missionaries by their charitable disposition and benevolence, permeated with evangelical spirit, attracted the outcastes-Malas and Madigas. They extended to them all assistance to hold their head high. Their contribution to the education was undisputedly great. Their helping had to the health, hygiene and economic upliftment of the untouchables was not less great. Here a serious attempt is made to trace their contribution to the all-round growth of untouchables. They displayed a genuine sympathy for the suffering of the underprivileged. The coastal districts of Andhra were dotted with missionary educational institutions, hospitals and workshops, some of which stand even today as living symbols of the indefatigable zeal of missionaries. Naturally, untouchables, the poorest of the poor were attracted by the kind missionaries. The cross became to them symbol of self-reliance and hope.[46]

Canadian Baptist Missionaries arrived in India already in 1868[47] and began a new and independent work in the very northern and coastal part of Andhra Pradesh in 1847. It is interesting to note that the independent missionary work among the Telugu speaking population by the Canadian Baptist mission was initiated by a Telugu Christian in 1870, named Thomas Gabriel. He began his work independently in Kakinada area. Only in 1874, the Canadian Baptist church decided to support his work and to integrate the mission into their own fold.[48]

There was another mission started by the Canadian Baptist in the northern part of Andhra Pradesh, i.e. northward from Visakhapatnam and eastward from the coast to Bobbili. It was founded in 1875 by the maritime foreign mission board in co-operation with the already started work of the Ontario foreign mission board, which worked in the area around Kakinada. The mission north from Visakhapatnam became known as the Canadian Baptist mission north, while the mission south from Visakhapatnam was the Canadian Baptist mission south.[49] The area of Canadian Baptist mission south was located around Koliar Lake and Kakinada. The work southwards down to the Krishna river. The salvation army has been founded by Rev. William booth in 1867, when he was preacher in London. In India, the mission began by F. Tucker in 1882. In Andhra Pradesh the mission work began in 1895 by Abdul Azeez, who settled in Vijayawada. Land societies were established to provide land to the converts. Today, the Salvation Army is also present in Hyderabad, Rajahmundry, and Nellore and Visakhapatnam.[50] The salvation army very dominant in Bapatla town where there is a big leprosy hospital and the salvation army is response to convert and educate the Stuwartpuram settlers who were previously call as criminal tribe.

The Christian missionaries from the United States of America and the continent were often subjected by the orthodox sections of caste Hindus and Muslims to criticism. Ulterior motives were attributed for their efforts to education of the Panchamas should under no circumstances be underestimated. The under-estimate their services to the education of the depressed classes is to fall into the pit of ingratitude, asserted some Christian localities in every coastal Andhra town reveals a high degree of sophistication, multi-stored buildings and more than average standard of life by Indian standards. Both husband and wife earn. Their combined income as teachers and other professionals far exceeds that of a class I officer. In this context, it is imperative to known that more than ninety per cent of the Christians were the off sprints of the Mala and Madigas, some two or three generations back. But for the benefits conferred by the white missionaries, it would have taken a century or more for the outcastes among Christians to reach their present status. Hewers of wood and drawers of water were transformed into teachers. Medical men, engineers and other professionals. The present day average Christians, whose ancestors were treated as untouchables and where barred even to enter into the public streets, are how holding their heads high. This is due to the fair play, service mindedness and sacrifices of the Christian missionaries. Braving the inclement weather, poor health conditions in which they worked, the Christian missionaries rendered yeomen educational services to the untouchables. The epitaphs of the missionaries in the Christian cemeteries in coastal Andhra, unfeelingly tell the missionaries' services to educate the most unprivileged sections of Hindu society.

Missonaries-Agricultural Development

India is a country mainly based on agriculture; three-fourths of the people of India are supported directly or indirectly by agriculture. The social organization of the village with land utilization as its base has been from the ancient times. The people of India considered the land as goddess and some described in detail the village as a unit in the economic development of India.[51] It is essentially the rural social solidarity and almost complete economic self-sufficiency one have enabled the village to survive repeated conquests and persist under every type of political control that has been imposed upon it. The same features of rural life very largely explain why the ordinary Indian village is much more concerned about the weather than with politics.

The people of India have contacts with Western world from the time immemorial. However, especially since British occupation of India, has profoundly affected on its Village industry and agriculture. Occasional voyages of Westerners for spices of other minor articles of trade developed into organized systems of cultivation and supply to meet the increasing demands of the west for indigo, jute, and cotton. Each extension of trade demanded an equal extension of protective measures. Private guards became public armies and complete political control was the inevitable outcome of profitable trade relations. Establishment of central government made necessary the collection of land revenue and, consequently, the recognition and regularization of the cultivator's rights in the soil. In Madras Presidency, the first revenues 'were collected on the native plan that is from villages as units. In 1780 the country was leased by the East India Company 'in large farms on nine-year leases.[52] But the renters failed and the estates were sequestered in 1788. In some areas, arrangements were made with local chieftains whereby the cultivator retained half the gross produce, the government got one-third, and the chieftain one-sixth. In other areas, an effort was made too collect revenue through the traditional organization by setting up the 'village-lease system' one of the conditions being 'that all the resident cultivators of a village should be jointly responsible for the revenue due on all the lands cultivated during the year.[53] But this attempt failed and what is termed the 'ryotwari system', the current prevailing type of land tenure, was introduced.

The East India Company's economic stake in indigo guaranteed its interest in scientific agriculture and government's interest in land revenue secured the continuation and expansion of its efforts to increase production. The opening of the Suez Canal and the establishment of coaling stations along the new sea route opened the markets of the world to India's products of the soil. Serious attention to the scientific problems involved in Indian agriculture is indicating in a British report by Voelcker in 1891. He very sensibly challenged the Westerner's uncritical condemnation of the Indian plough that he believe that in the great majority of cases the native system of ploughing is the one best adapted to the conditions, and that were a furrow-plough used, the result would be to lose a great deal of the precious moisture.[54]

In 1904, government established a department of agriculture and work was begun in research, education and extension. The chief practical results of these activities have been in plant breeding and seed distribution. Higher-yielding varieties have been development and the seed widely distributed. New varieties of rice, wheat, cotton,tobacco, sugar- cane ,jute, and peanuts development by the department are being cultivated in millions of acres, but in most cases the proportion of the area in the new variety to the total area in that crop is disappointingly small. For instance, with rice, the chief crop, the proportion is only 0.8%, with wheat it is about 7% and even with cotton only 12% improved varieties, however, are grown in 25% of the tobacco fields and in 75% of the sugarcane.[55] It area is significant that all cases of superior achievement are with the crops around which there are grouped many strongly organized European interests. These results of the plant breeding and seed distribution operations of a foreign government represent a tremendous net gain to the Indian cultivator because the consequent increase in production has been accompanied by only a relatively insignificant increase in cost.

In all other directions, however, progress has been much slower. With cattle, for instance, it has not been possible to effect much change because of religious prejudice against slaughtering the unfit; for no program of improvement through breeding can succeed where the prompt disposal of the unfit is impossible. Improved implements have been introduced, notably the iron plough, but their use has not become at all general. With respect to the western type of plough the questions in asked by the director of the institute of plant industry at Indore 'is soil inversion really needed in India.[56]

The fact that the early efforts of Westerners in scientific agriculture in India were all too often based on an assumed universal applicability of established European practices. In the use of manures, in irrigation practice, and in disease control, the way to larger profits has seemingly been demonstrated but the problem of application on the cultivator's own land remains largely unsolved. The department of agriculture has education, but it has failed, by and large, in application.

Foreign missionaries have generally been impressed with the poverty of India. The reasons seemed to them so obvious: the crudity and mechanical inefficiency of the implements employed and the 'backwardness' of cultivation practices. It has become almost a habit to characterize Indian agriculture in one phrase as 'scratching the ground with a crooked stick'. The honest, deliberate use of that phrase reveals the user as uninformed in the complicated technology involved in the manufacture of the Indian plough and in the mechanics of the preservation of moisture and soil tilt under a tropical sun, and quite lacking in the scientific attitude. Furthermore, missionaries have been handicapped in their efforts at agriculture improvement by inadequate financial support, insufficient time for careful consideration and planning, and by long furloughs which seriously interfered with the continuity of the undertakings. In addition, the discouragement of failures or of what seemed insignificant successes and the apparently complete failure to get Indian's to adopt some new practices no matter how successful, have proved very destructive of mission programs of agricultural reform. Discarded machinery in almost every mission station bears mute but impressive testimony to unsuccessful agricultural experiment. The Western missionary, too, in spite of great devotion to the task has been generally ineffective in efforts to change Indian agriculture.

Such was the situation in the mission we are studying when an agricultural survey was undertaken in 1923 by an experienced agriculturist trained in research. The surveyor demonstrated the poverty and landlessness of the Christian community and recommended concentration of attention on the correlation of subject-matter of class-room instruction in elementary science with everyday rural life. He recommended leaving all expensive research and technical agricultural education to well-established and not over-used government institutions. A further recommendation was for the establishment of a rural community school planned definitely for advancing all phase of rural life. This combined with a training school for village school teachers would provide for the encouragement of not only agricultural but also other rural activities in the villages, the very centres of agriculture.[57]

In 1931 a recommended school was established in Cumbum [Prakasam district] by the surveyor, a missionary trained in agriculture and education. How the teacher-training departments of the school, opened in accordance with the grant-in-aid rules and using the government course of study, quickly won a place in the community. Agricultural activities have been handicapped by inadequate resources, transfers of missionaries, and furlough interruptions, but certain lines of activity are worthy of note. The government agricultural department has been called in to demonstrate an improved peanut harvester and to give a course of lecture-demonstrations with the aid of their extension truck. Improved varieties of field crops have been grown on the mission farm. The growing of fruit and vegetables has been demonstrated and seeds and plants have been freely distributed. The profitable conversion of organic waste into agricultural fertilizer has been practiced and recommended. A system for the control of termites in the garden was developed and put into practice. The experimental installation of a conservancy system designed to preserve night-soil for fertilizer. Extension of the use of vegetables and fruits in the boarding home has also been described. Better irrigation practice has been observed. In short, accessible facilities, for improving agriculture, both government and mission, are being called upon in the hope that some innovation will prove practicable under local condition and attractive to local cultivators. But it must be admitted that measured in terms of change in village agricultural practice, the results of the mission program have been very meagre.

With respect to the depressed classes, however, there has been definite change. The depressed classes children in the boarding home have learned the art of cultivation and the value of using in the diet many vegetables, some new to the area. In the process, a healthful attitude toward manual labour and growing plants has been fostered. By showing caste farmer visitors the innovations and explaining the superiority of the practices to which they themselves are contributing, depressed classes experience a feeling of achievement which has definite psychological value.With most of the Christians coming from the depressed classes from Andhradesa are suffering from periodic famines. The early missionaries were so moved by the tragic plight of the people that most of them distributed gifts regularly to the poor and helpless. They tended to be lenient with the converts and not insist on regular offerings; in fact, the Hermannburg missionaries felt impelled to help the Christians when they left work to attend worship services on Sunday. The same was true of the period of catechetical training.[58] In 1892, Director Ermont Harms visited Nayudupeta [Nellore], he found that more than 100 catechumens in the compound receiving instructions. All the families are there, sleeping in the church, the school and the porches of the missionary bungalows. Harms realized some were probably there to receive material help. Other had planned to come long before his but could not leave their employment. Now that famine and lack of rain had put most of people out work, they took this opportunity to receive instruction and, incidentally, receive enough food to keep them going for a while.[59]

It was once the aim of many missionaries in India to gather Christian converts into agricultural colonies for protection from persecution, for economic betterment, and to facilitate further instruction. These have usually failed and the reasons commonly assigned are indolence or inexpertness of the settlers, insufficient finance or supervision, or inadequate land facilities. But a more plausible reason is disrupted social organization. The colonists, torn from affiliation with widely separated villages, strangers to one another, are suddenly faced with the problem of setting up an entirely new community organization. Accustomed to a very narrowly circumscribed and strictly controlled role in village life they find the task of establishing and directing a new organization beyond their capacity furthermore, the exchange of services with other village artisans is upset and fresh arrangements in the new area are handicapped in many ways. Being new-comers, they find the market for their labour restricted; consequently, they must pay cash for the services they require. In the case of one colony, however, these difficulties have been overcome and the settlers are prospering in Coles Dharmapuram. Here the lands is unusually good, the sponsor has been very generous in granting financial assistance and the location within one mile of the city of Kurnool has made accessible a large market for spare-time labor.[60] This has accelerated the development of individualism and obviated the necessity for much of the traditional village organization. As a matter of fact, the problem of a new socio-economic organization has objection that mission agricultural colonies are socially disruptive still holds.

The same factor operates to impede progress in the utilization of new areas opened to cultivation by government; only in such instances there is no selective force in operation in the choice of settlers. As a consequence, the community is more likely to contain representatives of every rural occupational class and is, therefore, in a much more favourable position with respect to the problems of community organization. Disrupted community organization remains, however, one of the chief obstacles to the financial productiveness[61] of many large irrigation projects in India and will continue so to operative until some way is found to solve these social problems.

Harms visit instituted a saving and association with the initial capital investment of 3000 marks and recommended that as much land as possible be secured for the people. Although he did not feel the day of large industrial schools had arrived in the mission, he urged the missioners to search for other ways to teach the native Christians new crafts to take the place they became Christian.He promised the congregation at Tirupati that he would raise funds in Germany for the purpose of buying land for Christians. But he expected them to show diligence and faithfulness by repairing their chapel.[62] Missionary Maneke reported that he bought land for his people and at the same time training them to support the poor and the windowed in the congregation.[63] While some missionaries felt that the outcaste, not being accustomed to ideas of independence and self support, had lost all sense of initiative, thrift, industry, and honesty, other felt that the Christian should be faced with the responsibility of contributing something just as he had given before his conversion. In times of festival and disease, most Hindu gave heavily to their gods. They must be trained to do so in the church as well as not expect hand-outs from the missionaries where ever needed. Part of the problem, of course, was that the native worker or pastor preferred his regular support from the mission rather than the people; this gave him greater freedom of action, for the people could not demand services of him when they did not pay for them. And he felt much more secure in the service of the mission.[64]

Missionary Warber, who had come to India in 1894, was the first to make a real attempt at a large agriculture undertaking to help the untouchable communities to help themselves. About two miles from Kodur, there was a river with an old dam and canal leading to rice-fields. This had fallen into disrepair and the fields were not being cultivated. Warber approached government and land was given to him on the condition that he should repair the dam and channel and pay the taxes. Although the other missionaries favoured the project since they were in the midst of one of India's worst famines.[65] It was a big project; and when completed he had so much I and that he distributed it among not only untouchables but also Sudras and Brahmins. Money was lent to outcastes for purchase of oxen and agricultural implements.[66] In 1909, the same missionary established farm school. The most successful of the schools was at Nayudupet. This mission had learned by previous experience that this elementary knowledge was necessary, if the outcaste was to hold on the land he bought through mission assistance. The value received from the crops raised on these farms was far greater than the amount spent. So, they became self dependent.[67] This system of self dependency soon spread to other areas. Unangst secured lands for outcastes in Sattenapalli and Bapatla taluks. High tide of the policy was between 1894-1899. Much land was reclaimed from primeval waste, and put for sale at public auction. Albrect in Palnadu, Dr.Uhl in Tenali, Repalle and Bapatla were leaders in purchasing this type of land for depressed classes. Dr.Uhl declared that, "hundreds of acres passed through my hands and most of them paid for by the recipients within 15years". He was able to help about 1000 people.[68]

Not only milk but sugar, too, is deficient in the Indian diet. Some of this deficiency could be repaired if the sweet juice of the Palmyra and date palms were used for that purpose. This juice is customarily allowed to ferment and then is sold as an alcoholic beverage called today. With the introduction of prohibition by Madras government in several districts, the way is open for utilization of the product of tapping either as a sweet drink or for the manufacture of sugar. Such a redirection of the utilization of a food resource should be a clear gain to rural India for the palms grows largely on soil that is not suitable for the production of other food crops. Furthermore, the change need cause little if any social or economic disruption since the chief work involved, tapping the trees, would continue unchanged and the manufacture of sugar would entail merely the revival of an indigenous industry and a more continuous use of apparatus now employed only seasonally for the making of cane sugar.

Indigenous leadership has been active in agriculture for many years in most effective ways. 'all matters relating to the production, improvement, trade and utilization of cotton are now dealt with by the Indian central cotton committee, an unofficial organization financed by a small tax on each bale of cotton, this committee has done a great deal for the regulation of trade and the conduct of research.[69] They furnished the capital cost and a large part of the recurring expenditure of the institute of plant industry at Indore where an effort is being made to co-ordinate of the various sciences that seem to have anything to offer for the improvement of the cotton enterprise.

During two great famines of 1897 and 1900, the missionaries did tremendous work in relieving starvation and giving employment. The latter famine was more severe in Guntur area. One half of the hill tribes were said to have died. 95% of cattle perished. The Lutheran mission carried on relief work among 1, 00,000 people. A sum of 4,700 English pounds was sent by Lutherans in America to aid the people in this area. Harpster directed the central famine camp in the three southern taluks where he was serving at the time, employed 4,613 people, who earned total of Rs. 10,212 on various construction projects paid for by both the government and the mission.[70] Similarly, Schmidt in Rajahmundry helped in famine relief. The situation was so bad that people were prepared to offer children in exchange for a morsel of food. This missionary bought lands and distributed money for their proper use.[71]

This lack of co-ordination in research and extension has been one of the chief reasons for the unsatisfactory progress in applying the findings of scientific agriculture in India. Illiteracy of the rural population is a great obstacle to extension activities the royal commission on agriculture states it as their conviction. That no substantial improvement in agriculture can be effected unless the cultivator has the will to achieve a better standard of living and the capacity, in terms of mental equipment and physical health, to take advantage of the opportunities which science, wise laws and good administration may place at his disposal if this conclusion be accepted, the improvement of village life in all directions assumes at once a new importance as the first and essential step in a comprehensive policy designed to promote the prosperity of the whole population and to enhance the national income at the source. The rural problem, should be attacked as a whole, and at all points simultaneously.[72]

The Howards, both economic Botanists who have made enviable records in government service in India, write even more comprehensively of 'the supreme importance of dealing with the Indian village and its fields as a single subject.[73] They deplore the piecemeal research of the past organized around scientific disciplines, and call for a co-ordination of all sciences in a concentrated effort to solve the main problems of Indian agriculture. Extension work is being handicapped by being divided into many independent movements. All these agencies, government and unofficial, as the Howards recommend, should be guided by a single coordinating body.

The proposed co-ordinate program will lack comprehensiveness if it fails to include the Christian agencies; missions will lose an opportunity for participation in integrated community activity if they adopt an attitude of aloofness; the peculiar needs of the underprivileged classes will suffer if missions relax their special efforts in this direction short of actual rehabilitation of the entire group.

Missionaries –Development of Education

The coming of Christian missionaries to India was as part of the worldwide phenomenon. Christianity arrived in India even before the European colonial powers did. The arrival of early Christians in India took place in the 1st century AD with the arrival of Apostle Thomas, a denomination of Syrian Christian community.[74] But the arrival of Portuguese, along the West coast of India, brought many problems to Syrian Christians, who had settled already on the Malabar coast. As a result, for a long time india was a bone of contention between the supremacy of Syrian and Portuguese bishops. Finally, the Roman Catholic Church established its supremacy under the Portuguese patronage.[75] As soon as the Portuguese had gained a hold in this country, Franciscan, Dominican, Jesuit and other Roman Catholic missionaries began to arrive and organize institutions in different parts of the Portuguese possessions for the evangelization of what they called 'pagans' and 'heathens' of this country.[76] In the same way, subsequently, protestant Christian missionaries first arrived in south India, including the Madras Presidency, in 1706 when two young Germans began their work at a Danish colony on India's South-eastern coast known as Tranquebar. These early missionaries, Bartholomaeus Ziegenbalg and Heinrich Pluetschau, brought with them a form of Lutheranism that emphasized personal piety and evangelistic fervour. They had little knowledge of what of expect from the peoples they were about to encounter. They were entering a foreign culture with scarcely sufficient preparation, but with the optimistic view that they would succeed in their task. For the missionaries, the ultimate goal was the propagation of gospel. Vast resources were contributed by various missionary societies in several parts of India, as in Europe and America, in order to establish such as hospitals, orphanages, and food-distribution centres.[77]

Before the present Cuddapah district, of the South Western part of Andhra Pradesh, passed under the British rule, the private persons looked after education. The traditional or orthodox educational system was continued for many years not withstanding political disorder and socio-economic changes in the society. This conventional system was limited to the rich people like the priests and the feudal and land lords, Brahmins, and some of the wealthy trading and artisan classes. The lower castes, common people and girls were excluded from the domain of education. This education was imparted in common places like temples, monasteries, mutt's[78] mosques and residential houses. Those people, who were unable to send their children to these schools, preferred 'pial' schools, which were run under the shade of trees and on the pials flanking the thresholds of houses. Here the three R's were taught by rote method without giving much importance of critical learning. The curriculum was narrow and limited. The teachers were lacking in sound education and in training methods. There were no required printed books or material. Geography, religion, philosophy, elements of science, mathematics, English and morals were the main subjects of the curriculum whereas the modern subjects like history, political science, and science and technology were neglected. There was no uniformity in the curriculum and much variation is there from place to place. Although the main aim of the missionaries was conversion and preaching of gospel, they thought that educational institutions could be an important means of proselytisation. These educational institutions paved the way for communication and dissemination of knowledge with different classes of people. As a result, missionary schools were cropped up and picked up momentum in all important towns of the district in order to provide Western knowledge.

When the education was receiving scanty attention of the government in India, the Christian missionaries took initiative in the spread of education to the extent their resources permitted in the Madras Presidency, including the Kadapa district. In other words, origin of the present system of education in India is to be sought in the activities of early Christian missionaries. Activities of the Christian missionaries in the field of education began with the opening of two charity schools at Madras in 1717 by the Society for the Promotion of local Christian Knowledge (SPCK), one for the Portuguese children and the other for the local Indian children. In the same way, the primary motive of these missionaries was the spread of Christianity they also took steps to promote secular education among the people of the Kadapa district. Now, let us briefly trace the role and services of various Christian missionaries in the field of education in the Kadapa district before the Magna

Carta of Indian education system, that is, the woods dispatch (1854) was given effect to, from when the education received an increased attention of the state.

Several branches of the Christian missions were started in Kadapa district by the beginning of 18th century. They started in the district with the aim of spreading education as a means to popularize the gospel among the people.[79] The principal missions that were engaged in this task were the Roman Catholic mission, the London mission society, the American Baptist mission Arcot Mission, the society for the propagation of the gospel and the Hermansburg evangelical society.[80] The London missionaries of Kurnool district was used to visit the Cuddapha jail and preach the gospel to the prisoners who belonged to Mala caste in Rudravaram of Sirvel taluk, then in Kadapa district, "received the word with joy". Under his influence several Mala families of surrounding villages joined the Christian religion.[81] Similarly, society for the propagation of gospel, American Baptist mission, Roman Catholic Mission preached gospel and a wakened the communities of Malas, Madigas and Kapus or weavers (who ate, drink and intermarry with the Hindus) in the Satiapuram village near Proddatur in Kadapa district and provided educational facilities on the one side and on the other relief measures during famines.[82] Under the influence of Roman Catholic mission around 500 people that belonged to weaving and Reddy communities gathered at Satiapuram and took Christianity. Later, Christianity spread to Nagarajupalli, Oratoor and Jangalapalli villages. According to 1871 census the total number of Roman Catholics in the Kadapa district was 877. They were consisting of weavers and Reddies.[83] The London mission society started its branches at Kadapa in 1822. The church of South India and the Roman Catholic missionaries propagated their theological concepts to the people of all the ceded districts, including the Kadapa district.[84] The protestant missionaries like Rev. Hands and Rev. Willam Havell worked virulently for their activities in the district during the 19th century.[85]

The role played by Christian missionaries in the progress of education was rather epoch making in the district.[86] For instance, Society for the Promotion of Christian Knowledge (SPCK) was the first one in the direction to start some charity schools at Kadapa in Kadapa district with the support of European settlers of the place. This was the first instance to show the impact of Western education on the region.[87] By the year 1835-36 six school were run by the missionaries at Kadapa of the region. The missionaries started one Tamil school at cantonment area and closed the existing school at old Kadapa. The teacher was transferred to adjacent village, Peddamukapalli. The strength of the pupils in the missionary schools was increased. The teacher at old Kadapa namely Chathre started one school at Yerramukkapalli in the Kadapa town. Geography and grammer were also practiced in some schools. By 1837 only three schools were left among six schools in Kadapa town.[88] A boarding school for orphans was started by the London mission society at Kadapa in 1845[89] The notable thing was at Madanapalli, then in Kadapa district, the wife of Jacob Chamberlin started one school for the students of all communities. After the completion of seventh form the students of this school were sent to Madras to pursue their matriculation. When Wood's Despatch (1854) recommended the grant-in aid facility for private schools, the government had accepted to implement it. The missions took advantage of it and opened Anglo-vernacular or middle schools in the district, along with other Neighbouring district. There came up two such schools by 1875, which were kept under the government's inspection.[90] The Society for the Propagation of the Gospel (SPG) utilized this opportunity and started many schools in the district. For instance, Rev. W. Howell and Rev. Spencer Higgins, Rev. H.O' Neill, and Rev. J. Hands[91] were some of the outstanding missionaries, who worked in Kadapa district for the promotion of education and Christianity.

The girls, education was possible through Christian missionaries only. This can be observed in several places of the district. For instance, by 1820, some girl's schools were started in the Kadapa district due to these missionary efforts.[92] Later, in 1860, the London mission society started one girls' school at Kadapa.[93] The London mission maintained a caste girls school at Jammalamadugu. This school was patronized very much as a result that its premises were being extended. The mission board school was started at Kadapa and drawn one hundred forty Christian girls students from all parts of the district. But later it was shifted to Jammalamadugu in A.D. 1898 as the lady missionaries migrated due to the lack of hygienic conditions in the Kadapa town. Similarly, the S.P.G. Mission had maintained about forty elementary school at Kalasapad. It had two hostels one for 30 Christian boys and another for 39 Christian girls.[94] Among the total number of students on the rolls of the S.P.G. school, more than thirty percent are girls. The same trend continued in the beginning of 20th century also.

In this way the Christian missionaries not only did their yeomen theological service but also contributed for the development of education in the economically drought prone, under developed and educationally backward people of the Kadapa district. It was due to their pivotal role, the common people, especially the neglected, marginalized, depressed. And subordinate section of the district were able to get their due economic support and educational facilities. Consequently, this helped such sections of people of the district to understand the mal administration and ill effects of the colonial rule and got consciousness from different dimensions. As a result, the people of the district played a crucial role during the periods of different phases of national movement to attain independence to the Indian nation. If one can observe and analyse the details of the freedom struggle of the district, suffice it to say that this scenario became an eye opener and ideal to other districts and parts of Andhra in particular and south India in general.

Women Evangelical Missionaries

An attempt is made here to put it on record, the services rendered by women missionaries who broke the isolation of Indian women and brought them into the main stream of life. The pioneering women missionaries entered into the zenana familiarized the Indian women with the common formal education and brought them out into public life. The need of the presence of woman missionary was realized by the Lutheran church towards the eight decade of 19th century. The missionaries in India found it difficult to approach the Indian women who were confined in zenanas or women's apartment from which they were not permitted to leave unless accompanied by some male member of the house. Even for Indian men it was very difficult to approach the women-folk. For foreigners, it was much more hence; the missionaries in India began to apply to the Lutheran church in America to send women missionary so as to have accessibility to Indian women offering their services. Still the missionaries needed the service of woman missionaries to labour by the side of the ordained male missionaries and their wives. The decision of sending woman missionary had its own long history.[95]

For the first time, the issue was raised in December, 1879 when Mrs. Emma Victorio Von Noxendorf offered her services to the foreign missions committee. The committee replied in the negative "resolved that the Rev. Dr. A. Spaeth, chairman of the committee inform her that we have not yet progressed far enough in our school work to spend out a woman teacher, but hope to be able to do at some future time". Thus, the questions of spending a separate woman missionary were ruled out for the present.

A similar application was received from Miss Agnes I. Schade, then a teacher in the orphan's farm school at Zelienople. This was in 1889 but still the church committee hesitated. It asked the missionaries on the field to give their opinions on this issue of spending woman missionary. All of them declared in favour of spending at least a single lady as woman missionary. Still the committee decided to delay the matter to ascertain the mind of the people at home. In an editorial in May 1890 issue of "the foreign missionary", every friend of the mission was invited to write on a postal card his or her view on the matter of spending out woman missionaries. Replies were favourable meanwhile Miss Kate S. Saddler daughter of Rev. Dr.B. Sadlter of Baltimore also volunteered to serve in India mission. Finally, at its meeting in June 1890, the committee resolved to begin zenana work and called miss Agnes I. Schade and Miss Kate S. Saddler as "assistants in the mission work in india".[96] After the announcement of the first woman missionaries, the committee distributed a circular explaining the circumstances of taking up the zenana mission among the Telugus and "that the special interest and co-operation of our devoted women in this work is solicited." The circular further explained the meaning of zenana. "The word zenana, is used by the Hindus to designate that part of the house, particularly among the wealthy classes which is assigned to the female members of the household-the wives, mothers and daughters of the Hindu families. This part of the dwelling is considered as the most secluded and inaccessible, to which no stranger and above all, no man is ever admitted. Zenana mission then in general designates that mission work which is carried on in the zenana; but how can the gospel ever enter these places if no missionary or evangelist, no minister of gospel, is ever admitted into them, and the inmates are forbidden to meet with Christian their preaching stations and churches.[97]

On October 17th, the women of the Lutheran congregations of Philadelphia and its vicinity met. Ninety women representing fourteen congregations assembled in St. John's church and supported the idea of spending women missionaries.

Ecclesiastical Work among Hindus

The missionaries began the work with persuasion. Caste, the major factors in Indian society with its hierarchical structure, became one of the major impediments. Church was received well by Brahmins in the beginning and later by Sudra, Mala and Madiga communities. The church could get more converts from these communities. It did appeal to the Muslims also. Relatively, it was more women in all the communities that became either converts or sympathizers than men.

Father Heryer, the founder of the mission was successful in baptizing a Muslim woman and later (1849) four men and two women of Sudra community in Palnadu region. The wives of the missionaries broke the isolation of native women and tried to establish a close rapport with them. The ecclesiastical work began with visits to the homes, maintaining educational and vocational institutions and imparting religious instructions along with the formal syllabi. The efforts of the early women missionaries resulted in the emergence of early converts and bible women.

It was the needle that first opened the zenanas of India in general and Guntur district in particular to the gospel. Rev. Mr. Rowe mentions in everyday life in India about the visits of Mrs.Uhl and Mrs. Rowe to the Hindu homes. The entrance was through home education. From Mrs. Ella Unangst's report a glimpse of the work can be seen. In October, 1885, she entered into the Hinduhomes of Guntur. She observes "many are glad to be taught fancy work and while teaching them sewing, we endeavour to impress the great things needful upon their minds. I have been led to think out work has not been entirely in vain, for some have asked about God."[98] This makes it clear that women missionary could raise curiosity among Hindu women about new religion. Mrs. P. Lucy was the first Indian Christian to enter the homes of Hindu women in Guntur. She was a convert from Sudra community and had received good education in Madras.[99] Bible women, the native converts, was responsible for familiarizing the new religion to the natives. By 1892, there were about 80 bible women visiting homes in the villages, towns and spreading the gospel.The accounts of missionaries also speak about the communal background of the converts and about the conditions at the time of conversion. The Brahmin and the Sudra homes were the first to respond to the call of Christ Kotamma, who learn first of Christ in the hospital, was the first convert of the hospital from Ponnur also an old women and her daughter were converted.It is interesting to notice the reactions of men towards conversation. They never thought their women could learn anything about the new religion. The first recorded results of work among the women were the receiving of girls into the home Mrs.Uhl. all three were Sudra girls-Mahalakshmi, Koti and Ratnamma. These later entered in to the mission work.There was one more convert Parvathamma who stood up on the hospital chapel and explained the gospel. Some women cured in the hospital became faithful and turned into bible woman. There were accounts of how a woman of the barber caste and dancing caste transformed themselves into Christians. After the baptism of a woman of the weaver caste, a relative of hers remarked that she too would like to be a Christian but if she did become one, all her people would follow her and then what would become of their business and caste.[100] There is an Interesting episode of a converted woman who had troubles with her step son regarding property. She asked the removal of her name from the church, roll. She was told "once a Christian, always a Christian in the eyes of the law". She continued her faith, won her case, returned to the church and brought her sister with her to bebaptized.[101]

The records tell us that in a number of places, families were being baptized. So the woman need not stand alone. Wherever there were cases of deserted women, they were accommodated in convert Homes. The zenana work was begun in Tenali in 1906. But the work of the Bible women was begun much early. The teaching of the songs in the homes was considered as the best way of presenting Christ. One woman learned about 30 songs. Among the native converts, B. Meenakshamma of Sattenapalli deserves merit. She worked first with her husband in congregational work and after his death as evangelist. She was a popular missionary and was attracting a large crowd of Hindus in street meetings. Even in old age, she was invited and when at home, she gathers her converts around her for more teaching.[102]

There is an interesting episode of the dangers the sympathizer of Christianity had to face. One goldsmith man attended the funeral of a Christian woman and was so impressed with the way it was done that he wanted to follow the way it was done that he wanted to follow Christ. His caste people found it out and one day made him blind by applying some medicine.[103]

Ecclesiastical Work Among Muslims

It is interesting to find that the Lutheran Mission was equally successful in gaining converts from Islam. Miss Dryden opened school for Muslim girls for the first time in February, 1884. It started in a rented building in Chinna Bazar, Guntur. As their own clan's man was appointed as the teacher. As their own clan's man was appointed as teacher, the parents were ready to send their girls. At the beginning, there were only 16 students but soon the number touched 60. As Miss Dryen was ignorant of Urdu, the teacher began spending his time on Arabic and Koran. When this was checked, there was a drop in attendance from 60 to 20. Miss Dryen overcame this difficulty with the help of a Christian teacher by name Mrs. Harriet who was conversant with Urdu language. She began Bible teaching in this school. Mrs.Unangst, assisted by an Anglo-Indian woman who knew Urdu, began visiting the Mohemmadan women in the zenanas in 1884. In her first report itself, she said that she could have many more homes if she would only teach sewing, and not the Bible, as the Muslim women were not inclined to listen to the Bible.[104] In order to remove prejudices Dr.Kugler began treating many Muslim patients in their homes.

As the Muslim zenana work was not much successful, an experiment was made in 1886 by adding an embroidery department to the school. Thus, an attempt was made in 1886 by adding to teach the Muslim women embroidery in gold and silver thread on velvet after the Mohemmadan fashion. After a few years, a trained Muslim woman came from Madras to teach this work. The Muslim women gladly came to learn and there was no objection to listen to the Bible stories even. There was also a financial incentive to learn the work as they were paid about two Annas a day.

The school was able to send handsome exhibits to the World Fair held in Chicago in 1883. The articles sent were sold and many more orders were received. This school also became self supporting.[105] 24 women earn their living in embroidery." Among the Missionaries who gave their time and energy in supervising the work. Mrs.Harpster was the most active. A large and handsome display of work was sent from this school to the Fine-Arts Exhibition in Madras. Six first prizes and two second prizes were received.[106] thus, the Industrial Schools started for Mohemmadan girls proved to be successful. The first prize giving was held in 1885 when the Sub-Collector presided. Many Mohemmadan men were present. The Muslim women could not attend it because of the presence of men. In contrast to this, the prize giving in 1893, the function was attended by the Muslim women and children, as men were not invited.[107]

Though similar schools were started in Mangalagiri and in Bapatla by Miss Dryen and Dr.Kugler, the schools had to be closed because of the lack of teachers in Urdu. The craze for Mohemmadan embroidery died out by 1903. It proved to be difficult for Mrs. Scholl who had charge of sales in America, to dispose of the products of this school. Hence, it was decided to close down the embroidery department.

The second phase started with Miss Rollier taking charge of the school of five standards. The children were paid a, small sum as an incentive to come to the school, thus replacing the old system of the wages hitherto earned by women in the Industrial school, thus replacing the old system of the wages hitherto earned by women in the Industrial school. Miss Rollier was appointed to study Urdu because it was felt that the missionary should speak to the Muslims in their own language. Miss Rollier introduced new developments. Besides, the old Mission school, a new school was opened at Sangadigunta for Muslim girls. She began her personal visits and started regular zenana work. Further, she started two Sunday schools, one for Muslim girls and another for boys.[108]

The Government opened a training and Model school for Muslim women and children in 1907. The Municipality also started a separate school for Muslim girls where the study of Quran also began. In spite of the drop out due to competition, the Chinna Bazar School continued to flourish.Miss Thomas returned to the Guntur, after qualifying herself in examinations, appointed G. Rachel in the zenana as a Bible teacher and trained Mrs.Raghavachari, New Headmistress for Chinna Bazar School. She was far sighted enough to train six younger Telugu girls in Urdu, by sending them to Bangalore. Further, Miss Thomas opened zenana work for Muslims in Chiral and a boarding school for Christian girls in Narsaraopet. But still she was giving a part of her time to the Mohemmadan work. Miss Edna Engle Was appointed to study Urdu in 1921. She opened a school for girls in Islampet. Mrs.Gali Naomi had made Chinna Bazar School a success.[109]

A new Urdu school was started in 1926 with a view to impart Urdu. The six girls, sent to Bangalore, were called back and were asked to attend the Mohemmadan training school in Guntur. Besides them, four Christians began learning Urdu to become Bible women. The school continued for five years till it was closed when Miss Engle left for the furlough. From this school, 29 women learned Urdu. The direct result of the school was the extension of work in new places. A new school for girls was started in Chirala. Bible women were sent to different places one to Narasaraopet, another to Ponnur, two assigned to Chirala and two more to Guntur.[110]

The work among the Muslim women was appreciated very much. Rev. V. Satyanandam was appointed to do Evangelistic work among men, but under the women's committee.[111] By this time the Muslim men began to interfere with zenanan work and the schools. Christian teachers were called back and pastor Satyananadam was sent to North-India to study Urdu and Islam. Sunday schools and the reading room were also closed down with the changing attitude. The missionary realized that it was better to send the Bible women for the spread of gospel work rather than running separate schools. Commenting on the role of caste, we find an interesting observation made by Rev. John C. Perry from Sattenapalli: the difficulty of caste is our greatest obstacle, and unless we look to Christ and regardless of difficulties, try to follow him closely, there will be a Madiga, a Mala, and a sudra Christian church, as soon as American help is withdrawn.[112]

Christian Missionaries-social Awakening

Social awakening is connected with mobilization and modernization of the society in all means. In the era of modernization liberty, fraternity and equality are given the importance. This awakening emerges in gradual and steady process in all the human societies. The social consciousness awakening and political identity in Tamilnadu gradually emerged as a continuation of the politico-social movements that took place in India owing to the impact of Western political thoughts and growth of English education. As a prelude to the social awakening, the spread of political consciousness worked as a contributory factor. The introduction of Western education, judicial system and administrative measures and reorganization paved the way for the rise of a new middle class initially this group consolidated itself into political associations in case based society like Tamilnadu. As time went on, the caste-Hindus who formed a pre-dominant social group in the state along with the depressed section worked against the Brahminocracy. It resulted in the rise and growth of non-Brahmin movement. Though the two movements forged head on parallel lines, which ignited the people towards pro-new trends, which ignited the people towards progressive thinking.

Spread of Western Education

The socio-political awakening in Tamilnadu was due to the variety of factors which functioned under diverse circumstances. The Western education initiated new awakening amongst the people and it came to be implemented in Tamil Nadu through administrative measures and missionary and voluntary enterprises. The earliest educational system known as Gurukula system was beneficial mainly to the upper caste Hindus. When the English East India Company was in power, certain forces persuaded to introduce an educational system based upon the West. The efforts of some of the civil officers of the company, the activities of the Christian missionaries and the rise of a new consciousness among some of the enlightened Indians prepared the ground in favour of Western education prepared the ground in favour of Western education. Seeing the pitiable condition of the rural masses who were mostly illiterates, the company's government in India came forward to impart education. By the Character Act, of 1813, the Governor General of India was obliged to allot a sum of not less than one lakh rupees per year for creating scientific knowledge among the people of India.[113] As a next step, the Macaulay minutes of 2nd February 1835 directly put an end to the native system of education.

In collaboration with Raja Rammohan Roy, the native reformer, Macaulay implemented English and thereby Sanskrit was replaced. It united the Indians to some extent and promoted the growth of national awakening in India. The English language promoted communication activities between the people of different regions of India.[114] Due to the English education, in Madras there was a close association of Tamils, the Malayalees and the Kannadigas which, in turn, contributed to a cultural and Dravidian affinity. Thus, English helped to cut across the linguistic barriers and served as the lingua franca for the multi-lingual people of South India. This rendered invaluable help to the elites of south India in discussing at Madras the common problems relating to the political developments and social emancipation and gradually to create changes among the rural people. In fact, the knowledge of English helped the people to read the works of Western philanthropists and political thinkers like Edmund Burke, Herbert Spencer, John Stuart Mill, Jon Locke, Voltaire, Roussseau, Thomas Paine, Count Cavour and Mazini.[115] It should be noted that these political thinkers in their works emphasized self-reliance and political and social rights. The elites of all sections, who studied the history of the French revolution history of modern governments, were influenced by the ideas of democratic and constitutional reforms and aspired to test them in their own countries.

The Charter Act of 1813 was freely allowed the entry to Christian missionaries who extended their various activities to the nook and corner of Tamil Nadu. It is said that very often the meetings of missionaries were held at the premises of district head-quarters under the patronage of the collectors. Because of poverty and social degradation many of everything possible for the uplift of the former. The association of the people with the missionaries helped the former to read and study the literary works and books of the missionaries on the social set up of India. The people read the worthy books such as caste in India, Hindu manners, customs and ceremonies, original inhabitants of the Bharathavarsha or India, slavery and agricultural bondage in South India in the 19th century. Further the works of Christian writers and missionary scholars like Alexander Butt, Charles Grant, Willam Carey, Marashman, Bishor Robert Caldwell, Henry Whitehead, Gustava Oppert Abbe Dubois, Hutton and Francis Buchanan analyses the Indian problems in detail and exposed the prevailing discriminative social setup.[116] Some of them with the assistance of Indians compiled grammar books and dictionaries in English and vernacular languages. They were highly valuable for the emerging middle class. Further, the Christian Sundry publication such as the Madras Mail, The Harvest field, International Review of Missions, The Madras Christian College

Magazine, The Foreign Field, Kingdom overseas, etc., extended the knowledge on the socio-economic and political problems of the caste-ridden society in TamilNadu.[117] The people who read them condemned the Hindu superstitions and social practices based on Manudharma and thereby they cultivated a sense of self respect and self consciousness. It clearly shows that the works of the missionaries touched the hearts of the downtrodden people.

Service of Christian Missionaries

The Christian missionaries were the first and for most in encouraging the educational activities in Tamil Nadu. In 1837, John Anderson, a missionary of the church of Scotland opened at George town in Madras, a school known as 'General assembly school' which later developed into Madras Christian College in 1841. Elphinstone, the governor of Madras, opened the High school of Madras where education of an advanced nature was imparted. This school later developed into the Madras Presidency College, with the commencement of universities and vernacular schools on the basis of Charles Wood's dispatch of 11th July1854, the Missionaries actively entered the field of educations. They also understand that education was one of the fields where the spadework could be done to improve the conditions of the backward people.[118] As a first step, they attempted to provide social rights to them in the caste-ridden Hindu society. They recruited the degraded, and the condemned men and woman of the Hindu society in their houses as domestic servants and in other jobs, which gave them closer association. They freely allowed the poor and illiterate men to approach them, and treated them on particular with the high caste people.

The advocates of Christianity served the poor people even people during the natural disasters like famines and droughts which hit Tamilnadu between 1865 and 1880. The Christian mission society, London mission society, young men's Christian association, young women's Christian association and Anglo-Indian association of Southern India vigorously preached their new socio-religious philosophy of social order. They rendered valuable service by influencing public opinion against social abuses like degradation of woman and caste system. They initiated a number of welfare measures in Tamilnadu for the uplift of the Shanars, Panchamas and other deprived sections of the society.[119] The missionaries did a lot for the poor land labourers, bonded serfs and helpless victims who were nurtured in bad-circumstances. As a result, the poor and the destitute, acquired a new dishonest drunken and immoral. They slowly became worthy members of the society, acquiring a new sense of human dignity. Colonies were laid for them, where they lived freely and fearlessly. Welfare schemes were extended to the non-Christians too and also universal brotherhood was shown practically to them. Their kindly touch and cheerful service gave hope to the hopeless lives, and led them to the path of progress. The constant criticism of the missionaries against casteism, Brahmanism made the orthodox Hindu elites change their attitude not only ideologically but also practically in removing the social barriers and the social evils.

Thus the agencies of Christian faith by giving basic necessities educated the bottom-line people. The gradual development among the backward classes, mad them embrace Christianity where they experienced love and respect. The proportion of Indian Christians who were able to read and write, in due course exceeded that of the Brahmins, the hereditary went ahead of all of them. Although they contended that the intellectual character had laid great emphasis on the principle of 'equalitarianism', it did not reach all sections, especially the backward classes. Therefore they urged the government to make educational institutions accessible to all classes irrespective of castes. On account of their persistent demands, the government schools were thrown open to all.[120] Further the British government in the 1890s made primary education compulsory for all, and came forward to render scholarships, stipends and other forms of materials support to the children belonging to the backward sections during the training periods. The Madras government report that in 1901 those who studied in high schools, middle schools and colleges were mostly Christian students belonging to the poor sections. By 1910 their position further improved, and in the districts of Madras, Madurai, Coimbatore and Tirunelveli, the literacy rate of the depressed class increased considerably.

Humanitarian Measures of The British

The all-human minded organizations brought to some extent the neglected sections of the society on equal with the people of other castes. Even afterwards, the British government, by talking drastic measures, tried its best to redeem the suffers from the shackles of complicated and problems which embroiled on the basis of caste system, age-old customs and religious practices. In this context the government undertook progressive measures to widen their knowledge and to provide opportunities for them to stride into a new society, which was expected to be casteless. In reality, when the British rule was firmly established in India, it evolved a new economic system and technology and had a new approach to the social and cultural problems. As a consequence, society witnessed a transformation from the old economic system like Zamindari and Mansabdari to a new one. The introduction of transport system such as railways, buses and tramways in cities and digging channels and laying roads, and the establishment of modern industries necessitated labour force among the lower castes. Such a trend developed their consciousness. It also helped them to achieve solidarity. Further, the common restaurants helped to slow down the caste inequality and caste distinctions. In the different British and French colonies outside India there was a great demand for labour force to work in rubber plantations, tea and coffee estates and agricultural operations. The introduction of modern transport system, cheap postage and innovation of the printing press, improved the communication system greatly helped the free movement of labourers, who acquired a new outlook on life. Gradually, their economic and psichronological foundation, which was based upon untouchability was totally transformed.[121] The work in class of Tamil districts emigrated to foreign countries and those became economically well off and on the return home, gave all possible lead to the rest who were still poor. The British administration and the new bureaucratic setup helped to uproot all the traditional social barriers in the long run.

The government then concentrated in removing the other disabilities suffered by the people. Decided to assert civil equality in public institutions in this endeavour, through a press note, it declare that all public institutions maintained at the cost of government should be easily accessible to all classes without any distinction. In the same spirit, the British government also passed the caste removal act c 1850 in order to eradicate casteism on humanitarian considerations. It highly encouraged the people to mingle with one another. The beneficiaries of the British laws had staunch faith in the British administration. Most of them embraced Christianity in order to protect themselves from the wrath of the caste-Hindus in Tamilnadu. At the same time they also face certain problems like inability to inherit their ancestral property. To remove this problem, the government enacted the religious disability act of 1850 which allowed the Christian converts to inherit their ancestral properties as a civil right. This civil measure slowly hit the foundation of the sacred domain of Hinduism which was strongly built upon the age old practices.[122]

The government also came forward to remove other civic disabilities. On 26th July 1859, the Travancore government under the instruction of British resident of Madras government granted permission to the women of depressed classes including the Shanars. Further in the same year the government enacted district police act by which in every village at least two or more family members of depressed classes were posted as Talaaris and vettis who's service as village police. They were respected as government officials. In 1862, the government enacted the Indian Penal Code replacing the existing Brahmanic code of Manudharma which upheld caste system and encouraged discrimination. The new British code clearly pointed out that everyman is equal before the law. Even the Brahmins were not exempted from the capital punishment, which was absent under the Manu code. Thus inequality prevailed in between man and women were legally checked and no difference was allowed between the socially backward and the forward people. In 1884 the revenue department asserted that slavery was abolished completely in British India. As a matter of fact, the civil laws and other progressive measures, undertaken by the British created a great awakening among the working class and poor people.[123] Krishnaswami Iyer remarked that the "British legislation has done a great deal and perhaps all that is possible for the legislature to do for the downtrodden classes.[124]

References

1. Frank F. Conlon, A Caste in a Changing World: The Chitrapur Sarasuiat Brahmans, 1700-1935 (Berkeley, 1977).
2. David Washbrook, 'The Development of Caste Organisation in South India 1880 to 1925', in C. J. Baker and D. A. Washbrook (eds), South India: Political Institutions and Political Change 1880-1940 (Delhi, I 975), pp. 150-203.)
3. Angus Stewart Woodburne, The Indianization of Christianity, The Journal of Religion, Vol. 1, No. 1. (Jan., 1921), pp. 66-75.)
4. Rigveda 1-89-1.
5. Hugald Grafe, History of Christianity in India Vol. IV, Part II (Bangalore: Chai, 1990) 221.
6. Koji Kawashima, Missionaries and a Hindu State (New Delhi: Oxford University Press, 1998) 55 -80.
7. P. Thomas, Christians and Christianity in India and Pakistan (London: George Allen and Unwin Ltd., 1954) 195-223
8. Stephen Neill, The Story of Christian Church in India and Pakistan (Madras: CLS-ISPCK, 1972) 106-109.
9. Stephen Neill, The Story of Christian Church in India and Pakistan (Madras: CLS-ISPCK, 1972) 106-109.
10. P. Chenchiah, "Christianity and Hinduism", NCCI Vol. XLVIII, No. 3 March (1928): 119-138.
11. K.T. Paul, The British Connection With India (London: SCM, 1927) 21-70.

12. J.W. Gladston in his case-study of the conversion movement among lower castes in Travancore has elaborated the details. Refer J. Waston Pickett, Christian Mass Movement in India (New York, Abingdon Press, 1933) 58-85, 265-312.
13. P. Thomas, Christians and Christianity in India and Pakistan (London: George Allen and Unwin Ltd., 1954) 188-189.
14. Arthur Mayhew, Christianity and the Government of India (Delhi: Gian Publishing House, 1988) : 165–166.
15. Studdert-Kennedy Gerald, British Christians, Indian Nationalists and the Raj (New Delhi: Oxford University Press, 1996) 116-119.
16. E.C. Dewick, "India, The War and the Gospel", NCCR Vol. LXII, No. 10 October (1942): 399-405.
17. Tara Chand, op. cit.: 238-239.
18. S. Dharmaraj, Colonialism and Christian Mission: Post Colonial Reflections (New Delhi: ISPCK, 1993) 34.
19. S. Dharmaraj, Colonialism and Christian Mission: Post Colonial Reflections (New Delhi: ISPCK, 1993) 34.
20. A.M. Mundadan, History of Christianity in India Vol.1 (Bangalore: Theological Publications in India, 1982) 21.
21. Tisserant, Eastern Christianity in India (London: Orient Longman, 1957) 10.)
22. S. Immanuel David, "Save the Heathens from themselves" The Evolution of the educational policy of the East India Company till 1854, ICHR Vol. XVIII, No. 1 June (1984): 19-29.
23. *Ibid.*
24. Jacob S. Dharmaraj, Colonialism and Christian Mission: Post Colonial Reflections (New Delhi: ISPCK, 1993) : 19.
25. Julius Richter, A History of Missions in India (Edinburgh: Oliphant Anderson & Ferrier, 1908) 30. .: 221.
26. Jacob S. Dharmaraj, Colonialism and Christian Mission: Post Colonial Reflections (New Delhi: ISPCK, 1993) : 58.
27. C.P. Mathew &M.M.Thomas, The Indian Churches of Saint Thomas (New Delhi: ISPCK, 1967) : 48.
28. T.C.Joseph, "The Myth of the Colonial Connection", The Sunday Statesman September 20, 1987: 4.
29. C.P. Mathew &M.M.Thomas, The Indian Churches of Saint Thomas (New Delhi: ISPCK, 1967) : 48.
30. T.C.Joseph, "The Myth of the Colonial Connection", The Sunday Statesman September 20, 1987: 4.
31. T.V. Philip, "Christianity in India during Western Colonisation: Conflict, Reconciliation or Adjustment", ICHR Vol. XXI, No. 1 June (1987): 20.
32. Poikail John George, "Racist Assumptions of 19th Century Missionary Movement", IRM Vol. LIX, No. 235 July (1970): 271-283.
33. Jacob S. Dharmaraj, "A Brief Review of Alexander Duff, English Education and Colonial Connections in 19th Century India", ICHR Vol. XXV, No. 2 December (1991): 82-83.

34. Arthur Mayhew, Christianity and the Government of India (Delhi: Gian Publishing House, 1988) 163.
35. A.C Perumalil, the Apostle of India, 1971, p. 67.
36. S.Thangundla, the structure of the church in Andhra Pradesh, Rome, 1975, pp. 116-119.
37. Martin Luther Dolbee, Jr. A history of Lutheranism in the Andhra Desa (the Telugu territory india) 1842-1920, (New York. 1959), p. 35.
38. *Ibid.*
39. Sherring:History of Protestant mission in India, (1884), p. 20. Also see Campbell's British India, (1839 place of publication not mentioned), p. 250.
40. Stock, Eugene: The History of the church Missionary society (London, 1899), Vol. I, p. (1884), p. 20. Also see Cam[bell's British India, (1839 place of publication not mentioned), p. 250.
41. *Ibid.* Also see A Article by Dr. David Raju& K. Gangaiah in A.P. History Congress proceeding XVII Session (Tirupati, 1993).
42. Heyer, C.F.: Account of his first voyage, 1841-1846 (Philadelphia, year of publication not mentioned, pp. 82-83, Heyer's letter written in Guntur, India (1844, Philadelphia) also throws much light on his work in Guntur. See also Martin Luther Proben Jr. Op. cit.. pp. 81, 82.
43. Dolbeer Jr.op.cit. p. 60.
44. *Ibid.,* pp. 68, 69.
45. James, M. Baker: Contending the Grade in India Baltimore, 1947, pp. 47,48.
46. B.S. Murthy: Depressed Oppressed: Forever in Agony, (New Delhi, Year of publication not mentioned), pp. 16-18.
47. The first Canadian Baptist missionary named A.V. Timpany arrived at Madras on 16-04-1868 and was received at Nellore by the American Baptists in the Sothern coastal area of Andhra Pradesh. He began to work in Ongole area.
48. N. Surya Rao, The History of the Geological Training Institute at Kakinada, Andhra Pradesh, 1882-1964, pp. 1-5 (unpublished thesis) and G. Beaulah Pearl Sunanda, an Insight into the History of the Canadian Baptist Mission in Andhra Pradesh (1874-1924), pp. 12-15.
49. G.Beaulah Pearl Sunanda, an insight into the history of the Canadian Baptist mission in Andhra Pradesh (1874-1924), pp. 18-21.
50. Mannam Samuel, work of salvation army in Andhra Pradesh, religion and society 1990 p. 57.
51. W.H. Wiser, the Hindu Jajmani system, a social-economic system interrelating members of a Hindu village community in services. (Lucknow: Lucknow Publishing House, 1936), pp. 192.
52. Madras Presidency, administration report, 1921-2, p. 84.
53. Madras Presidency, op. cit., p. 86. A.T. Fishman, 'agriculture in the American Baptist Telugu mission', Baptist missionary review, XXII (June, 1926), p. 224.
54. J. Augustusvoelcker, Indian agriculture in its physical Aspects, 1891. Reprint, Journal of the Royal Agricultural Society of England, Vol. II, Third Series. Part 1, p. 12.

55. G.L.C.Howard, Indian Agriculture (London:Oxford University Press, 1927), pp. 38-42.
56. G.L.C. Howard, op. cit., p. 48.
57. A.T.Fishman, 'Agriculture in the American Baptist Telugu Mission', Baptist Missionary Review, XXII (June, 1926), p. 224.
58. Strasser, DieTaufe in der Geschichte der deutschenevangelish-lutherschen Mission, Leipzing, 1925, p. 86.
59. Harms, Geschichte der Hermannsburg Mission in India, manuscript, 1935, p. 191-193.
60. Andhra Christian council, proceedings, 1934, p. 47.
61. The former project [Lloyd (Sukkur)] which was opened for irrigation in 1932 did not yield any revenue this year as against Rs. 25 laks in the preceding year while the latter project (Cauvery-Mettur) which was completed during the year under review, yielded a net revenue of Rs. 198, 000 only.' The Indian yearbook, XXV (Francis low, editor), 1938-9, p. 343.
62. Harms, geschichte der Hermannsburg mission in India, manuscript, 1935, p. 175-176, 230-231.
63. Hacciuss, hannoverschemissions geschichte, Hermannsburg, 1914, second half, p. 274.
64. Foreign missionary annual, evangelical Lutheran joint synod of Ohio, 1930, p. 8.
65. Harms, geschichte, op. cit., pp. 318.
66. Martin Luther Dolbeen, Jr. A history of Lutheranism in the Andhra Desa (the Telugu territory, India) 1842-1920, (New York, 1959), p. 105.
67. *Ibid.*, p. 306.
68. *Ibid.,* p. 309.
69. G.L.C. Howard, op. cit., p. 29.
70. *Ibid.,* p. 308. also see Richter: A History of Missions in India (New York, 1908) p. 239.
71. Martin Luther Dolbeer Jr.: op. cit., p. 308. also see Harpster: Among the Telugoos (Philadelphia, 1902) in p. 28.
72. Royal Commission on Agriculture in India, Abridged report (Calcutta: Government of India, 1928), p. 89.
73. G.L.C. Howard, op. cit., pp. 84-5
74. Richard D.N. Dickenson, The Christian College in developing India, Madras, 1971, p. 1.
75. M. Ramadevi, "Intellectual Awakening in Andhra with special reference to Christian Missionaries, 1857-1920, " Ph. D Dissertation submitted to S.V. University, Tirupati, October 2001, p. 11.
76. K.S. Vakil and Natarajan, Education in India, Bombay, 1966, p. 46. The term 'pagano' is derived from the latin word 'pagus' which means 'village', and the word 'heathens' is derived from the latin word 'heaths' which means 'jungles'.

77. Dyron B. Daughrity, "Hinduisms, Christian missions, and the Tinnevelly Shanars: A Study of Colonial Mission in 19th century India", Ph.D. Dissertation submitted to the University of Calgary, Calgary, Albert, 2005, p. 1.
78. Bh. Sivasankaranarayana (ed.), Andhra Pradesh District Gazetteers, Cuddapah, Hyderabad, 1967, p. 595.
79. Y. Vithal Rao, Education and Learning in Andhra under the East India Company, secunderabad, 1979, pp. 256-262.
80. J.D.B. Gribble, A Manual of the Cuddapah District in the Presidency of Madras, reprint, (originally published in 1875), Hyderabad, 1992, pp. 348-354, see.also N Gopalakrishnamachetty (com). Manual of the Kurnool district in the Presidency of Madras, Madras, 1886, pp. 193-194.
81. *Ibid.*
82. Ibid, p. 194.
83. J.D.B. Gribble, A Manual of the Cuddapah District, p. 352.
84. J.Mangamma, Andhradesam Lokraisthava Missionareelaseva (Services of Christian Missionaries in Andhra) (Telugu), Hyderabad, 1992, p. 4.
85. *Ibid,* pp. 41-45.
86. C.F. Brackenbury, Andhra Pradesh District Gazetteers, Cuddapah District Gazetteer, reprint, (originally published in 1915), Hyderabad, 1993, p. 172, see also P. Manikyamba, "Role of Education in the Emergence of Andhra Movement in South India, 1828-1913", Proceedings of the South Indian History Congress, Dharward, 1991, p. 199, and K.H.S.S. Sundar, "Valasavidya Vidhananmuanuc Hitamataprame yamu (Telugu), Proceedings of the Andhra Pradesh History Congress, Tenali, 1994, p. 112.
87. General report of the board of revenue, 1826, p. 283, quoted in Bh. Sivasankaranarayana (ed.), Andhra Pradesh District Gazetteers, p. 596.
88. J. Mangamma, Andhradesam Lokraisthava Missionareelaseva, p. 4.
89. Bh. Sivasankaranarayana (ed.), Andhra Pradesh District Gazetteers, p. 598.
90. RPIMP, 1856-1857, pp. 23-24 (TNA).
91. J.D.B. Gribble, A Manual of the Cuddapah district, p. 351, see also T.V. Manjulathadevi, "Promotion of Education by the Christian Missionaries in Rayalaseema in the early 19th century", p. 91.
92. T.V. Manjulatha Devi, "Promotion of Education by the Christian Missionaries in Rayalaseema in the early 19th century", Ithihas, Vol. XII, July-December. Hyderaba, 1984, p. 89.
93. Sunitha Busy Reddy, "Education of Women in Colonial Andhra (1800-1920)", Proceedings of the Andhra Pradesh History Congress, Warangal, 1990, p. 171.
94. C.F. Brackenbury, and Andhra Pradesh District Gazetteers, p. 172.
95. George Drach and Calwin F. Kuder. The Telugu Mission of the General Council of the Evangelical Lutheran Church in North America (Philadelphia, 1941), p. 268.
96. *Ibid.,* p. 269.
97. *Ibid.,* pp. 272-273.

98. Swavely. (Ed.) A hundred years of Andhra country. A history of the Indian mission of Luthern church in America (Madras, 1942), p. 253.
99. *Ibid.,* p. 255.
100. *Ibid.,* p. 256.
101. *Ibid.,* p. 256.
102. *Ibid.,* p. 257.
103. *Ibid.,* p. 257.
104. Swavely, (Ed.), op. cit., p. 262.
105. *Ibid.,* p. 263.
106. *Ibid.,* p. 263.
107. *Ibid.,* p. 263.
108. *Ibid.,* p. 264.
109. *Ibid.,* p. 265.
110. *Ibid.,* p. 265.
111. The annual report of the Foreign Missionaries of the United Luthern Church in America for the year-1935 {Baltimore, Maryland, 1935}, p. 31.
112. *Ibid.,* p. 27.
113. Atmanand Misra, Grants in aid of Education in India, Madras, 1973, p. 9.
114. Modern Rationalist, (monthly), Madras, February 1983, p. 11.
115. Sukbir Choudry, Growth of Nationalism in India 1857-1980, New Delhi, Vol. 1, 1973, pp. 17.
116. S. Manickam, Studies in Missionary History, Madras, 1988, pp. 145- 146.
117. *Ibid.,* p. 146.
118. Triloknath, Politics of the Depressed Classes, Delhi, 1987, p. 26.
119. *Ibid.*
120. *Ibid.,* pp. 78-85.
121. Celestin Bogule, Essays on the Caste System, Coimbatore, 1971, p. 82.
122. G.A. Natesan, The Depressed Class of India, new Delhi, 1977.
123. P. Nagoorkani, Struggle for Social Justice in Tamil Nadu 1916-1939, (Unpublished Ph.D. thesis), Madurai Kamaraj University, Madurai, pp. 41-42.
124. G.A. Natesan, op. cit., pp. 126-127.

Chapter - V

Christian Missionaries in Kurnool

Kurnool is a city in the Kurnool district of Andhra Pradesh state in Southern India. It is the administrative seat of the district. Kurnool is the gateway to Rayalaseema and the largest city in the area, with a population around 6, 69, 000. From 1 October 1953A.D. to 31 October 1956A.D., Kurnool was the capital of Andhra State. It has many educational institutions and is also a major hub for Banking and Insurance companies. Kurnool district lies between the Northern Latitudes of 14-54 and 16-18 and the Eastern latitudes of 76-58 and 79-34. The district of Kurnool is bounded on the North by the Tungabhadra and Krishna rivers as well as Mahaboob Nagar District. On the East by Prakasham district. On the West by Bellary district of Karnataka state and on the South by Anantapur and Cuddapah districts. Kurnool District is a district in the state of Andhra Pradesh, India, located in the west-central part of the state on the Southern banks of the Tungabhadra and Handri rivers. The Kurnool town is currently the headquarters of the district. Telugu and Kannada are the widely spoken languages.

According to "A Manual of the Kurnool District in the Presidency of Madras" the name Kurnool is derived from Kandenavolu or Kandanavolu (a Telugu name by which it is referred to in the inscriptions and literature of the past), pronounced as Karnoolu. During the time of Western Chalukyas in11th century A.D., the Odderas carted stones for construction of a temple at Alampur and halted at the present town of Kurnool before crossing River Tungabhadra. The locals supplied oil for greasing carts here and the place came to be known as Kandenavolu (A street called Bandimetta is present in Kurnool near Tungabhadra river) which subsequently became Kurnool.

According to another legend, during the regime of 'Santamoola' an Ikshwaka ruler, Kurnool town was built by Paraskandanaga, accordingly, the town came to be known as 'Skandanaprolu'. It is said that the Sanskrit word Skandanaprolu got changed in to 'Kandanavolu' as time passed by. Besides, a town named 'Nagar Kurnool' of Mahaboob Nagar District was also built adding another angle to the meaning.

In some of the inscriptions, Kurnool is referred as Kannadu or Karu Nadu (Karu means black; Nadu means territory). Some scholars argue that Kurnool derived its name from Kallu which means stone and Nadu which means territory.Kurnool is also said to have been derived from Skandanavolu, the city of Skanda or Kumaraswamy. The worship of Skanda in Andhradesha is very ancient. The cities were also named after Skanda, the chief God of the Devas. Kurnool is also called "Qamarnagar"(The Moon Town). The area of Kurnool district is commonly fall in the zone of "Thrilinga desa". It is so called that the'Thrilingas' are located in Sri Kalahasti in the south Chittoor District, Srisailam in the South-East of Kurnool District, Draksharamam in the north East of Srikakulam District.These three places are considered to be the boundaries of the Trilinga Desa and the language commonly spoken in these three areas is Telugu.

During the 18th century Kurnool formed the jagir of a semi-independent Pathan Nawab, whose descendant was dispossessed by the British government for treason in 1838. The Nawab's former territory became a district of Madras Presidency, with Kurnool as its capital. The district surrounded the princely state of Banganapalle. After India's independence in 1947, Kurnool became part of the state of Madras, created out of the former Madras presidency, and Banganapalle was added to the district. The eleven northern districts of Madras state became the new state of Andhra in 1953, and Kurnool served as the state's first capital. In 1956 Andhra Pradesh was formed by combining the Andhra State and Telangana region, formerly part of Hyderabad state. In 2014 again the state of Andhra Pradesh is further divided in to Telengana state and Andhra Pradesh state.

In Kurnool there are 52 muslim shrines located around Thungabhadra and Hundri rivers. A very famous and lengthy K.C. Canal starts from Sunkesula in Kurnool and ends in Kadapa. In Kurnool city there are a number of ancient temples, churches and mosques. Kurnool city, known as the gateway to the Rayalaseema region, on the banks of the Rivers Thungabhadra and the Hundri was the capital of the first linguistic state in free India, Andhra State from 1 Oct. 1953 to 31 Oct. 1956. Kurnool District comprises 3 Revenue Divisions, 54 Revenue Mandals, 53 Mandal Parishads,

One Municipal Corporation, 3 Municipalities, 899 Gram Panchayats (Notified –7, Non notified – 862), 920 Revenue Villages and 615 Hamlet Villages.

Kurnool has freedom fighters like Vuyyalawada Narsimha Reddy, Gadicharla Harisarvothama Rao. Zilla Grandhalaya Samstha (ZGS) and the District Central Library (DCL), Kurnool, building near the old Bus stand is named 'Gadicharla Harisarvothama Rao Smaraka Bhavanamu". It is the second district, apart from Nellore, Bejawada Gopal Reddy 'Andhra state' and Nedurumalli Janardhan Reddy, which has contributed two Chief Ministers to Andhra Pradesh: Damodaram Sanjeevaiah 1st Dalit Chief Minister of India and Andhra Pradesh), Kotla Vijaya Bhaskar Reddy, 10th Indian Prime Minister P.V. Narasimha Rao was elected as Member of Parliament from Nandyala constituency with over 6 lakh (600, 000) majority, a world record.

KURNOOL DISTRICT MAP

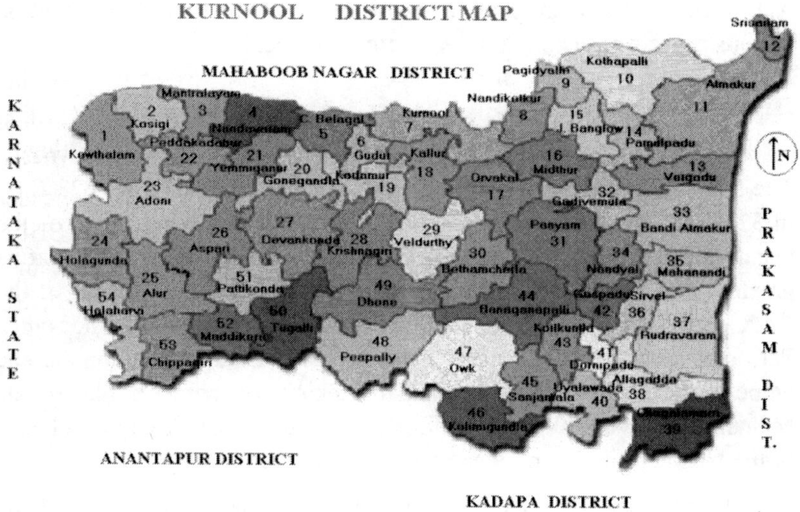

Nallamalas and Erramalas are the two important mountain ranges in Kurnool district running in parallel from North to South. The Erramalas divide the district into two well defined tracts from East to West. Between Erramalas and Nallamalas lies the Eastern part of the district comprises Nandikotkur, Pagidyala, Kothapalli, Pamulapadu, Atmakur, Velgodu, Jupadu Bunglow, Midthur, BandiAtmakur, Gadivemula, Nandyal, Mahanandi, Panyam, Banaganapalli, Owk, Koilakuntla, Rudravaram and Chagalamarri Mandals. This tract is crossed by the crest of Krishna and Pennar, watershed at the North part of the Pagidyala Mandal at about 1000 above the sea level. From this height the ground slopes to the South along the river Kundu till it traverses into Pennar valley. Major part of its tract is predominantly black cotton soils. The eastern part and north western parts comprising Koilakunta, Nandyal, Allagadda, Kurnool, Nandikotkur, Alair, Adoni and Atmakur, have predominantly black cotton soils. South eastern parts of the district, Dhone and Pattikonda, have red soil.

Kurnool district offers many places of tourist interest. The district houses many places of religious importance, like Mahanandi, Ahobilam, and Mantralayam, etc. The historic Konda Reddy Fort is located in the heart of Kurnool town. This has an underground hidden pathway (suarang) of about 25 km to Allampur (a neighbouring town). Srisailam temple that has one of the Jyothirlingas and attracts millions of pilgrims from different parts of the country, falls in Kurnool district. Kurnool is a simple town with some interesting places to visit. The ruins of a royal fort dating back to the medieval kingdom of **Vijayanagara**, which flourished from the 14th to the 16th century AD. Several Persian and Arabic inscriptions of the region throw light on various aspects of historical interest are found here.

History of Kurnool

The early history of Kurnool dates back to the history Nanda dynasty. The Nanda Empire was established by Mahapadmananda (345-323 B.C) in 323 B.C. Pataliputra was his Capital City. Of the Nine rulers of the Nanda dynasty. Dhananda was the last ruler and the Nanda Empire at its greatest extent under Dhana Nanda (circa 323 BCE). The sources of the study reveal that the Kurnool area was reasonably important in the Nanda Period and the Mauryan Period. 'Chowdeshwari Purana' mention that the emperors of the Nanda dynasty ruled this region. The names of places like, Mahanandi, Nandikotkur and the like confirm this point. After the collapse of the Nanda Clan, Kurnool came under Mouryan dynasty.

The Mauryan Dynasty 322 B.C - 189 BC:-Under the power of the Mauryans, the rise of Chandragupta Maurya by 322 BC established the first Mauryan Empire. Chandragupta Maurya with the help of Chanakya (Kautilya) ruined the Nanda Empire and laid the foundation for the great Mauryan Empire. Chanakya was one of the important ministers in the court of Nandas. It is believed that Chanakya was maltreated by Nanda king and then he vowed to ruin the family of Nanda dynasty. They formed their own army and succeeded in forming the Mouryan dynasty. The minor and mojor Edicts of Ashoka Mourya, are **inscribed on the rocks of** Yerragudi.The village Yerragudi is situated eight miles away from Gooty on the southern border of the Kurnool district, and is eighty miles north-east of Siddapur.

Clearly it was a site of some significance since both the Major and the Minor Edicts are to be found here. No remains of a town have yet been discovered in the area, but it is possible that a frontier town may have existed at the site, with a route leading through it to the south Indian kingdoms.

Subsequently the Shatavahanas (230 BC-220A.D) are the subordinate rulers of Mouryas . The Shatavahanas initially ruled the area between the rivers of Krishna and Godavari. The Pûrânas listed 30 Andhra rulers are known from their coins and inscriptions. It is learnt that the Shatavahanas ruled Kurnool. 'Satanakota', a village in Nandikotkur mandal confirms this point. The strategic position led to the formation of a small settlement on the spot which subsequently came to be known as Kandenapalli, Kandenolu and Kandenavolu, the city of Kandena or for the grease. The site which was used as a halting place by the Vadderas in those days is still known as Bandla Metta, Bandla means carts and Metta means headquarters or halting place. Today this is a street in the Old city of Kurnool. Now the name of this place is better known as "Bandimetta". In some of the inscriptions, Kurnool is referred to as Kannadu or Karu Nadu with Karu meaning black and Nadu meaning territory.

In 7th century AD and 8th century AD Telugu Cholas, Kalyani Chalukyas and Velanati Cholas ruled Kurnool. Later it came under the rule of the Yadavas and because of this 'Yadavaneni' of that period is called now as, 'Adoni', the monumental scripts seen in the areas of Adoni and Parla testify this point.The Eastern part of Kurnool was under the rule of Kakatiyas (1100A.D-1474 AD). The monumental scripts of Kakatiya Prathaparudra are seen at Damagatla Village near Nandikotkur even today. It is also learnt that some part of Kurnool was ruled by the Reddy Kings. Harihararaya I and Bukka Raya I, the founders of the Vijayanagara Empire in 1336AD occupied Kurnool from Reddyrulers. The Konda Reddy fort was believed to be built by Achyuta Devarayalu, belonging to Vijayanagar Empire and stands even today as the splendorous example of the architecture of those times. Konda Reddy Buruju is a part of Kurnool Fort and also the only part left out of the magnificent fort. The Buruju was a sentinel and was used as a prison. Chronicles has it that, a revolutionary named Konda Reddy was imprisoned by the Nawab of Kurnool when he tried to oppose him.

Many a time Konda Reddy (1597A.D-1643A.D), the last ruler of Alampur defeated Kurnool Nawab who was a subordinate and an associated with rulers of Golconda. After a prolonged battle Konda Reddy was captured and imprisoned in the fortress. Because of his valour and untiring resolve to fight the Muslim rulers, the fort came to be known as Konda Reddy

Buruju. He escaped from the fortress digging a tunnel across the River Krishna to Alampur and ultimately lost his kingdom to the Golconda Kings.

Kurnool was under the rule of Bahmani Sultans (1347A.D.–1527A.D.) and Moghul emperors (1526A.D.–1858A.D.) for about 150 years. Mohammad Quli Qutub Shah, son of Ibrahim Qutub Shah, King of Qutub Shah dynasty (1518A.D.–1687A.D.) invaded up to Nandyal and occupied Kurnool by force from Basavanta Raya, King of Kurnool. In 17th century the Kurnool fort which was under the control of Gopalaraju, was successfully occupied by the force by the Sultan of Bijapur. Abdul Wahab Khan, the first Nawab of Kurnool, ruled Kurnool for about 16 years before he died in 1618. His tomb can be seen ever now as a beautiful construction on the banks of the river 'Hundri'. It is called 'Goal Gummaj'.The Goal Gummaj has been there for 100 years and is presently under the supervision of the Archaeological department. After the death of Abdul Wahab, his brother 'Mohammad' came to power. However, the last Nizam of Hyderabad, the last Qutub Shah defeated the king and Kurnool came under the power of the Moghuls.

In 1618 A.D. Aurangazeb sent "Ghaziuddin" to occupy Nandyal and Kurnool by force. These two regions were called 'Kammur Nagar'. After occupying these places, Ghaziuddin changed their name into 'Ghazipur', after his name. At the end of 17th century Kurnool was given to Dawood Khan as a Jagir. After his death in 1715AD his brother Ibrahim Khan became his successor. The Minister of Afsar Jahi murdered Ibrahim Khan on 24-09-1727A.D. Later, 'Salabat Jung' occupied this place and kept it under the supervision of his knight Syed Mohammed Alam and Ramanayudu, the Zamindar of Gadwall.

In 1799A.D. after the fall of Tippu sultan at Sri Ranga Patnam, the Mysore territories were divided between the Nizam and the English. Kurnool was left to the share of the Nizam at 66, 600 Pagodas per annum. This was fixed by Hyder Ali. In 1800A.D. the Nizam of Hyderabad Ceded (surrendered) the Districts of Kurnool, Cuddapah, Ananthapur and Bellary to the British Govt. From then onwards, Kurnool was brought under the rule of the British Govt. The British began to have supremacy over Kurnool making thee the Nawab was rule Kurnool as their subject. Though Gulam Rasool Khan, the Nawab of Kurnool at that time, (1839A.D.) was very loyal to the British, they conducted a trial on him, on a small suspicious note, arrested and sent him to the fort of Tiruchirapalli, and killed him there. They sanctioned a monthly pension of Rs.700/-to Dawood Khan Bahadur, the grandson for maintenance of the family. His daughters were granted life pensions only.In 1913 A.D. Dawood Khan died and his four sons namely: 1. Rafiul Mullah Bahadur. 2. Amir Ul Omar. 3. Suleman Jha. 4. Ghazi Ul Mullah settled in various fields. Rafiul mullah Bahadur worked as a deputy collector in the Madras Presidency. Thus, in the history of Kurnool, the reign of the Nawabs came to an end with the arrival of the British in India.

Christian Missionaries

The persisting effort to work for the uplift of the poor and marginalized of the society amidst the opposition is derived from The Ten Commandments (Exodus 20:2-17) "You shall not covet your neighbor's ***house; you shall not covet your, neighbour's wife, nor his male servant, nor his female servant, Knor his ox, nor his donkey, nor anything that is your neighbor's."*** Moses with the Ten Commandments by Rembrandt (1659A.D) and its gist ***"love your neighbour as you love your God ...."*** is explained in the parable of Good Samaritan.... Jesus asked them "go and do likewise". Therefore, for a Christian, social service is not an option but essential part of his day-to-day life.

Jesus Christ was always the part of the humanity and part with the poor and marginalized but did not ignore the rich. By taking the side of the poor and downtrodden and by raising voice against prevailing injustice and the authority of the ruling class, Christ had to pay the price for accepting his crucifixion. Thus, social worker, according to Christianity, must continue to have vision of just society and work towards the realization of the basic Christian values, accompanied by both a faith dimension and spiritual aspect.

Mere humanism will not suffice the integral development of the community. The Christians are aware that those guided only by humanistic values and social work principles and scientific methods will achieve their social work objectives but they will fall short of continuous commitment and selfless services.

The commandment to love your neighbour as you love yourself is the inspiration for starting charitable services by the Christians. But close examinations of the work reveals that it can create 'a feeling of benevolence and superiority on the part of giver and sense of inferiority among the recipient. Thus experimenting community model and to practice of equality, fraternity the shift of work especially among funding agencies have changed to Development. The economic development has helped the country to progress but the rate of people below poverty line did not diminish significantly. This is possible in the practice of distributive justice which

Christians strive for and many of the Christian institutions visualized this through Jesus summoned His twelve disciples and gave them authority over unclean spirits, to cast them out, and to heal every kind of disease and every kind of sickness . . . 'And as you go, preach, saying, 'The kingdom of heaven is at hand.' 'Heal the sick, raise the dead, and cleanse the lepers, cast out demons. Freely you received, freely give'

Almost all missionaries regarded their work as imitating Jesus' actions, but also directly fulfilling his instructions to those who considered themselves his disciples. Wellesley Bailey and the Mission to Lepers, and other missionaries and societies explicitly reiterated that their work with leprosy sufferers was biblically prescribed. For instance, Reverend Edward Guilford, serving in Tarn Taran, India, with the London-based Church Missionary Society, affirms in a May 1890A.D speech at Exeter Hall describing the efforts of the Mission to Lepers. (Quoted in Bailey, 1899A.D, P. 112):

As stated earlier that it was in 52 AD., St. Thomas introduced Christianity in Kerala in South India. However, Christianity was limited to the South West Coast of India, i.e., within the boundaries of Kerala State only until the arrival of the Portuguese in India in 1498 and later by East India Company from England in Seventeenth Century. The dynamic spirit of missionary activity began in different parts of India including Andhra and other parts of the State during these periods. Although the first contacts of the Telugus with Christianity were established at the beginning of the 16th century, the seeds of salvation have not taken deep root among them during the first three centuries in the Nizam's Dominion. The reason could be political, the attitude of the Telugus towards Christianity and the lack of missionaries to spread the Faith.

On September 1, 1798 Lord Wellesley made the Nizam of Hyderabad to accept the Subsidiary Alliance on the death of General Raymond on March 25, 1798. The Nizam was the first one to come under this 'Subsidiary Alliance'. Once this was concluded, the Nizam Ceded the districts of Bellary, Cuddapah, Anantapur and Kurnool to the English which are known as Ceded Districts in the history of Andhra Pradesh. In 1947, when India gained its independence, the Nizam of Hyderabad wished to remain independent without joining the Indian Union. He was adamantly jealous of his independence. There was unrest and fear in Hyderabad for the non-muslims. As things were getting out of control, Hyderabad was given an ultimatum by the Government of India to join the Indian Union. On September 13,

1948, the Hyderabad army surrendered to the Indian troops under Major General Chaudhuri.

Most of the Roman Catholic Missionaries were Doctors. This medical knowledge helped them much in their missionary work. Once a Zamindar who was the nearest relative of Nawab of Kurnool brought his daughter for treatment to Roman Catholic Bishops. That daughter after listening to the teachings of the missionary went back to her home and sent her servant to bring that missionary to Kurnool. Meanwhile the daughter of Nawab was died, later her parents got baptised. The servant took baptism and later named as Paul and started preaching the Gospel of Jesus Christ and reached Cuddapah. There he changed one Brahmin by name Thimmaiah and baptised him. Later he also treated the ill health of the daughter of Nawab of Cuddapah and as a gratitude the 'Siddavatam' Zamindary was donated to one of the Christian missionaries.

In the early Christian Church history Nandyal area of Kurnool District also figured much in Andhra Pradesh. During 1810, few ladies from Nandyal travelled to Proddutur in Cuddapah district. When they were witnessing one Church worship organised by Catholics, they were much impressed by the order of service and started enquiring about Christ and Christianity. Later they embraced Christianity and went back to their homes and converted many of the Hindus along with their family members. But these families through strongly attached themselves to Christianity did not make any efforts to propagate the religion. By the year 1847 the Christian population in Cuddapah District was 700, in Kurnool 400 and in Guntur 700. In the year 1839 the British occupied Kurnool and the Nawab of Kurnool 'Rasool Khan' was put in Tiruchirapalli Jail on the pretext that this Nawab was webbing a conspirasy against the British. When he was in the Jail he was given some biblical literature. He read the literature and later converted to Christianity. Afterwards, Mr. Stocks succeeded John Goldinghome as District Collector. He also took lot of interest in Gospel Preaching especially in Kurnool area and made possible for the SPG Mission to start work in those areas. He was also responsible for inviting Father Higher to start Lutheran Mission in Guntur District.

Since the year 1872 the Bellary Missionary Rev. Eduru Lavis was visiting the places like Adoni, Alur, Anantapur, Dharmavaram and Penugonda. From 1868 onwards he made Adoni, Gooty and Bukkapatnam as his outstations. They travelled from village to village teaching women sanitation, cleanliness, sewing and godliness and they established schools for girls in Anantapur, Bukkapatnam and Dharmavaram. They travelled from village to village teaching women sanitation, cleanliness, sewing and godliness and they established schools for girls in Anantapur, Bukkapatnam and Dharmavaram.

The methods and techniques adopted by Telugu Baptist Mission in preaching the Gospel positively helped to spread Christianity quickly to various parts of Andhra Pradesh especially among Telugus. These Missionaries not only concentrated in evangelical work but also took interest in the establishment of schools in these regions. In 1879 they started one High School at Ongole. Later, High Schools were started in Nellore and Kurnool. Even today these educational institutions are functioning and progressed as Colleges. Today all the Telugu Baptist Churches got united and formed as one United Church under the name of 'Samavesam of Telugu Baptist Churches (STBC) in 1962. There are more than 550 Churches in this Union.

At the time when Wittford stayed at Cuddapah one dalit by name 'Aakula Nancharu' from the village known as 'Rudravaram' of Kurnool district who got baptised through a missionary when he was in jail worked for propagating Christianity in Kurnool area. He was responsible for requesting the SPG Missionaries to send one Preacher to Cuddapah. When they sent the Preacher to Cuddapah, through him the relatives and friends of Akula Nancharu and his village people converted into Christianity. In this way the mass conversions in Kurnool district took place through SPG Missionaries.

Educational Policy in Andhra: The establishment of British rule in India marks the beginning of a new age in Andhra as in other parts of the country. It also marks the introduction of a new political, social and educational system in the region. The British were more successful in helping to revolutionize the intellectual life of India through the introduction of modern education. But the spread of modern education was not solely the work of the Government, the Christian missionaries and a large number of enlightened Indians also played an important part. During the pre-British period, literacy was neglected, social and religious evils became rampant and indigenous education was on its way out. The deterioration in educational standards and the irrelevance of the curricula is only an index of the prevailing social condition in India, and Andhra was no exception to this general rule. The present paper is an attempt at understanding the British educational policy in Andhra region of Madras presidency.

Traditional educational System: Traditional education in India revolved round the teacher. Though no fee was collected from the pupils, the teachers used to accept charities and collect donations during the harvest season. The living conditions of the teachers were far from satisfactory and they lead a hand to mouth existence. Caste prejudices denied the privileges of education to vast numbers of men, but for people of upper caste the doors of education were always open. Priestly class was allowed some elementary knowledge of arithmetic for common accounting purpose. The traders, merchants, businessmen, shopkeepers, money lenders, village headmen, tax collectors, accountants, big cultivators and such other people considered education essential for their children.

The systems of education were no doubt different from the modern systems – defective or unscientifie; they served the needs of the time. The major defects in the traditional educational system were the absence of proper standards of teaching, extreme narrowness of the subjects taught and little encouragement to originality in thought. It also did not attempt to inculcate the habit of scientific and critical thinking and the spirit of enquiry among the students. There was no education authority to lay down uniform standards in regard to qualifications of teachers, syllabi, periods of study etc.

Attitude of English education : At the time of British conquest, at the lowest level there were village pathasalas or primary schools to impart elementary education. The conditions of schools were miserable. Government did not take interest, that is why there was no system, no uniformity, and lack of well-conceived plans to regulate the schools. Most of the pathasalas were held in temple premises, in religious institutions, on the verandas, in huts, even in cow sheds or under trees. Besides arithmetic, religious and mythological stories and tales from the Ramayana and Mahabharata were taught. On the whole, the village pathasalas met the demands of the society, and the teacher, with all his ignorance really served useful purpose.

The East India Company did not think of the necessity of introducing any system of education in their conquered territories for three to four decades after the conquest of Bengal and Bihar. The Charter Act of 1793 was under consideration, some Englishmen raised the question for giving Indians some kind of education. Wilberforce felt convinced of the need for an educational system based on utility for both the ruler and the ruled. Charles Grant pleaded, in a philanthropic way, for educating the Indian people.

The East India Company after sixty years of its domination in India took little interest in the education of its subjects. Missionaries and their supporters and many humanitarians soon began to exert pressure on Company to encourage and promote modern secular westernized education in India. While the humanitarians, including many Indians, believed that modern knowledge would be the best remedy for the social, economic, and political ills of the country. The British tried to activate the intellectual life of India through the introduction of modern education. A humble beginning was made in 1813 when the Charter Act incorporated the principle of encouraging learned Indians and promoting the knowledge of modern sciences in the country. The Act directed the company to spend the sum of one lakh of rupees for the purpose.

But even the petty amount was not made available by the Company authorities till 1823. Macaulay's act of 1835 gave the official seal to the introduction of English education. Lord William Bentinck proclaimed that the great object of the British Government ought to be promotion of European science and literature among the natives of India and that all funds appropriated for the purpose of education would be best employed on English education alone.

This reflects upon the attitude of the company towards the diffusion of western education in Andhra. Sir Thomas Munro Governor of Madras was the first to formulate a scheme for the establishment 40 collectrate schools and 300 Tahasildary schools in the whole of Madras Presidency. The court of directors sent a dispatch to the Madras government which urged the necessity for higher education in preference to elementary education in order to train a body of Indians to take part in the civil administration of the country. Accordingly the government established the Madras University High School (1841), which later developed into the Madras presidency college, and a number of provincial schools of which one was located at Rajamandry in Andhra.

School Education: Government had more number of middle and high schools than primary schools under its control. It started a few schools for girls and for the people in the early 19th century. Provincial schools and Taluq schools of 1850's were the only important schools under its control. After this Act, Christian missionaries came to India more in number to spread Christianity through the educational institutions. In 1844, Lord Hardinge announced that a candidate with knowledge of English, would be preferred for government service. The missionaries started a number of schools with the main object of converting Indian students to Christianity. The government encouraged those missionary schools by giving grants-in aid. The government did little to improve the indigenous elementary schools or to increase their number. This was left to private and the missionary's effort. Among the schools which were the outcome of private effort was the Taylor's School in Narasapur. The missionaries also established a few schools in Krishna, Guntur and Nellore districts. The Church Missionary Society under the leadership of Rev. Noble established a school at Machilipatnam in 1843, with the intention of importing western education. In 1864 it was upgraded as a college.

The woods Dispatch of 1854 provided a comprehensive outline to the system of education. In spite of these developments, educational activity in Madras Presidency in the period before the Woods Dispatch of 1854 was very limited when compared to the other provinces. In the meanwhile in 1857 the Madras University was established. This gave sufficient impetus for the development of higher education in Andhra. In 1873, the Madras Government started a second grade college at Rajahmundry and this was upgraded later as a degree college in 1877. The Hindu college at Visakhapatnam and the Khallikota College at Berhampur were established in 1878 and 1879 respectively. It is very interesting to note here that most of the schools and colleges that were established in Andhra were confined to the coastal area. This may be due to the economic prosperity of the region.

The education that was impacted by the above referred institutions had two special characteristics. One was that it was almost entirely education in Western culture, sciences and philosophy. The other was that it was an education imparted through the medium of English language. Both these had their effect in shaping the thought and character of the new educated class. They got steeped in the learning and in the political, economic and social ideas and ideals of the west.

The Christian Missionaries established a large number of schools in various parts of the Madras Presidency. These missionaries believed that modern education would destroy the faith of the people in their own religion and lead them to adopt Christianity. The Government of Madras, known for its proselytizing propensities, diverted part of the educational grant to missionary schools under the name of grantinaid to help converting operations. In addition to this serious attempt were made to introduce the Bible as a text book in the educational institutions, contrary to the orders of the Court of Directors. The main mission of the missionaries in spreading Western education was to convert Indians to Christianity.

Higher Education system: The higher education began to make much progress in the third quarter of the 19th century. Universities were established in Madras, Calcutta and Bombay. Admission to the Indian Civil Services was through a competitive examination held in London. The brilliant among graduates of Indian Universities were expected to sit for the examination and get into the Civil Service. The assurance given through the Proclamation encouraged the Indians educated youth to pursue such a course. But the authorities created many obstacles in this connection. The age for admission to the examination was fixed at nineteen. It was too low an age for an Indian to complete his university education in India and proceed to London. The Coconda Literary Association submitted a memorandum to the Secretary of State for India on this issue. Alongside of this demand for rising the age limit was the one for holding the competitive examination simultaneously in England and India, so that the Indians might have equality of opportunities with Englishmen.

But these demands were kept in cold storage. Besides, that admission to the other branches of Higher Civil services, like Police, Engineering, Medicine, etc., was closed to the Indians. In 1861, the Secretary of State for India declared that "the Natives of India of native parentage are unsuited for Military and medical appointments". Thus the pledge that the Indian service or the Indianisation of Higher Civil services was reduced to splinters.

The Madras Native Association argued in 1859 that the distribution of grants-in-aid to missionary schools was inconsistent with the principle of religious neutrality as the grant was used for the teaching of Bible and the tenets of Christianity. It also objected to the Government officials associating themselves with missionaries.

The governor of Madras, Trevelyan, in his remarks on the petition of the Madras Native Association defended the payment of grants to mission schools on the ground that a similar system existed in England and that it would not be possible for the government to bear the entire expenditure on education. He was not convinced by the arguments that the people in a poor country like India could not afford to start private institutions and that in consequence government grants would go to mission schools which had plenty of resources at their disposal. In this connection it may be stated that the missionaries started their activities in Andhra in the early 19th century.

Women's Education: Women's education was very backward in Andhra. The rise in the status of women in india is a matter of recent development and is due mostly to the influence of Christian Missionaries.

Visakhapatnam had the distinction of establishing the first women's school for adult Hindu girls in September 1868 under a non-missionary agency. Subsequently, girl's schools at Dowleswaram in 1874 and in other places were established.

By 1905 four out of every five villages were without a school and seven children out of every eight were growing up in ignorance and darkness and with all the moral and material helplessness that followed. As if to make matters worse the British government had raised the school fees. The journal Rasikollasini deplored the system of school fees and term fee and criticized the recommendation of the finance committee to reduce grants-in-aid to private schools.

Company Educational Policy: The development of education was not uniform in all the districts in Andhra. Some districts and municipalities where enlightened officers and zamindars did some good work became centers of educational activity. The fertile delta districts of Northern Circars were more advanced educationally due to the economic prosperity, enlightened zamindars, missionaries and earlier contacts with the British administration and administrators than the economically backward Ceded districts. Thus, the spread and impact of Western education differed from town to town, district to district and Northern Circars to Ceded districts in this period.

For all the tall claims that it made, the government of india under the company did not really take any serious interest in spreading Western education in Andhra. Even the limited effort that was made was the result of several factors that had little to do with Philanthropic motives. The most important reason was the government is anxiety to economise the cost of administration by getting a cheap supply of educated Indians to man the large and ever increasing number of subordinate posts in administration and British concerns.

Another motive behind the educational policy of the company sprang from the belief that the educated Indians would help to expand the market for British manufactures in India. Lastly, Western education was expected to reconcile the people of India to British rule. The British thus wanted to use modern education to strengthen the foundations of their political authority in the country. It is evident from the above discussion that Andhra suffered a lot, like other parts of India under the Company's rule. The administration completely Europeanised. The governor and the Governors council reigned supreme over the presidency.

In India the Christian Missionaries established their residential areas in the initial stages. They introduced their religious practices in their teaching. Giving prime importance to forming an understanding with the local Telugu literature, they decided to come out with a policy on religious customs. Christianity could not reach the forward castes easily. Missionaries faced many problems in their effort to change the problem. Villagers were given more priority than towns in establishing the Christian Churches. Christian religion was able to attract the rural and the poor to some extent and added to this, natural calamities like drought, infectious diseases, and ill health made the Missionaries busy in rescuing operations, with their commitment of service. They provided educational and medical facilities, and set rehabilitation centers and thus tried to draw the attention of the local people with their service attitude.Though the Missionaries worked in different service sectors, they simultaneously worked for a common cause of religious expansion with their mutual understanding and awareness. They did not interfere in politics. But the big change that the Missionaries brought in society is an incredible achievement indeed!

The personal life style of the Christian Missionaries was very simple and modest. They maintained disciplined lives with good standards of life. They worked hard and they proved by their example that it is not wrong to work hard and in fact it promotes good health. They explained to people the importance of economy in a family. They taught how to live happily with low income. In the society of that day, they organized industrial exhibitions. They conducted and supervised Harvesting festivals of that time. They made the Church and the society achieve self-dependence. The Christian Missionaries encouraged woman-education. The Christian Missionaries started their efforts to spread Christianity through women. They provided opportunity for all to get education irrespective of racial caste, religious and regional differences.

Missionaries in Kurnool

Most of the Roman Catholic Missionaries were Doctors. This medical knowledge helped them much in their missionary work. Once it so happened that one Zamindar who was the nearest relative of Nawab of Kurnool brought his daughter for treatment to Roman Catholic Bishops. That daughter after listening to the teachings of the missionary went back to her home and sent her servant to bring that missionary to Kurnool. Meanwhile that daughter died without taking baptism from the missionary. Later her parents got baptised. That servant also later took the name as Paul and took baptism.

When this servant refused to worship the Zamindars' Gods he was sent out from his job. Later, he became a catechist and started preaching the Gospel of Jesus Christ and reached Cuddapah. There he changed one Brahmin by name Thimmaiah and baptised him. Later he also treated the ill health of the daughter of Nawab of Cuddapah and as a gratitude the 'Siddavatam' Zamindary was donated to one of the Christian missionaries.

Nandyal area of Kurnool District also figured much in the early Christian Church history in Andhra Pradesh. During the year 1810, few ladies from Nandyal travelled to Proddutur in Cuddapah district. When they were witnessing one Church worship organised by Catholics, they were much impressed by the order of service and started enquiring about Christ and Christianity. Later they embraced Christianity and went back to their homes and converted many of the Hindus along with their family members. But these families through strongly attached themselves to Christianity did not make any efforts to propagate the religion. By the year 1847 the Christian population in Cuddapah District was 700, in Kurnool 400 and in Guntur 700.

During the year 1830's one person by name 'Aakula Nancharu' who belonged to a depressed class from Andhra area was a village youth and he was a cotton merchant. He had a great desire to know about God. He travelled many places in search of truth and finally he reached famous Temple at 'Ahobilam' which is situated near Allagadda of Kurnool district in Rayalaseema region. When he entered the temple, the Brahmins identified him as a Dalit and when they prevented him from entering the temple he protested them. Thus, there was some quarrel and law and order problem. Immediately the police kept him in a jail. One Christian missionary visited his jail and preached him about Christ. After his release he started thinking about what the Missionary preached to him. Later he went to Cuddapah and met the missionaries and requested them to send the teacher to his village. As a result of his efforts, a teacher was sent to his village and he started preaching the gospel of Christ in that village and converted thirty families into Christianity. Thus, this was the way how missionary work for the first time commenced in Telugu area.

In the year 1839 the British occupied Kurnool and the Nawab of Kurnool 'Rasool Khan' was put in Tiruchirapalli Jail on the pretext that this Nawab was webbing a conspiracy against the British. When he was in the Jail he was given some biblical literature. He read the literature and later converted to Christianity.

Kurnool is a place with the look of a unique island surrounded by water on all sides. The river Hundri flows on its South and the Kurnool – Kadapa canal on its West.This is the confluence place of two rivers Tungabhadra and Indravati. Kurnool is the only district head quarters of India which is situated on the confluence of two rivers. Kurnool was once a hamlet of Kallur village but it has grown into a Corporation now. The Nallamala and Erramala mountain ranges in the district run parallel from the North to South. The ranges divide the district into two tracts crossed by the Krishna and Pennar rivers. Between the Erramalas and Nallamalas lies the Eastern part of the district comprising of:

1. Kodumur,
2. Nandikotkur,
3. Pagidyal,
4. Kothapalli,
5. Pamulapadu,
6. Atmakur,
7. Velgode,
8. Jupadu Bungalow,
9. Miduhur,
10. Bandi Atmakur,
11. Gadivemula,
12. Nandyal,
13. Mahanandi,
14. Panyam,
15. Cementnagar,
16. Banaganapalle,
17. Srisailam,
18. Owk,
19. Allagadda,
20. Koilkuntla,
21. Rudravaram,
22. Chagalamarri,
23. Yemmiganur,
24. Adoni,
25. Devanakonda,
26. Pathikonda, and
27. Dhone .

In the olden times, there was a big wall around the town of Kurnool of which only a bastion still remains. The famous Konda Reddy Fort was constructed without using mortar. In 1800AD Nizam Ali Khan Asaf Jah II, ceded the districts of Kadapa, Kurnool, Ananthapur, and Bellary to the British Government, and the name Ceded Districts was appended to these four districts. Kurnool has a rare distinction of being known as the first capital of the new State of Andhra Pradesh, formed on the first of October, 1953AD.

Dalit movement in Kurnool

Sixty three years of freedom for India has not bought freedom in a real sense for Dalit's who are still staggering way behind. Around 200 million Dalit in India continue to face widespread caste-based discrimination, extreme forms of violence, chronic hunger and poverty, and have been living denied of even basic entitlements and minimum facilities. Despite many State provisions safeguarding their rights, the community has been subjected to systemic subjugation of rights.

Kurnool district is one of the most backward areas in Andhra Pradesh. It is a part of Rayalaseema region in Deccan Plateau. It falls rain shadow region with scanty rainfall from June to September. Summer is very hot and temperature rises up to 44 Degree Centigrade and there is acute shortage of drinking water and people have to walk miles together to get a pot of drinking water. Agriculture is the main occupation of people in the villages of this region.

In our district the Dalit people are living far away from main village. The total Dalits are controlled under one of the land lords in the village and he dictates the Dalit people. Dalit are called the Scheduled Castes, Madiga (cobblers) Malas (Pallbearers; persons who helps to carry coffin at a funeral) the untouchables who have been suppressed and downtrodden for ages. They have been bounded labourers of the upper castes landlords. They are mostly illiterates and poor. The percentage of literacy among these people is below 5%. A few are educated by the missionary schools.

These people are made to suffer by their men and local landlords and the police. They don't know proper rights about their Rights and Laws. Because lack of education and awareness. Tribal women are also living in the hill areas and they are unable to converse with others because of their caste conditions/traditions. So far they don't know Government Programmes. Their main occupation is to prepare the cheap Liquor illegally by Forest Products. Because of this they are beaten by the police and put behind the bars several times.

The main occupation of the target people is agriculture labour. This depends on monsoon rains from June to September. When these fail there will be drought and famine. The villagers suffer from drought and famine every alternate year. As agriculture is seasonal there will be agriculture work for six months in a year. The rest of the time people are without work, most of the agriculture land is owned by the high caste land lords and others are agricultural labourers who get meager daily wages ranging from 100-150 rupees per day which is not sufficient to maintain their large families. So they migrate to urban areas to work in factors. As most of the industries are dependent on Market demands. This region has not developed industrially. During the period when there is no work they approach the village land lords to borrow money at heavy interest. When they fail to repay the loan money the landlords will forcefully take their lands. Sometimes the bonded labour is continued from generation to generation.

The social conditions of the dalits are poor and pathetic. Being untouchables they are forced to live in small hurts at the outskirts of the village. They don't enjoy good roads and sanitation and drinking water facility. They cannot freely mix with other upper caste people. Their children are discouraged from receiving education in village schools. The upper caste land lords do not want schools for Dalit children. The upper caste land lords tell their parents not to educate them. If they are educated, the landlords think, they may not be in their control.

Dalit are not awakening politically, even they do not know what their rights are and they cannot freely express their right of vote at the time of elections. They are strictly instructed/warned by the land lords to whom they have to vote by swearing on their gods and goddesses. Many times they are asked to obtain from voting and someone will vote on their behalf. So rigging is quite common in villages. Now Government has made provision for their election by reserving certain seats for the Scheduled Castes and Scheduled Tribes both men and women. Even after Dalit are elected they remain political labourers in the hands of upper caste land lords and fraction leaders.

Dalits are not fully aware of their civil and political rights on account of their ignorance and lack of education. Even if some know they are afraid of thinking aloud for fear of the upper caste landlords. They are not well organized to assert their rights there is no one to make them realize of their rights and privileges given by the constitution of the Government. The economic concessions like subsidies, Margin Money and Bank Loans are enjoyed by the upper caste land lords by forcing the poor Dalits to sign on the relevant documents.

Bonded labour is prohibited by the Government but it is still practiced in a suitable way. Most of the people in villages are not even aware of this. A few know about bonded labour, they are helpless as there is no one to report to government and take legal action against the offenders.

Child labour is abolished by the Government of India as well as state Government. But there is no one to implement it. It is due to the poverty and child labour is available very easily. So there must be a third party who acts as watch dogs and the report the matter to Government for taking necessary action. The poor parents must also be helped economically for the loss of income. The Government effort to rehabilitate the child labour proud to be a failure. Only a few non-Governmental organizations could do something in this regard. Low Wages most of the agricultural labours are the illiterates and they are not well organized to represent to the government.

Untouchbility was abolished 50 years ago by an Act of law. Under prevention of Atrocities Act, it is an offence to abuse any one by caste name. but this is quite openly violated everywhere and no action is taken as the victim is afraid to register a case against the upper caste land lords or political as there is no one to support the victim and file case in court of law. Under the law the dalits cannot even eat snacks and food and drink coffee or water in hostels as any other citizens. But in some villages these dalits were forced to wash the plates and glass after they drink and as they are still treated as untouchables. There is no one to report and file case and pursue it the end.

Even after Independence in India the Dalits are forced to live at the outskirts of the villages. Dalits are not allowed to build houses in the locality of the caste people. Nobody dare enough to defy the practice it is still continuing. The Dalits cannot directly take water from the village wells. Some people will bring water from the wells and pour water in dalits water conditions. It is still practiced in our entire mission village. Village barbers do not give haircut, their clothes are not washed by village washer –men, they are not allowed to enter Hindu temple etc.Even in towns and cities these dalits are denied houses for rent.

In certain parts of Kurnool District the practise of 'Basivisystem' is still in vogue. The women in certain section of the Dalit community are forced to practice prostitution as it has come from generation to generation. Many parents give away their daughters to the temple at a very young age and these girls cannot marry and they have to remain unmarried by practicing prostitution. This practice is regarded as something holy and divine. The Government is trying to wean away these women by granting lands and other self employment facilities. Due to their ignorance and connivance of the land lord they are unable to extricate themselves from the practice.

Dalits are not allowed to exercise freely their franchise at the time of elections. Generally they are guided by the land lords to vote for certain persons and political parties of their interest. Mostly it is done by threat or by swearing in before the picture of a deity or goddess. Most of the dalits are threatened from approaching polling booth to exercise their votes if they don't listen their master. They are asked to remain at home and somebody will vote on his behalf. This kind of rigging in political election is quite common and nobody dare enough to give complaint against their master.

Missionary Movement in Kurnool

The American Baptist Missionary union of United States of America, sent pioneer missionaries to India. Rev.Samuel S.Day started the first mission station at Nellore. Now the missionary grown immensely into a big banian tree spreading its branches all around Nellore, Ongole and Kurnool covering about nine districts in the present Andhra Pradesh. The land of Telugus was chosen as the project for the Evangelical work by the American Baptist missionary Union. The real purpose of religion is not only to bring about a spiritual reformation of the individuals but also to inculcate a sense of discipline and sincerity in the lives of individuals and community as whole. The American missionaries gave properties, educational institutions and hospitals which they thought would help best to express the love of Christ. They not only preach but practiced the gospel in the form of helping the people in various ways which were termed as the 'institutions of the church'.

The aim of the missionary movement is to bring the people to Christianity and Lord Jesus by preaching the word of God. The missionaries discovered that they had to make the people literate fist to understand the gospel well and also they had to train the native preachers to assist them in evangelistic work. So they started a schools along with the mission work. A fist school was established by Rev.Samuel S.Day in 1840 in Nellore. The American Baptist mission sent John E Clough to Ongole in 1865. It is he who provided a programme, a policy and direction to the American Baptist Telugu mission.

John E Clough and Rev. D.H. Drake visited Kurnool in 1875 and formed the Kurnool field. A church was organized in Kurnool on December 23, 1877, Rev. F.E.Morgan and his wife worked in the Kurnool field from 1885 to 1897. The mission House was constructed by them in 1882.Rev. E.E.Sillimon succeeded the Morgans in 1885. Rev. G.N.Thomssen worked in field from 1892 to 1895. Rogers Memorial Gospel Hall was erected in 1893.

Rev. William Arthur Stanton and his wife took charge of the Kurnool field in January, 1892. He is the hero of the missionary work in Kurnool upto 1932 a long period of 40 years.The American Baptist Mission [ABM] Lower Secondary School was upgraded in to high school on fifth January, 1905. Lord Ampthill, the then Governor of Madras gave permission for the high school. The old little school was not suitable to the high school. Cole's Memorial High School, Kurnool was established in 1905. Narasiah was the headmaster of the school. It brought of different classes together on the same footing. The school had kept up its reputation in sports during the year 1916. The Pentlands Shield in 1916 as prize for field and track events for the second time.

The vision and fervent services of Stanton laid the foundation for the upliftment of downtrodden in different villages of Kurnool district. He started A.B.M. High school at Kurnool in 1905. In 1923 he opened Night Schools in the surrounding villages of Kurnool. Dr.Jonathan Ackerman Coles, a missionary, built buildings for A.B.M.High school and named it as the Coles Memorial High School, a Coles hostel for boys, Emilie Coles Memorial [ECM] school and hostel for girls. The Coles memorial high school was upgraded into senior colleges in 1969. Earlier in 1917 he laid the foundation to built the famous Coles Centennial Church. He established two village Colonies in the name of Coles Anandapuramu, Dharampuram with provision for their self-maintenance.

Stanton's have served the Telugus of Kurnool for a long period of 40 years and on 19thMarch, 1934 they left Kurnool for their motherland. On 4th March, 1954 at the age of 86 years W.A. Stanton slept in the lord. It is an imaging event in the history of Kurnool town in South India that the American Baptist foreign mission, U.S.A. has done through beneficence of Coles and Miss Emilie Coles, whose magnificent monumental structures for worshipping God and institutions for the uplift of the poor and the downtrodden in south India among the Telugus of Andhra Pradesh through the lifelong services of the chosen and dedicated services of the American missionaries, Dr. William Arthur Stanton for Baptist mission field church-work and Prof. Rev. Burnard fames Rockwood for academic higher educational industrial institutions, which rapidly covered the purpose with in the country of hard labour and dedicated services resulting ina million of believers.The ColesMemorial High school in Kurnool could see the light of the day celebrating its own Hundred Year service [1905 to 2005] to the people of Kurnool.

Religion, mainly Hindu religion played a dominant role in systematizing the tradition and culture of the past. Modern outlook of Hinduism is that it is a way of life or Dharma. However, Hinduism is generally treated as a popular religion which accommodates all philosophies from Atheism to Poly-theism.Mahatma Gandhi has made a curious statement about Hinduism, "it is a religion searching for Truth through non-violent means. A man may not believe in God and still call himself a Hindu."

Nehru feels that the, "Hinduism as a faith is vague amorphous and many- sided - all things to all men. It is hardly possible to define it, or indeed to say precisely whether it is a religion or not in the usual sense of the word." In short, it is a wholesome meal of all sorts of philosophy encompassing the Aryan and the Dravidian cultures, Vedic period, worship of select gods and goddesses and finally the caste system that has been influencing the way of life among the Hindus till now.

Caste system among the Hindus prevailed with remarkable difference as Forward castes, Backward castes and the Panchamas. The Panchamas constituted mostly the Malas and the Madigas. The fate of Panchama Class was very pitiable and their was the last place in society. By stamping a class of people as totally untouchables, the then society left the affected Panchamas lead horrible lives. People belonging to the Madiga community were the worst affected in Kurnool. Mala and Madiga are the names heard most among the untouchables. Along with them there are sects and sub-sects. Indian constitution called these castes 'Scheduled Castes'. Mala and Madiga are spread all over India. Adi Andhra is the common synonym used for them.Madiga is a social group or caste group of Andhra Pradesh, Karnataka, Maharastra etc. found almost in all Indian states with different names. The people belonging to this community are most oppressed and exploited in the society. The term Madiga is derived from Sanskrit word **Maha-Adiga** which can be loosely translated as **great and oldest.** They form the largest segment of what is considered to be the **Dalit** castes of Andhra. They are also no parallel in north India. They are manual leather workers in some parts and agricultural labourers in some regions of Andhra Pradesh.

According to Thurston "the Madigas are the great leather working caste of the Telugu country and corresponds to the **Chaklians** of the Tamil area." The Madigas sometimes call themselves **Jambavas** and claim to be descended from **Jambu** or **AdiJambavudu** who is perhaps the **Jambavan of the Ramayana.** The Madigas also claim to be the children of Mathangi. Tudimella is the place of origin of the Mathangi. In the Hinduism**, Matangi** is aspect of Devi (in other words, the Mahavidya) who is patron of inner thought and speech. She guides her devotee to the uncaused primordial sound. Matangi is said to be born as a Chandala or 'outcaste' (lit. outside the Hindu caste system). Her father was a Chandala who was raised as a Brahman (see Ramayana). This is likely to suggest Her origin as a tribal or non-Vedic deity.In the Manual of the Kurnool District of 1886AD, N.G. Chetty states that "the Madigas belong to the left hand caste and often quarrel with the Malas (right hand caste)". **Rev. H. Huizinga** explains the lifestyle of the Madigas as, "they live in hamlets at a respectable distance from the villages of the caste people by whom they are greatly despised. Their habits are squalid in the extreme and the odor of Madiga hamlet is revolting. .They perform all the lowest kinds of service for the caste people especially bearing burdens and working in leather."Inspite of discharging their duties, they were called untouchables. Yet, while walking on the roads treaded by the forward caste people, these labelled untouchables used to take extreme care to see that their foot marks were not there by wearing the broom stick round the waist, and sweeping their foot marks away. In order to avoid spitting on the streets of the forward caste they used to carry a small pot of clay. These people were forbidden from learning the Vedas, the prime education of the day. Forward caste people had a strong notion and feeling that the Panchamas were not qualified to learn the Vedas. According to the Hindu Dharma rules, anyone who violated the rules would be punished severely. If any Panchama overheard the Veda Chantings secretly, learnt and uttered them, his tongue would be cut to pieces. If by chance they came to know that a Panchama overheard deliberately the chanting of Vedas, they would pour boiling lead (metal) into his ears so that his ears would become dead forever. In the social dharma of those days it was the responsibility of the king to see that the rules of the class and caste were strictly adhered to he bring their rules to practice. As observed in this context it can be said that the so called untouchables (the Panchamas) had no protection from the king against the atrocities meted out to them in society.

The untouchables had no permission to enter the temples and it was the strong belief of caste Hindus that the entry of the Panchamas would taunt even the presiding deity inside the sanctum-sanctorum of the temple. These Panchamas were also called 'Chandalas'. Even though our father of the Nation Mahatma Gandhi ceremonially called them "Harijans," people belonging to God, their plight did not change a wee bit. Since they had no permission to enter the temples, they worshipped rural deities of worshi p.

The life style of the untouchables was pathetic. They had no awareness regarding cleanliness nor was there any guidance from any side in this matter. They did not even know the minimum requirements for cleanliness like bathing, combing the hair, and applying oil. They used to eat vegetarian as well as non-vegetarian food. They gave shape and form to the gods/ goddesses of their choice. They gave shape to their gods by drawing circles of Red colors and white on the walls of their houses. The Malas worshipped Sunkulammas, llamma and Lachumamma as their goddesses while Poleramma, Maremma and Ankalamma were worshipped as Goddesses by the Madigas. There was a new trend in their way of worshi p. They used to offer different kinds of pulses and grains, and oil besides animals like goats, sheep and as sacrifice to their deities. They used to worship potent powers of Nature and Animals. These deities are worshipped in almost all the villages of Kurnool district including the town of Kurnool.

Christian Missionaries and Evil Society

In the Indian society of the past several evil practices were observed. These vices were deep rooted in society and made the civilized society bow its head in shame. On observing these bad practices it can be said that they were the most uncivilized ones. The Sati, Child marriages, Child murders(infanticide), Dowry, Polygamy, Polyandry, Burning the Lepers Alive, The Plight of the Widows, Devadasi System are examples of such barbarous socials in the vicious circle of which women were made scape-goats.

A great missionary movement took place in 19th century AD. William Carey an English Baptist missionary, came to India at the end of 18th century AD and laboured in 19th century AD and started a Theological School at Serampore. In mid 19th Century AD, Mr. S.S. Day(1) first American Baptist missionary labored in Andhrapradesh. Later on, Dr.John Clough, Dr. Drake and Rev. Jewett were the significant missionaries that witnessed for Christ in this area. The history of the establishment of the church in Kurnool is connected with the "Lone Star Mission". In 1805A.D.Rev.and Mrs. Sutton were sent by the General Baptists of England to start work among the Telugus. However, Sutton was shifted to Orissa. In 1835A.D. Rev.Samuel S.Day and his wife were appointed to work among the Telugus. Their study of the language began at Srikakulam, continued for a while in Madras, and finally settled at Nellore. After his ill health, the Jewetts arrived at Nellore in 1849A.D. bringing in a new life to the "Lone Star Mission." The progress was too slow to continue. In 1853A.D. in the Annual General Meetings held at Albany, the question of abandonment of the Telugu Mission came up as only five converts had been won in a long span of 17 years. Dr. S.F. Smith, a participant there, was deeply affected, and as if by divine intervention, composed the prophetic poem, "The Lone Star" at midnight. This poem inspired one and all there, and in 1854 A.D, Lyman Jewett and his wife with three other native Christians came to Ongole and climbed up the nearby hill and prayed. He saw Ongole as the centre of a great missionary movement. Lyman Jewett was called the prophet of the most High. John E.Clough was sent as a missionary to work with the Jewettes. Clough began to study the Telugu language and initiated baptism to 124 persons in Ongole. Before the great famine, the number grew to 3,000 within ten years in Clough's service. In 1874AD, Clough(1) wrote a letter to the A.B.F.M.S. in which he expressed his prophetic view of establishing a Mission station in Kurnool area. The prophecy is recorded as follows: *" Either in the city of Kurnool or on the line of this Railway, in one of its numerous towns we should have a station as soon as possible"*. In 1875 A.D Rev. Clough and Rev. Drake made a tour via Dornal and Atmakur. In Atmakur they baptized 46 converts. In 1876 A.D. Rev. Drake came to Kurnool and opened the Mission station.

The primary purpose of the missionaries was to initiate baptism to local converts thereby spreading the Gospel of Christ among the believers. However, the missionaries came to the Kurnool region highlighting the point that Jesus manifested himself in human form to fill their lives of the untouchables with light dispelling ignorance, to change their uncivilized life styles and grant them a new way of life. They further explained that it was he who spilt his invaluable blood on the sacrificial altar of the cross to redeem the entire human beings from all their sins and curses and protect them as their Saviour. Thus the arrival of the Missionaries created a new chapter in the history of Kurnool. The role played by the missionaries in bringing about a social change of that day and in making the common people get rid of their Superstitions and become well-educated, is a real SAGA of progressive achievement and it is highly laudable indeed! In this regard the hard work put up by the missionaries in various fields in Kurnool district needs to be studied extensively.

In the ancient Indian history and in its social constitution, the order of Class was considered the most standard one. This order of class was based upon the different types of profession which again got transformed into various types for over 3000 years as and when tradition and culture as one spread its vicious pangs on the innocent ones.

It is said in Purusha Sukta of Rig-Veda, the earliest of the Vedas that from the head of Brahma the Adipurusha arose the Brahmins, Khsatriyas from his shoulders and Vysyas from his stomach and Sudras from his feet. In addition to the four communities came into existence the Panchama Varna. Besides this, the Hindu society was divided into different castes and sub sects, full of social inequalities.

In Kurnool town, Hindus, Muslims, Jains, and Buddhists used to coexist. Mala and Madiga belonging to the lower castes also started living here. They resided near the Konda Reddy fort, and slum areas like Vaddepet, Budhawarpet and later spread to Bangarupet, Dharmapet, Indiragandhi Nagar, S. Nagappa Street, and Bagathsingh Nagar.

Among the evil social practices rampant in those days. The Sati was the most inhuman and barbarous one. When the husband dies, along with the corpse his wife is burnt alive by force along with the corpse is called the Sati. This evil practice was in force in the Hindu society of those days. In those days North India was under foreign subjugation. The most powerful kingdom set up by the invaders was the Sultanate of Delhi. But in Rajputana, the Rajputs had defiantly preserved their writ by resisting the Delhi Sultans. One such Rajput kingdom was at Chittor. The unsurpassable beauty of the Rani of Chittor, named Padmini made Allah-ud-din Khilji lusty. (1347A.D.) He saw Padmini in the mirror and wanted to possess her by wily means. But the Rani and her women servants committed SATI in a huge pyre.Hand-prints in a temple symbolizing women who died performing Sati.

In the evil social practices of those days In this connection an important observation was made by William Carey (a Christian missionary serving in Bengal) that in the process of the burning pyre in the funeral rite, it was customary on the part of the deceased person's wife to continue sobbing and crying in a desperate helplessness sitting by the corpse amidst flames touching the sky and get herself cremated alive. Taken aback by this heinous scene he grew sensitive about it and published the incidents in his papers 'Darpan' and 'Indian Friend (Bharathiya Mitra) to let fellow visitors from abroad know about it. The sati was the most inhuman one. When the husband dies, burning his wife alive along with the corpse is called the Sati. This evil practice was in force in the Hindu society of those days.

There are many monuments erected in the middle- ages which are dedicated to those women who committed Sati (Jauhar) when their honour was in danger of being violated by Saracenic princelings. These temples are called Sati-Mata mandirs. Raja Ram Mohan Roy, a great social reformer of that time, worked very hard to put an end to this evil practice, helped in the process by the Christian Missionaries. In 1829 A.D the then British Governor General William Bentinck observed that almost 10,000 women were burnt alive due to the evil practice all over India, and made ordinance thereby prohibiting the evil practice of Sati. The abolishing of Sati system is one of the greatest contributions of Christian missionaries to India. December 4 marks that day in 1829A.D. when Sati system - traditional Hindu practice of a widow immolating herself on her husband's funeral pyre - was banned across the country.

While notably Raja Ram Mohan Roy spearheaded the campaign, alongside him were Christian missionaries like William Carey who vociferously questioned the practice and fought for its ban. It was Carey's relentless battle against Sati for 25 years which finally led to the famous Edict in 1829A.D. banning widow burning. The cobbler turned Baptist missionary was also the first man who led the campaign for a humane treatment for leprosy and ended the practice of burning them alive.

The Serampore College, the oldest Christian organization in India, founded by missionaries Joshua Marshman, William Carey and William Ward in 1827A.D.William Carey was a great social reformer, when he witnessed Sati, the worst evil which prevailed at that time, was horrified and dismayed". The 'Serampore Trio' joined other social reformers like Raja Ram Mohan Roy, and each on their own capacities vied to abolish this inhuman practice, " he told Christian Today. It was not an easy road. Carey came through a lot of pressure and agitation by traditional Hindus who validated the act by citing ancient Hindu scriptures. "But, Carey was not to give U P. He studied the Vedas and sacred texts for months to be fully conversant to debate the learned pundits," says Dr.Lalchungnunga, the Principal of Serampore College. During his campaign against Sati, Carey found that nearly 300 widows were burnt alive around Calcutta and 10, 000 all over India within a short span of time. Traditional Hindu practice of a widow immolating herself on her husband's funeral pyre - was banned across the country. Sadly, the Hindu practice of polygamy compounded the problem even more. On one occasion Carey documented 33 wives of one man burned alive at his funeral. This practice made children orphaned without father and mother. Carey fought against all these, publishing articles and books, resolutely opposing this practice. Both Carey and William Wilberforce persuaded the Governor Lord William Bentinck to carry a regulation to abolish sati system on December 4, 1829 A.D. declaring Sati as illegal and criminal. In addition to abolishing Sati system, Carey also protested against the other cultural institutions that oppressed women they are, polygamy, female infanticide, child marriage, euthanasia and forced female illiteracy. The versatile English minister also built a system of elementary schools with over a hundred such separate schools for girls. The government of India released a Stamp in commemoration of Dr. William Carey in 1993 A.D.

Child Marriages: In those days there was a tradition of getting the new born baby (child) married even though foreign invasions compelled this practice; the missionaries did their best to root out this practice. In rising the marriageable age of a girl to 10 in the Hindu marriage Act in 1860A.D.the missionaries were influential. By 1891A.D. the marriageable age of girl rose to 12 years. Child-marriage is another 'blessing' of the mediaeval age and it was born from the same compulsions that perpetuated Sati. Child-marriage was not prevalent in ancient India. This custom originated in the medieval ages. In the turbulent atmosphere of the mediaeval ages, law and order was not yet a universal phenomenon and arbitrary powers were concentrated in the hands of a hierarchy led by a despotic monarch. In India the Sultans of Delhi who held the place of the despotic monarch, came from a different type of culture. They were orthodox in their beliefs with a fanatical commitment to their religion and a ruthless method in its propagation. Intolerant as they were to all forms of worship other than their own, they also exercised contempt for members of other faiths. Women as it is are at the receiving and during any war, arson, plunder, etc. During the reign of the Delhi Sultans these were the order of the day and the worst sufferers were Hindu women. During these dark days were spawned customs like child-marriage and selection of women from the rest of the society, wearing of the Ghungat (veil). This age also perpetuated customs like Sati. Looking upon the birth of a female baby as an ill omen, they even condescended to killing new born baby girls by drowning them in a tub of milk. Amidst the feeling of insecurity, the presence of young unmarried girls was a potential invitation for disaster. Young men and women of marriageable age are bound to be choosy. This difficulty could be avoided when the marriage was between two children or babies where there was no question of their having any sense of choice as to who their partners in life should be.

The caste hierarchy also perhaps had its role to play in perpetuating such a system. Caste which is based on birth and heredity does not allow marriages between members of different castes. But as youngsters whose emotions and passions could be ruled by other considerations might violate this injunction. Out of the necessity to preserve itself, the hereditary caste system could have helped in nourishing the practice of child-marriage.

Among other subsidiary considerations which could have helped to preserve this custom might be the belief that adolescent boys and girls would indulge in loose moral practices. This consideration would have - been more relevant in the context of the puritanical and orthodox environment of the bygone ages. The practice could also have been perpetuated, especially among- the economically weaker sections, by the consideration of keeping marriage expenses to the minimum. A child-marriage need not have been as grand an affair as adult marriages.

Sati, Child-marriage, Ghunghat, etc were largely caused by the arbitrary tyrannical rule of the Sultans of Delhi. The temperament of these Sultans was a result of socio-cultural reasons. They had imbibed these tyrannical traits along with their religion from the Arabs who display traits like fanaticism and short-temperament to the extreme. The reasons why these traits should exist among those Arabs who originate from the Saudi Arabian Peninsula are to be found in their harsh natural environment.

The issue of child marriage had for long remained a thorny issue in British India. The British missionaries and officials expressed their horror of pre-puberty marriage could now be publicly questioned, a definite proof that the British Indians explained as only the first marriage to be followed by the Garbbadan (consummation) ceremony immediately after the attainment of puberty. In 1860A.D. the criminal code set the age of consent for both married and unmarried girls at ten years. The issue reappeared in the 1880A.D and in 1891A.D the criminal code was amended to rise the age of consent to twelve years. . However, there were no convictions under the Act until thirty years later. By then there were new reasons to re-examine the age of marriage in India.

Devadasi System: Devadasi system in South India, the biggest and the worst tradition was the Devadasi Practice. According to this, a virgin from a family was offered to God in betrothal and marriage. However, she was forced to follow the evil practice of Prostitution, and treated as the combined property of one and all. In Kurnool, this kind of Devadasi practice is known as Basivini practice. This is a deep rooted uncivilized practice in society. The Devadasi system started as a tradition in Medieval India, a few centuries ago. At this time the temples and Kings were the main patrons of the arts and girls from upper caste families were dedicated to be trained in the performing arts, care for the temple, and take part in its rituals and ceremonies. These girls were called Devadasis which means servants of god. This was a highly respected way of life and great piety was attributed to the girls who remained unmarried to serve the deity. The status of the Devadasis changed when the status of the Hindu temples fell with invasions that dethroned the patron kings. It is said that the women were also misused by the rich and powerful and the upper caste families ceased to dedicate their daughters to the temples. As temples became poorer the Devadasis fell into a life of poverty, misery and abuse. It is here that the system became one where girls from the lower castes were made Devadasis. However, these women were no longer patrons of the performing arts but used by the men of the village.

Christian Missionary Services in Kurnool

Jesus instructed the apostles to make disciples of all nations (Matthew 28:19-20). This verse is referred by Christian missionaries as the Great Commission and inspires missionary work. **The kind of service rendered by the Christian missionaries in Kurnool district is priceless.** Be it a church, or an educational institution, a colony or a small village - each one of them stands testimony to the quality of service willingly rendered by them. Charles W. Eliot quote, "Be unselfish. That is the first and final commandment for those who would be useful and happy in their usefulness. If you think of yourself only, you cannot develop because you are choking the source of development, which is spiritual expansion through thought for others." American University President of Harvard University for 40 years, 1834A.D.-1926A.D.

It is precisely in this observation that one gets deprived of words to explain the success achieved by the missionaries in bringing words into action. It is they, who made a good beginning for modern education in India, laid firm foundation in the field of medicine, introduced innovative technology in the agricultural sector, created ultra-modern trends in society and achieved remarkable progress in the operative field of science.

The unselfish and relentless efforts of the missionaries have come to stay with the needy in a natural course of time and there is no second opinion to the fact that Christianity is now looked upon with conviction and great veneration in India. They worked hard to weed out social inequalities rampant in the past, developed moral values among people, made them understand the value of economy, and set an example to others by leading simple lives by themselves. It can be easily understood that their precept is seen in their way of living by example which is ideal and worth-following, not only to the Christian community but humanity at large.

After the **London Mission Society** had first arrived at **Nandyal, S.P.G., A.B.M.,** and **Roman Catholic Mission** entered **Kurnool.** These organizations rendered great and noble service for the progress of education and medicine, thereby gaining prominence unsought among the people. Untouchability, Devadasi tradition, child marriages, child abortions were a cruel practice of the ancient Indian society. The missionaries fought against these social evils bravely, encouraged widow marriages and created awareness among the people. Thus, their lives full of self-sacrifice leave an indelible impression in the annals of Indian history of reformation. Though the Missionaries worked in different service sectors, they simultaneously worked for a common cause of religious expansion with their mutual understanding and awareness. They did not interfere in politics. But the big change that the Missionaries brought in society is an incredible achievement indeed.

Influence of the Missionary Service in Social Sector

The personal life style of the Christian Missionaries was very simple and modest, They maintained disciplined lives with good standards of life, They worked hard and they proved by their example that it is not wrong to work hard and in fact it promotes good health, They explained to people the importance of economy in a family, They taught how to live happily with low income, In the society of that day, they organized industrial exhibitions, They conducted and supervised Harvesting festivals of that time, they made the Church and the society achieve self-dependence, The Christian Missionaries encouraged woman-education, The Christian Missionaries started their efforts to spread Christianity through women, They provided opportunity for all to get education irrespective of racial caste, religious and regional differences, They started "Janana" School. Through these Janana Schools, they used to educate women in their houses as they could not go to school. They used to teach the Bible as a part of the education.

By adopting this method, they were able to weed out social inequalities to a good extent. They worked hard to eradicate non-remunerative slave labor, and worked for the up lift of women, with the help of several social reformers, they worked hard to do away with child marriages and increase their marriageable age. They brought pressure upon the Government to enforce laws to annul child marriages and widow marriages. The service rendered by the Missionaries in preventing girl-child killings of that day is unforgettable. All said and done, at first the Christian Missionaries were able to check untouchability to some extent.

Society of Propagation Gospel, an organization, established a Bank at Nandyal-SPG Christian Co-operative Bank.SPG society established a Co-operative bank at Muthyalapadu. This is a Christian Co-operative Bank.R.C.M. Rehabilitation centers of **Abhayagiri** Leprosy Orphanage Centres Leprosy Patient Centres.**R.C.M 'Premagiri'**-H.I.V/Aids attacked patients-orphanages for them. **R.C.M. Orphanage/Rehabilitation** centers for cancer patients by RCM. **R.C.M. Destitute** Girls Orphanage. **R.C.M. Rehabilitation** Centers.St. .Damien Leprosy Centre Kurnool (Premagiri) 1988 A.D. **R.C.M.** Guardian Angels Orphanage Alur 1995 A.D. Centre for the Mentally Retarded 1995 A.D. Centre for Physically Handicapped Pedda Kottala 1995 A.D. St. Joseph Orphanage Peddakottala1995 A.D. St. Ann's Social Service Society(3) Peddakottala1995 A.D. Orvakal St. Elizabeth Orphanage 1999A.D. St. Ann's Social Service Society(4) Peddakottala1995 A.D. Sinai Divine retreat centre Premagiri 1999 A.D. Maria Nilayam Caliper workshop Premagiri 1999A.D. Care and Support Centre for HIV/AIDS Premagiri 1999 A.D. R.C.M. Carmel Child labour School Kosigi 2003 A.D. **Owk** Christ the King Orphanage 2004A.D. St. Ann's Social Service Society(2) Peddakottala1995 A.D. Infant Jesus Home for HIV affected children 2009 A.D. **R.C.M. Orphanages** for physically and mentally challenged people run by Mother Teresa charities and Maria Dawn Rehabilitation Center for the old people. The **'Sick Room'** run by **A.B.M** for patients suffering from Cholera. **Y.M.C.A.** Society doing social service at Kurnool. With the help of the above mentioned societies/organizations the Christian Missionaries were able to render service to people coming from different classes/Castes irrespective of religion. They were able to attract the People of Suppressed castes and those of forward communities equally well with their unselfish service.

Service in Medical Field

Owing to lack of proper understanding several infectious diseases used to multiply dangerously in the Indian Society of that day. These contagious diseases and drought were very common in those days. However, the Christian Missionaries brought an awareness of various diseases among the common people and tried to eradicate them. Native people began to follow the type of cleanliness observed in Missionary hospitals. Most importantly, personal discipline and cleanliness were given top priority in the medical and educational institutions of "Roman Catholic Mission". Though the objective of the Christian Missionaries was spreading religion, their service motto and a feel to help others was directly evident. Besides this, when contagious diseases were rampant and natural calamities occurred, funds were collected from abroad by the Missionaries to give succour and comfort to them. Several orphan boys and girls were brought under the shielding protection of the Christian Mission. The Missionaries originally were dedicated in the service of mankind. They provided medical Service to the Hindus and the Muslims equally alike. Since Service oriented attitude was taught in the schools, women did not hesitate to work as Doctors and Nurses. Missionaries sacrificed their lives in the service of patients affected with epidemic diseases. In 1903 A.D. when the plague epidemic spread across Madanapalli, the Missionaries while rendering service to the patients became victims of the disease themselves. Several Missionaries died due to Cholera in Kurnool. Each Missionary who came to serve the Cholera-affected patients, was infected and some of them died too.

Medical Dispensaries: St. Werburgh's Mission Hospital- C.S.I. Nandyal, Muthyalapadu Medical Dispensary-S.P.G, Giddalur Medical Dispensary-S.P.G, St. Teresa Hospital, Kurnool –R.C.M, 1923 A.D. Devamatha Hospital 1974 A.D. Adoni, Maria Maatha Health Center 1978 A.D. Adoni, Community Health Center, Atmakur (SCB) 1992 A.D., Krupa Bhavan Boarding for Handicapped Girls (CPS) 2004 A.D., ASHA – Drop in centre HIV/AIDS 2007 A.D., Rehabilitation /Mercy Centers (5) for patients suffering from AIDS and LEPROSY-R.C.M. Societies. Maria Don Orphanage for Mentally challenged and old age home. St. Francis Sick Room, Kurnool –A.B.M. The present governments which are implementing social welfare Schemes such as free distribution of Tablets that control Cholera and those reducing fever are in fact learnt from the practice of the Missionaries only.

Service in the Education Field

In the field of education, the Missionaries introduced the latest method by giving up the traditional and ancient Gurukula system of education and enabling equal representation from all classes of society. Even though it was decided not to make Bible Preaching mandatory, the main aim was to preach Christian religion. They set up schools for the poor boys and girls, habitation Schools for women who would not come out of their houses, and professional schools for those without basic education. They administrated plans for schools, in those days the topics/subjects for study were Grammar, History, Geography, Social Studies and General Science. The Christians treat Sunday as a Holiday. This observation of "Sunday Holiday" by the Missionaries is in force even today.They appointed teachers by giving them special training. They gave Women education a new fillip by opening and spreading special schools for girls and Janana Schools for women. They were the first to introduce education to children in English medium. The mission schools developed further by receiving grants from the government. Irrespective of caste, religion and class differences, Schools, Libraries, Reading Rooms, Technical Educational Centers were made accessible to one and all. Since the method of teaching was in English medium in Missionary schools, students were not only able to gain good control over English but get access to western knowledge also for further development. With this good grasp of western knowledge educationists of modern times to drive school evils away and progressed with a firm determination of mind to build modern society. "Coles Industrial School" in Kurnool earned prestigious name as the top most one in the entire Kurnool district. The first women who passed out from Indian universities were Christians only. Several educational institutions were set up by the Christian Missionaries.

Missionary Educational Institutions In Kurnool

Society for Propagation of Gospel [SPG – CSI]

Educational Institutions:

S.P. G. Girls High School, Muthyalapadu 1857 A.D.

S.P.G. Elementary School, Muthyalapadu 1857 A.D.

S.P.G. Upper Primary School and High School for Boys Muthyalapadu 1858 A.D.

S.P.G. Model Primary School, Nandyal1883 A.D.

S.P.G. Upper Primary School, Nandyal 1884 A.D.

S.P.G. High School, Nandyal, 1884 A.D.

C.S.I. Elementary School, Nandikotkur 1911 A.D.

Christ Church Elementary School (S.P.G.), Giddalur 1912 A.D.

C.S.I. Holy Cross Elementary School, Nandyal, 1916 A.D.

S.P.G. Elementary School, Govindapalli 1921 A.D.

Christ Church Upper Primary School(S.P.G.), Giddalur 1939 A.D.

S.P.G. Upper Primary School, Govindapalli, 1946 A.D.

S.P.G. Girls Boarding Home, Govindapalli, 1946A.D.

S.P.G. Boys Boarding Home, Govindapalli, 1946 A.D.

C.S.I. Upper Primary School, Nandikotkur, 1972 A.D.

C.S.I. Holy Cross Girls Upper Primary School, Nandyal 1986 A.D.

Christ Church High School (S.P.G.) Giddalur, 1988 A.D.

C.S.I. High School, Nandikotkur, 1982 A.D.

C.S.I. Holy Cross Girls High School Nandyal, 1996A.D.

American Baptist Mission Educational Institutions:

A.B.M. Castey Girls High Schools 1891 A.D.: Rev. Thomson declared this school open in 1891A.D. This School building was constructed opposite the Bungalow of Kurnool Nawab. This school was constructed for the sake of Hindu girls living in Kurnool. O. Vishranthamma was the first Head mistress of this school. At present, this school is closed.

Coles Memorial High School 1905 A.D.: This is the first Christian school established in Kurnool. Kurnool Missionary Dr. W.A. Stanton set up this school in 1905A.D. Initially it got permission from the British Government as A.B.M. High School. Later, with the financial support of Dr. Coles, it got fully established and got recognition as "Coles Memorial High School".

Reading Room and Book Room: The reading Room and Book Room were constructed by Rev. Thomson and they are now part of Cole's Memorial College.

Coles Industrial Vocational Middle School 1919A.D.: Dr. W.A. Stanton constructed Coles Industrial School in 1919A.D. At present this school is closed and in its place "Rockwood Memorial High School" is being run. Coles Junior College 1969 A.D.The old hostel for the Hindu students is now rebuilt as 'Coles Junior College'. In 1969A.D, Prof. S. Jeevarathnam John was appointed as the first principal of this college.

S.T.B.C. College 1971 A.D.: Boys hostel of that time was modified as S.T.B.C. College with Dr. Jeevarathnam John as the first Principal, the college came into existence on 15-11-1971. A.D.

A.B.M. Elementary School Budhawarpet. 1929 A.D.: This elementary school was found for the suppressed class students in Budhawarpet, Kurnool with Sri. D.C. Lingaiah as its first Head Master.

Rockwood Memorial Hall 1953A.D: Rev. T.G. Gipson the last Missionary of Kurnool constructed this Building in 1953A.D.

Gipson Science Block (2) **1969A.D.:** This was constructed on 19 July in1969A.D.

E.C.M. Girls High School 1924 A.D.: This is the first High School constructed for girls living in Kurnool. This was founded by **Dr. W.A. Stanton** in 1924A.D. in memory of **Emily *Coles,* Sister** of ***Dr. Coles,*** and the donor for the construction of the school.

E.C.M. Girls Hostel 1924A.D: In 1924A.D. Dr.W.A. Stanton constructed this Hostel for the girl students of the High School (E.C.M). This is the first Hostel intended for girls only.

Baptist Girls Hostel: This was constructed in E.C.M. Compound for girls studying in various schools of the town.

New Boys Boarding Home: This is a Hostel for Boys, constructed in Rockwood High School Campus.

Rockwood Bungalow: The District Postal Department occupied this building for a monthly rent@150/-

Many Residential Houses were constructed for teachers, Principal, Head master and Peons of S.T.B.C. College and for those working in different A.B.M. Societies.

Dr. Stanton Bungalow was constructed in A.B.M. Compound.

Miss Findley's Bungalow was constructed in A.B.M. Compound. Residential Houses meant for E.C.M. High school, Head Master's residence, Warden and drivers were constructed.Head Master's residence in Rockwood compound was built.

Roman Catholic Educational Institutions in Kurnool

Teacher training centre, Kurnool. At present it is closed.

Sacred Heart Convent, J.M.J. 1913A.D.

St. Francis Regis Boarding for Boys 1917A.D.

St. Joseph's boarding for Girls, Kurnool (J.M.J.) 1917 A.D.

St. Mary's Elementary School for Boys1939A.D.

St. Joseph's Girls High School (1947 A.D.), Kurnool.

St. Mary's High school for Boys1970 A.D., Kurnool.

St. Mary's English Medium School, 1977 A.D.

St. Joseph's Girls Junior College, (At present it is called J.M.J. Girls High School) Kurnool, 1970 A.D.

St. Joseph's English medium School (SAB) 1973A.D.

Carmel Ashram of St. Joseph's and Little Flower (OCD) 1974 A.D.

St. Joseph's Girls Elementary School (J.M.J).

Roman Catholic Sisters Monastery Hostel, Kurnool.

St. Mary's Boys Hostel (S.G) 1984 A.D.

St. Mary's Junior College 1988 A.D.

Jesus Mary Joseph English Medium School for Girls1988A.D.

St. Ann's Convent 1989 A.D.(SAB).

Don Bosco Technical Training Centre SDB 1991 A.D.

Chaitanya Gruhini Training centre (SAS) –Luzern 1995 A.D.

Deepthi Bhavan 1999 A.D.

Krupa Nilayam (SJT) 1999 A.D.

St. Johns Major Seminary (HGN) 1999 A.D.

Don Bosco boarding Home for Boys 1999 A.D.

St. Joseph's Degree College, Kurnool.(2000A.D.)

Vimal Jayanthi Convent (DSS) 2000 A.D.

Kristhu Jayanthi Carmel Bhavan (CTC) 2000 A.D.

Missionaries of Charity (NC) 2000 A.D.

Congregation of Mother of Carmel (CMC)2001 A.D.

Vimala Provincial House (DSS) 2005 A.D.

Adoration Sisters (SAB) 2005 A.D.

Salesian Missionaries of Mary Immaculate(SMMI) 2006 A.D.
Shanthinikethan JMJ Care and Support Centre 2008 A.D.

Hand mades of Sacred Hearts of Jesus (ACI) 2008 A.D.

Adoni: St. Gabriels Convent 1848A.D. St. Anthony Girls High School 1979A.D.St. Anthony's Primary School 1936A.D.Anthony's Boys Boarding 1939 A.D. St. Anthony Girls Boarding 1993A.D.St. Anthony Girls Boarding High School1993 A.D.

Allagadda: R.C.M. Elementary Aided school Dorakottala 1945 A.D.

Alur: R.C.M Telugu Medium school 1930 A.D.

Atmakur: De Paul's English Medium School 1989 A.D. De Paul's Boys Home 1992 A.D.3. De Paul's High School 1992 A.D. Vincentian Convent 1992 A.D. Jyothi Nilayam Boarding Home for Girls 1994 A.D.

Banaganapalli: AuxiliumVidya Niketan English Medium School 1996 A.D. St.Joseph Boarding Home for Girls 1999 A.D. 3.Mother Theresa Boarding Home for Boys 2000A.D.

Bethamcherla: Mount Fort Boys Home (1) 1992A.D. St.Ann's Convent1994 A.D.. St.Ann's English Medium School, 1994 A.D. St.Ann's Girls Boarding 1994 A.D.

Chagalamarri: St. Joseph's High School 1948 A.D. St. Joseph's Telugu elementary school 1948A.D. St.Joesph's Boys Boarding 1990 A.D. St.Ann's Convent 1991 A.D. St.Ann's English Medium School 1991 A.D. Bishop Gorantla Johnannes Boarding School 1999 A.D.

Koilakuntla: Our Lady of Lourdes Convent JMJ 1968 A.D. St. Joseph's High School for Boys 1969 A.D. St. Joseph's High School for Girls 1969 A.D. DePaul's Boys Home 1992 A.D. DePaul's High School Telugu Medium 1992A.D.

Nandikotkur: Jeevana Jyothi Convent 1985 A.D. Velangani Maatha High School 1985 A.D.

Nandyal: St. Joseph's Elementary school 1964 A.D. St. Joseph's Upper Primary school 1964 A.D. St. Joseph's High School For Girls 1964 A.D. St. Joseph's Boarding for Girls 1964 A.D. St. Joseph's Junior College for Girls 1995 A.D.

Onteddupalli: RCM Aided Elementary School, 1927 A.D.

OWK: Maria Nilayam And Boarding 1978 A.D.

Maria Nilayam Convent, 1978 A.D.

PeddaKottala:(Dora Kottala): St. Joseph's Elementary School 1919 A.D. St. Joseph's Convent 1919 A.D. St. Ann's Convent 1919 A.D. St. Josephs High School 1989A.D.St. Josephs Elementary Telugu Medium School 1919 A.D.

POLUR: ElementaryTelugu Medium School 1912 A.D. St. Monikas Convent 1912 A.D. St. Monikas Girl s Boarding 1995 A.D.

Konda Bollavaram: RCM Elementary Aided School.

Pathikonda: St. Joseph's High School for Boys and Girls.

Yemmiganur: R.C.M. Girls High School.

The educational institutions founded by R.C.M. Organisations have given their students a social uplift by training them personality development in maintaining good self discipline, personal cleanliness and the like. R.C.M. has a unique method of imparting training in cleanliness and discipline.

The Bible is the foundation on which the Missionary literature has grown. Bible Societies and Tract Societies played a prominent role in spreading the Bible Literature, which is very sacred to the Christian Missionaries. The Christian Missionaries and the employees of the company (East India) wrote books like Primary Texts, Grammar Texts, Encyclopedia and Dictionaries for the benefit of learners of the language. Books related to Science, Philosophy, Technology, Economics, History and Moral Education came to lime Right through the Missionary literature. It was through translation, Edition, Publication, printing, distributing newspapers, and Books, that several people got their livelihood. A Missionary by name **Robert de Nobile** worked very hard in **Telugu** literature. The important books written by him in Telugu are:.Gnaana Samkshepam, Prashnotharalu, Punarjanma Akshepam, Vishvasa Sallapam.

BenjaminShultz, a German Missionary, worked very hard in Telugu literature after RobertdeNobile, he published 6 small books in Telugu during 1746 A.D.-1747 A.D. The Missionaries worked relentlessly to get into the depths of Indian literature. Protestant Missionaries like **Rev. Dr. William Carey, Joshua Marshman and William Ward** were among the first who took up the task of printing in India. The first magazines they started were**'Samachara Darpan'** and **'Friend of India'**. Rev. Dr. William Carey translated the Bible into 44 national and International languages. Not only this, Shultz translated the Indian epic 'Ramayana' into English language. The Missionaries subscribed script to various spoken colloquial languages and brought nearly 120 languages to practical use of people at large in

India. Telugu as a script was brought into use by them only. It was the Missionaries who brought out a book on Telugu grammar.

The prayer "Heavenly Father" which Lord Jesus Christ taught his disciples was translated into various Indian Languages including Sanskrit. 1000 copies of New Testament in Telugu were printed in Serampore of west Bengal. Telugu grammar was printed there only. Bible translations, Gospels, and speech on the mountain were largely prepared by Christian missionaries. A.D. Campbell prepared a dictionary in Telugu. The devotional songs written by Garden were printed in 1839A.D. Verses of religious literature called Christian hymns were introduced at all places. National and International Ragas were followed and arranged in such a way that even the very ordinary people could sing the prayers of worship happily in prayer meetings and at home.

Almost all the Kurnool Christian Missionaries have learnt the Telugu language. During the period of their stay in the district, they transcribed their experiences in the form of Books. Though their writings were related to Christian literature, they were useful to the Americans, The Britishers and the Germans. They were useful for Missionaries migrating from abroad to have comprehension of India.

References

Sherwani H.K. "The region of Abdullah Qutff Shah-economic Aspect –II, Journal of Indian History, Vol-XLII, Part III, December, 1964, p. 684.

Gleig, G.R., The life of Major General Thomas Munro, Vol, I, pp. 302-303.

Venkata Rangiah, M. The Freedom Struggle in Andhra Pradesh, (Hyderbad, 1956)Vol-I, (1880-1905), P.20.

Francis, W. Imperial Gazetters of India, Provincial series, Madras Vol. I, pp. 184-185.

Benson C.An Account of Kurnool District. pp. 4-5.

Mr. Stantor, The awakening of India pp. 7-72.

History of the Lone star for the year 1922, p. 74.

Report of the American Baptist Telugu Mission for the year 1928. p. 101.

Google links for Pagidyala, India.

Temples of Kurnool fort Dr. K. Maddaiah Sapthagiri - June 2003 A.D.

Narahari Gopalakrishnamah Chetty, 1886.

Prof. Sreenivasachari History of India Madras undated.

Hindiusm 1948 by A.C.Bouquet.

Caste and tribes of Southern India by Thurston, Edger .

Indian History by K.Krishna Reddy.

Indian History by K.Krishna Reddy.

Buddhist Remains of Andhra by Dr. K. IV Subrahmanaian.

Manual of Kurnool district by N.G Ranga .

Kandenavolu Charitham by Chokkavarapu Narayana Swamy.

Origin and growth of Kurnool Town by K. Devaraju.

Gladstone and Sunderesan, Church History of India and Pakistan, Madras: CLS, 1956, p. 49.

Smith George, The Conversion of India, Madras: CLS, 1958, p. 42-56.

Gladstone and Sunderesan, Church History of India and Pakistan, Madras: CLS, 1956, p. 118 (Gladstone and Sunderesan, Op. cit., p. 118.)

Manual of Kurnool District by 1886 by N.G Ranga.

Hinduism by A.C. Bouquets .

Castes and Tribes of Southern India by Thurston, Edger.

Castes & Tribes of Southern India by Thurston, Edger.

Castes and Tribes of Southern India by Thurston.

A.History of American Baptist Mission in Kurnool District by Rev. K. Daniel.

A History of American Baptist mission in Kurnool District -Rev. K. Daniel.

The crown of Hinduism by J.N. Farquher.

Out of the East By Rev. Dr. W.A. Stanton.

Renaissance in India by C.F. Andrews.

The Indian History by V.A . Smith .

An introduction to Indian church History by E.B. Firth.

An Introduction to Indian Church History by E.B. Firth.

Friend of India by William Carey.

The Renaissance India by C.F.Andrews.

The Renaissance in India by C.F. Andrews.

A History of South India by K.A.N. Sastry.

The Indian History by V.A. Smith.

Andhrula Charitha by.S.L. Hnaumantha Rao, Holy Bible.

Andhra Pradesh District Gazette by M.V. Rajagopal.

Hennessy, H.E., A History of India, 1526-1923, Bombay: Himalaya 1923, p. 21.

Gense, J.H., O p. cit., p. 296.

Menon, V.P., The Story of Integration of Indian States, Madras: Orient Longman, Madras 1961, p. 34.

Gladstone and Sunderesan, Church History of India and Pakistan, Madras: CLS, 1956, p. 49.

Smith George, The Conversion of India, Madras: CLS, 1958, p. 56.

Gladstone and Sunderesan, Church History of India and Pakistan, Madras: CLS, 1956, p. 118.

Y. Vaikuntham, education and social change in south india: Andhra, 1880-1920, p. 2.

P.N. Chopra, B.N Puri, M.N das, a Social, Cultural and Economic History of India, Vol. III, p. 223.

Y. Vaikuntham, opcit, p. 2.

P.N. Chopra, B.N Puri, M.N Das, op. cit, p. 223.

Ibid, p. 227.

Ibid. p. 228

P.R. Rao, history of modern Andhra Pradesh, p. 51.

Report on the Administration of the Madras Presidency for 1875-76, pp. 356-357.

Ibid.

K.V. Narayana Rao, the emergence of Andhra Pradesh. Bombay-1937, p. 8.

Petion of Madras Native Association dated 26.2. 1852 to the government of Madras, quoted as document No. 14 in the Freedom Struggle in Andhra Pradesh (Andhra) ed by M. Venkatarangaiah, Vol. I. Hydrabad, 1965, pp. 131-135.

Ibid, document, 51. P p. 210-211.

P.R. Rao, op. cit, P. 60.

P.R. Rao, op. cit, P. 60.

Y. Vaikuntham, op. cit, p. 14.

History of Christian Missionaroies in Andhra Pradesh by Dr. Mangamma.

Indian Christian of St. Thomas by Brownie.

Indian Christian of St. Thomas by Brownie

History of the Catholic Diocese of Kurnool 1701-2007-By Rev. Fr. Anthonappa

History of the Catholic Diocese of Kurnool 1701-2007-By Rev. Fr. Anthonappa Chowrappa

A History of American Baptist mission in Kurnool District -Rev. K. Daniel.

Kurnool Mandala Charithram by Dharani Ramachandra Rao

Holy cross cathedral, Nandyal souvenir 1905-2005, Catholic directory of Kurnool Diocese. 2009

Church, State and Christian Society by Geard. T.

Kurnool Jubilee by Rev. Dr W.A. Stanton and Rev B.J. Rockwood

Coles Memorial Junior College Centennial Celebrations, Souvenir1905A.D- 2005 A.D.

Kurnool Jubilee Souvenir by Rev. Dr. W.A. Stanton and B.J. Rockwood

Catholic Directory of Kurnool Diocese 2009.

Catholic Directory of Kurnool Diocese 2009.

History of the Catholic Diocese of Kurnool 1701-2007-Rev. Fr. Anthonappa Chowrappa.

William Carey by Pulukuri John.

The Andhra Churches by K.B.Simon, Supporting Church in Telugu Area by B.N. Nathaniel.

Chapter - VI

Summary and Conclusions

The History of planting and growth of Christianity, Christian faith and Christian Church in a vast, varied and complex Hindu society like India is a glorious saga of historical adventures, persecutions and challenges. The genesis and activities of Church of South India in the most backward and drought prone districts of Rayalaseema region of Andhra Pradesh is an another venerable milestone in the Indian Church history. The highly dedicated, selfless Christian missionaries thousands of miles away from their native land made their voyage in to tradition bound caste-ridden land with zeal to spread the message of Jesus Christ.

The Indian Church history seed was sown by St. Thomas in the First Century A.D. After the destruction of Jerusalem in A.D. 70 Christianity was separated from Jewish roots. The Christian Church stood out as a quite separate, mainly gentile community. After the assassination of St. Thomas at Madras, the Christians in India established religious relations with the Christians in other countries like East Syria, Mesopotamia and Pursia. They came from Pursia, settled down in South India and became Syrian Christians and converted weaker sections into Christianity. William Carey, a Protestant, originated modern missionary movement as its first missionary in Bengal. He was responsible for founding of Baptist Mission Society and settled in Serampur. Themissionaries at Serampur were pioneers in the translation of the Holy Bible into Indian languages. The landmark in the annals of Church history is the Anglican evangelists, Presbyterians and Methodists joined together to form London Missionary Society in the year 1795.

Kurnool district is one of the backward districts of Rayalaseema region in Andhra Pradesh, with a scheduled caste population of 17.81% out of total population in the district. In spite of the constitutional guarantee and safe guards to the Dalit Christians, they never had an opportunity to enjoy the privileges like social equality, access to economic standardization and participation in the political and public life. Atrocities and attacks on Dalit have become a common phenomenon in the district. The oppressive methods imposed on Christian Groups, once again establishes the upper caste dominance and political empowerment of caste Hindus in rural areas of Kurnool district. This clearly speaks, mere constitutional guarantees does not serve any purpose, unless and until the state and civil society feels it as a very important aspect to uplift of the Dalit. Hence, an attempt is made to study the role of Christian Missionaries in Kurnool and the growth and development of Christianity in Rayalaseema region of Andhra Pradesh.

The Church Union Movement in South India received a setback in the initial stages. But the proposal was strengthened by the South India United Church, the Anglican Church and the British English Methodist Church. All the Church bodies negotiated Church Union in South India but the British Methodists had the least difficulties in accepting it. The All India Conference on Church Union convened at Nagpur in 1931 brought together all those who were involved in the Church Union in South as well as in North India.

When the missionaries came to India they came unprepared in the medical work. They used only some domestic medicines like quinine and pain killers for their workers. Father Heyer of Lutheran Mission has realized the physical suffering of the people on account of lack of medical facilities in Andhra and studied medicine at Philadelphia at the age of 55 years. Rev. Samuel S. Day, the first missionary of American Baptist Church to Nellore used a surgical kit about the size of a modern high school student's dissection outfit.

The missionaries did not lag behind in extending medical services to the poor and sick people in Rayalaseema region. They established hospitals and other medical units in three areas and through these hospitals they not only treated the Christian converts but also opened service to others also so as to exhibit love and charity of Christianity to non-Christians.

Another impact of missionary activity in Rayalaseema was the introduction of female education. In fact, the London Missionary Society was the pioneer in the field of female education in Rayalaseema. The distress of women in Indian Society profoundly moved the hearts of missionary ladies and as such they for the first time started the efforts to wipe away the tears of ladies. They directed all their efforts to counteract the misconceptions about women and combating their ignorance.

The missionaries were of the opinion that educating a male person means educating an individual but educating a female means educating the whole family. Another important aspect of the encouragement of female education was that the missionaries thought that the educational activity among the females was an easy access to reach the homes of caste Hindus which was otherwise closed to them. First, the missionaries' wives encouraged the female children of their Bungalow workers and in course of time started a small school in 1880 exclusively for girls in Madanapalle. Another consequence of the Missionary activity was the upliftment of untouchables. In fact, the London Missionary Society was the pioneer in the field of welfare activities for the untouchables.

The missionaries besides their evangelistic work, also concentrated on education and social work. They established many schools orphanages & hospitals only for the sake of these weaker sections. A new epoch was envisaged among the untouchables who became independent in thought and thus could break the chains of "bondage" to which they were subjected hitherto and led for socio-economic emancipation.

The missionaries exercised profound influence on the minds of Rayalaseema people. Besides their role in education, they attacked the prevalent social and religious evils to better the social conditions. Besides the secular and sacred instruction in the educational institutions, the missionaries also gave proper nourishment to the students about the dangerous effects of the social evils and prepared them to fight against the superstitions, caste system, child marriages, infanticide, suppression of womanhood, Sati and other social evils in the society.

The early Church, London Missionary Society, operated in the four districts of Rayalaseema region, especially in Kurnool district for its religious, spiritual and other evangelical work like propagation of the word of Jesus Christ. Poverty ignorance, illiteracy and superstitious beliefs are the root cause of all the social evils including the absence of health, energy and vitality of Indians which has largely raised the mortality rate even in 20th century. If this is the state of affairs at the end of the 20th century it is any body's guess how it would have been the condition of the health of the people in the seventeenth, eighteenth and nineteenth centuries.

The Mala and Madigas from the ages were treated as dregs of the society. They were not allowed to use the main streets of the village. Their touch was considered to be polluting. Their occupations were considered to be defiling. They were not allowed to wear the same dress of high caste Hindus. They were not allowed to use slippers or umbrellas. Who they enter the village they had to carry their slippers in hands and to fold their umbrellas. Even the possession of such materials like foot wear, umbrella etc., evokes the worth of the high caste land owners. Men covered their loins with coarse cloth and above waist; they were prohibited to be anything. Women wore sarees exposing the portion below the knees and they were not allowed to wear blouses; they were not allowed to spit on the ground, which was considered to be defiling. They are used to tie a small spittoon around their neck so that they had to spit into that only. They had to give way by standing far away from the road, to a high caste man who is passing through that way. They were not allowed to enter the front yard of the high caste man's house. They had to talk on him only in the back yard of the house.Even today this system is continued. The Vetti system, Devadasi system and other systems are engaged in the society. The village people worshiped goddesses in Andhra Pradesh. The goddesses such as Maremma, Sunkulamma, Yellamma, Pedamma, Mutyalamma, Durgamma, Poleramma, and Mahankalamma are important to the backward communities in villages. The upper caste people worshiped the gods and goddesses such as Venkateshwara, Shiva, Vishnu, Laxmi, Parvathi and Saraswathi etc,. The Sankranthi, Dasara, Diwali, Ugadi and Holi festivals are engaged by the upper castes and the Dalit are used to watch the ceremonies and rituals of upper castes.

Another fruit of Andhra Pradesh was the formation of in Rayalaseema Region. In1950, Church Union Movement founded Rayalaseema Diocese covering the four districts namely Cuddapah, Kurnool, Anantapur and Chittoor. This Diocese is the outcome of the amalgamation of Churches belonged to four Missions viz., London Missionary Society; Church of India, Burma and Ceylon (CIBC) formed as SPG; American Arcot Mission; and Kanarese Church of Mysore Diocese all operating in Rayalaseema region.

The beginning of the activities of Church of South India - Rayalaseema Diocese could be attributed to the London Missionary Society with its two Dioceses known as Cuddapah Diocese and Anantapur-Kurnool Dioceses administered by two different Bishops under one administrative unit known as 'Telugu Combined Committee'. The Missionaries who started their missionary work in these areas served the needy with love, affection, hospitality, sympathy and benevolence. These missionaries were deeply moved by the ignorance and superstitions of the non-Christians around them. The selfless services rendered by the missionaries impressed the hearts and minds of these people.

The Social evils such as Sati, Untouchability, Child Marriages, Devadasi System, Dowry, Plight of Widows, Burning the Lepers alive were prominent across the length and breadth of Hindu society drastically affecting the lives of Women, Children and other suppressed categories causing inequality in socio-economic and religious conditions. The human character of the Christian Missionaries attending to the needy and depressed laid a strong foundation for them at the right hour of Indian History. The Missionaries started evangelized in different parts of Kurnool district particularly, Atmakur, Dornala, Kurnool, Nandyal, Adoni, Polakal, Nagulapuramu, Guduru, Joolakalu, C. Belagal etc. The Parishes established at Pattikonda, Devanakonda, Karivena, Kodumuru, Peddakaduburu, Nannuru, Lodipalle, Banaganupalli, Yemmiganuru and Nadikotkuru.

The services rendered by Christian Missionaries in Kurnool district are priceless. The Churches, educational institutions, colonies, villages that we see even today stand testimony to the quality of service rendered by them. Words often lose their power of explanation in relation to the success achieved by the Missionaries. It is they, who made a good beginning for the modern education in India, laid firm foundation in the field of medicine, introduced latest methods in the agricultural sector, created ultra modern trends in society and achieved remarkable progress in the arena of science. Christianity acted as a stimulus, an inner urge, creating in them a new dynamic force setting them on with a firm footage, leading to total transformation of personality and mindset. It led to self awareness and made the people conscious of their own collective identity. This kind of missionary service provided objective-based vision that went beyond one's village, clan or tribe and offered the world a divine opportunity to understand the service as the Christian message of love, equality and pardon and peace and justice.

The Christianity is one of the great religions of the world, which was established by Jesus Christ in Palestine in Asian continent. This is the most popular religion among the Islam, Hindu and Sikh etc. It gave equality in Socio-economic and religious context to the people. This Christianity spread from Palestine to India and given message about the Christianity to attracted the Dalit. Later Portuguese, the Dutch, the English and the French companies established their colonies in India particularly in Andhra. They were maintaining close relations with the Dalit in both Telugu states also.

The Missionaries such as Methodist Missionary, Indian Missionary Society, the Franciscan Capuchin Missionary, the Telugu Missionary Society, the order of Friars Minor Capuchins, Carmelites First Order (O.C.D), holy cross fathers (C.S.C), Mill hill Missionaries, Missionaries of St. Francis De Sales (MSFS) Missionaries of the poor, Politico Institute Mission Ester (PIME), Silesians of Don Boscov, society of the divine world (SVD), the society of Jesus (S.J), Brothers of sacred heart, catechist sisters of St. Ann (CSA), Assisi Sisters of Mary Immaculate (ASMI), Congregation of Mother of Carmel (CMC), etc.With their relentless efforts the Missionaries have seen Christianity attain regard and respect in India. Christian missionaries worked hard to weed out social inequalities rampant in the past, developed moral values among people, made them understand the value of economy, and set an example to others by leading simple lives by themselves. As such their way of living by example is ideal and worth of emulation not only for Christians but to humanity at large.

The services of The Christian Missionaries spread throughout the district of Kurnool. As an impact of their services, several Christian Missionaries, Organizations such as A.B.M., S.P.G, and R.C.M. took part in Social, Medical and Educational fields in overall uplift of society irrespective of caste and religion. This is a positive sign of action indeed auguring for total social reformation.

The education system in Andhra before the British was based on indigenous methods and was confined in most cases only to higher castes. Traditional education had a religious orientation and lacked rationalism and scientific attitude and failed to question social evils and practices. The East India Company was not in favour of introducing English education system in India. The company started taking interest in the spread of education from 1813 onwards. Macaulay's minute of 1835 gave the official seal to the introduction of English education.

The study of the history and culture of Europe influenced the Andhra to a great extent by broadening their outlook. The humanism, individualism and sense of reasoning broadened the outlook of the Indians in general and Andhra in particular. The people's outlook had undergone a sea change and they gave up their blind beliefs. They wanted to revitalize Hinduism by removing the abuses and blind beliefs that crept into Hinduism.

The effect of the Christian missionaries were of far-reaching consequences. Some appreciated, some tried to reform their own religion in the light of what they had learnt in the Bible classes and missionary institution, and others passionately clung to their ancestral faith. The idea of social service is certainly derived in part at least, from the principles of Christianity and their application in practice by its followers. The option for the poor is also a rallying call to focus the spiritual, cultural, and physical energies towards saving society from social injustice to bring up social equality.

Another important fact of missionary work in this area was that wives of the Christian Missionaries used to accompany their husbands with equal zeal and interest. They shared the joy and sorrows of their husbands in their service to humanity for many years. Bachelors and spinsters also came all the way as young missionaries to preach and serve the society.

The Hospital established in Kurnool District such as Maria Don Old age Home, St. Theresa Hospital, William author Stanton sick home. Not only hospitals, but also many schools and colleges were established in Kurnool district. Coles college, St. Joseph's School, ECM Girls schools, SPG Boys school, it is the first school in Kurnool district. St. Mary's school, St. Joseph's school, St. Joseph's (EM) school, Mary school, St. Ann's Girls high school, St. John's high school, St. Francis de Sales high school, St. John's high school, St. Ann's Girls high school, school etc are established in Kurnool District for Dalit children are working in different parts of Kurnool District. These hospitals, schools and parishes worked for the expansion of Christianity in Kurnool and Andhra.

In addition to the services of European Missionaries in this area good number of native clergy also did tremendous work in evangelizing the people. They not only accepted Jesus Christ as their saviour but also underwent theological courses, got ordained and served as Bishops and Presbyters. They served the Churches as Pastors, Presbyters and contributed for establishment of new Churches in their neighboring areas. The preaching of gospel by native presbyters also strengthened the evangelical movement and gave good results. The untouchables like Mala and Madigas in this area were attracted easily by the preachers belonged to the same community. The recruitment of Mala Pastors and Madiga Pastors and sending them to their respective caste villages was also another technique adopted by the Christian missionaries in Rayalaseema region. The Rayalaseema Diocese immediately after its formation realised the need for building up of leadership in the Church and identifying missionary zeal among the youth so as to make use of them for missionary work.

Realising the economic backwardness of the Dalit who were converted to Christianity and whose children were enrolled in Mission Schools, for their advantage, the missionaries started Boarding Homes, Hostels attached to the schools for both boys and girls. Further the Church also sanctioned monthly stipends, yearly scholarships to the students of missionary schools as a financial support for their studies.

Another impact of missionary activity in Rayalaseema region was the introduction of female education. The London Missionary Society was the pioneer in the field of female education in Rayalaseema districts. The distress of women in Indian Society profoundly moved the hearts of missionary ladies and as such they for the first time started the efforts to wipe away the tears of ladies. They directed all their efforts to counteract the misconceptions about women and combating their ignorance. During pre-independence period the whole village education was managed by the London Missionary Society Schools and later by Church of South India, Rayalaseema Diocese. Today with the change in government policy on education all these schools were taken over by the State Government and only management was left with the Church.

The Christian missionaries all over India have been rendering unselfish service for the welfare of the poor, destitute, innocent people of the country, braving all odds including threats to their lives, with a never disappearing smile of on their faces, hoping to see the downtrodden and suppressed humanity grin and laugh with fellow sisters and brothers of the country. The research questions and hypotheses find their answers in this systematic attempt to view the past as it was, and presenting the current situation with all its achievements and left overs and visualizing a near perfect future.

Lastly, Christianity in India has rich heritage from the first century onwards and there are several indigenous movements which helped Indian Church to survive in the midst of opposition from the critics of non-Christians in India. Though colonial powers gave a wrong picture about Christian faith due to their dominant nature, we should acknowledge their service to Indian church and society.

The remedy for all these maladies require that the offices and high positions in the church and its various institutions be divested of their power and influence, and be vested in the ideals of humility, selfless service and sacrifice. A radical change is also needed in the five-star life style of leaders who must live closer to the poor and project the image of the suffering and servant church. Further, it is necessary that the authority inherent in these exalted positions be used for the purpose of renewing the church for mission, evangelism, service and human social development.

In order to provide the spiritual foundations for the unity of the Church of South India, all the members from the Bishop to the ordinary lay person in the local congregation must try to seek and find Power in powerlessness; Exaltation in humility; Spiritual bliss in material poverty; Fullness of divine presence in self-emptying; New life in authentic suffering and sacrifice. This kind of attitudinal and behavioral change among all those who are at the helm of affairs would enable the Church of South India, Rayalaseema Diocese to regain the past glory and commitment. It is not too late to rededicate itself to fulfill the tasks ahead and achieve the goals of Spiritual, Ethical, Evangelical and Social Development in South India in general and Rayalaseema Districts in particular.

The Christian Missionaries from the United States of America and European Continent, have interspersed themselves into the Indian culture and evolved a new culture. The author's effort is to bring back to the memories of the services rendered by the Christian Missionaries in Rayalaseema region, especially in Kurnool district is like enjoying the tiny drop of ambrosial water for oneself from a great Ocean.

Index

N

R

S